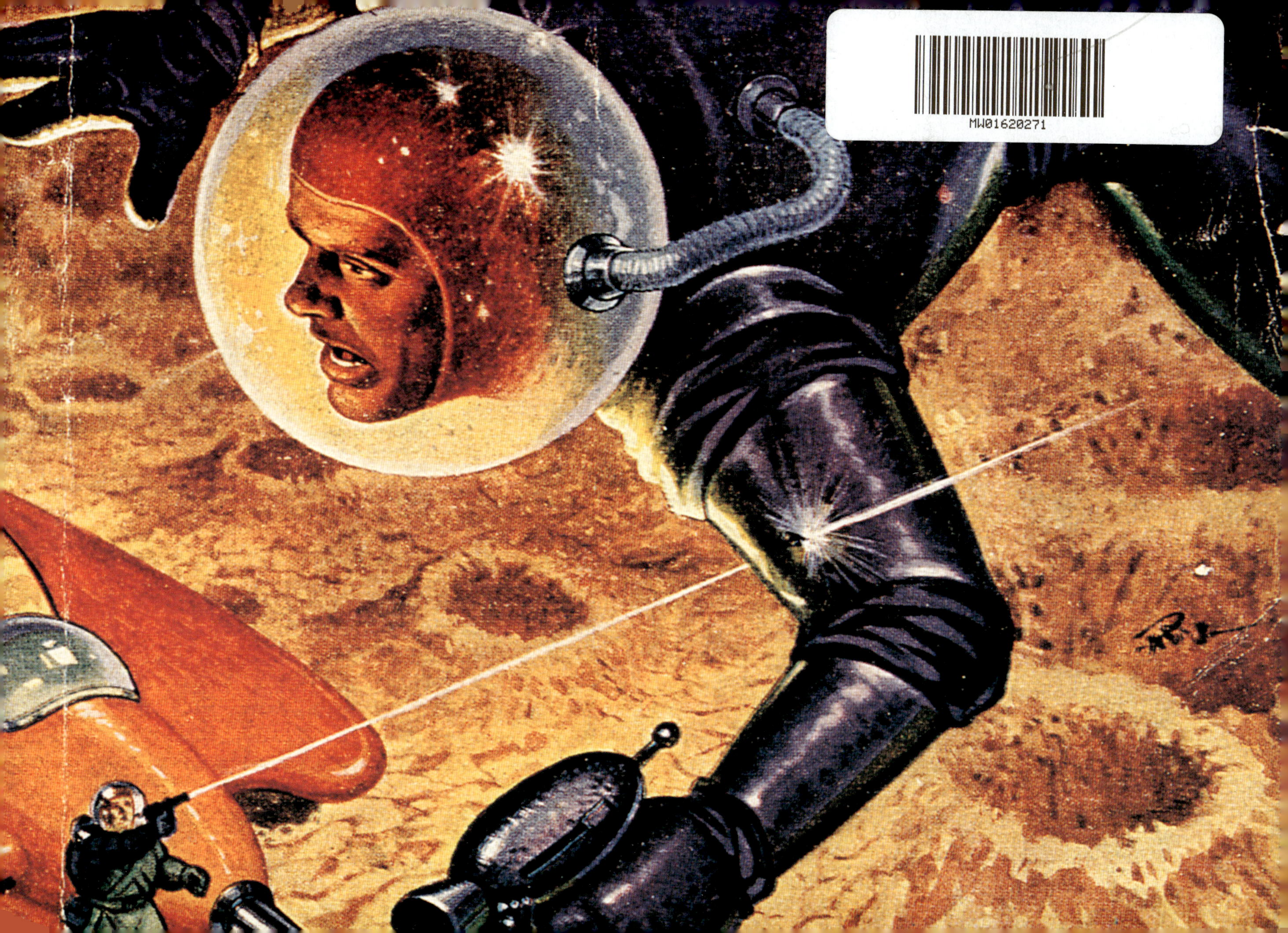

fotofolio

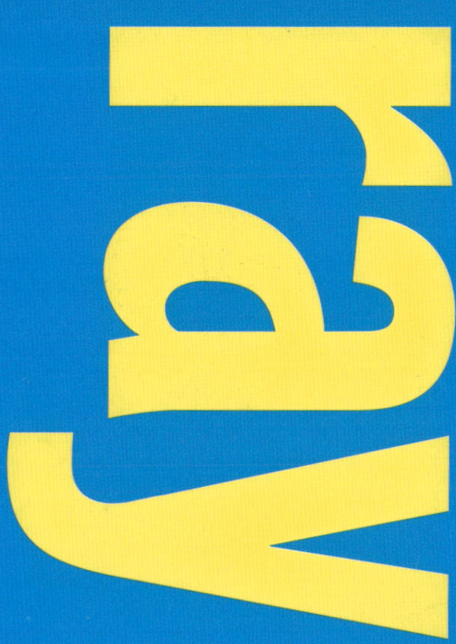

by Eugene W. Metcalf and Frank Maresca. Photographs by Charles Bechtold

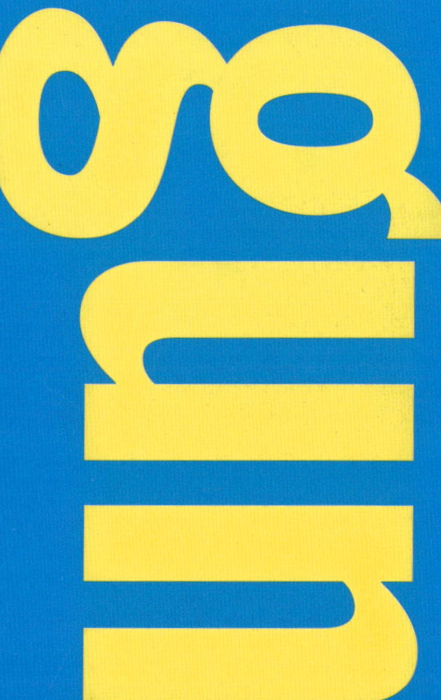

INTRODUCTION

Toy ray guns conjure a wealth of meanings and associations. Their outlandish shapes and fanciful colors evoke fond childhood memories of Buck Rogers and Captain Video, of backyard spaceships that blasted off for high adventure in the endless reaches of space. The stuff of fancy, toy ray guns are powered by pure imagination, by our almost unlimited capacity to wonder. Yet they represent other things as well. They are weapons intended to protect us from our deepest fears of the dark unknown, and they remind us of our vulnerability in the face of an endless and mysterious cosmos. Ray guns are testimony to the fact that we often imagine even the majesty of space as a backdrop for our conflicts and struggles, and that humankind finally set foot on the moon only as the result of a competitive, war-like "race" between two superpower nations. From the exuberant Art Deco disintegrator pistols of the 1930s, to the streamlined tin-litho sparkers of the 1950s and the darkly post-apocalyptic nitro-blasters of today, toy ray guns express and represent our dreams, fears, and fantasies.

BUCK ROGERS AND THE POPULAR DISCOVERY OF SPACE

The first toy ray guns were produced in the 1930s. Part of the Buck Rogers craze that swept the United States, they were an important by-product of, and influence on the popularizing of space that occurred in the early decades of the twentieth century. Our entry into the domain of space began during the 1920s and 1930s when an American scientist, Robert H. Goddard, began the first early tests of liquid fueled rockets. Disproving the theory that rockets could not move forward in space because there was no air to push against, Goddard discovered the basic principles of rocket science. Yet, ironically, it was not Goddard, the father of space travel, who first caught the public's attention and popularized space exploration. It was a far more fanciful and romantic character, Buck Rogers.

Anthony "Buck" Rogers was born in August of 1928 in an early edition of the pulp magazine, *Amazing Stories*. Introduced in the story "Armageddon 2419" by Philip Nowlan, Rogers was an air force officer who lapsed into a coma and awakened in the 25th century where he found America in ruins and the world dominated by Mongolians from inland China. Quickly discovering the marvels of this future world, including anti-gravity belts, rocket pistols, and space ships, Rogers and his cohorts, the lovely Wilma Deering and the intrepid scientist Dr. Huer, set out to free the world and battle evil and injustice.

At about this same moment the editors of the National Newspaper Syndicate began looking for a new adventure comic strip, and Philip Nowlan and illustrator Dick Calkins were commissioned to inaugurate a syndicated comic based on Nowlan's story. Anthony Rogers' name was changed to "Buck" to recall the popular heroes of America's Wild West and the new Buck Rogers comic strip made its first appearance in January of 1929. An almost instant success, it ran for over forty years. A radio adaptation was broadcast from 1932 to 1947, movies were made, and television versions of Buck's adventures appeared in both the 1950s and 1980s. Buck Rogers became *the* American space hero and one of the greatest pop culture heroes of all time. So insatiable was the public appetite for the daring space traveler that he spawned another popular space hero, Flash Gordon, who was created in 1934 by King Features to compete with the Buck Rogers comic strip. Like Buck, Flash soon became a comic book hero and radio star and, over the years, he appeared in movies and on television. By the end of the 1930s, Buck Rogers and Flash Gordon had transformed space into a popular and well-known adventure setting. More importantly, until the actual inauguration of the space race in the 1950s and early 1960s, these two fictional characters were probably responsible for teaching most people what they knew about outer space.

The introduction of the first metal toy ray guns by Daisy Manufacturing Co. was carefully planned to coincide with the developing popularity of Buck Rogers and became one of the most successful marketing campaigns in the history of the American toy industry. Daisy designers first convinced Nowlan and Calkins to redesign the hand guns, helmets, and holsters portrayed in Buck's adventures so that they could be exactly duplicated by Daisy. In February of 1934, after the Buck Rogers comic strip and radio show had developed a significant following and a strong market potential for Buck Rogers toys, Daisy introduced their first Buck Rogers gun, the XZ-31 Rocket Pistol. Before the introduction of the XZ-31, Daisy had already convinced the J.L. Hudson department store in Detroit to make "Buck Rogers in the 25th Century" their Christmas theme, and to install a large rocket ship and set of Martian figures in their toy department. Daisy then used these same props when it finally introduced its Buck Rogers gun at the prestigious American Toy Fair.

Despite initial skepticism about the XZ-31 (many toy buyers at the toy fair thought Buck Rogers was a cowboy!), Macy's Department Store in New York City agreed to promote the gun in exchange for a one week exclusive on its sales. Using the rocket ship and extra-terrestrial figures from J.L. Hudson, Macy's promotion was so successful that, on the day the guns went on sale, over 2,000 people stood in line outside their doors to buy the Rocket Pistol. As the week went on the crowds grew, and in order to keep Macy's supplied, Daisy kept trucks on the road every day from their Michigan plant.

Following this first week promotion, the XZ-31 was shipped to stores across the country, including Gimbel's, Macy's rival department store in New York City. As soon as Gimbel's received their guns, they cut the price below the forty-nine cents which Macy's had been charging. This started a price war between the two stores. Within a few weeks Gimbel's was pricing their guns at two for nineteen cents—substantially below their cost! Prices of the Rocket Pistol changed almost hourly in each of the stores, except when one of them ran out of toys, at which time the other store raised its price. While this was going on, Daisy exacerbated and profited from this situation by sending people into whichever store had the lowest price and buying back its guns which were then sold to the other store. According to Cass Hough, Daisy sales manager at the time, "during those first two weeks the Gimbel's and Macy's toy departments looked like a cyclone had struck, and people were still lining up to buy (Lesser, 168–227)."

Soon almost every toy store in the country was clamoring for shipments of the XZ-31 and Daisy could not get enough steel material or cardboard boxes to keep up with the production demand. For Christmas that year, Daisy developed a Buck Rogers holster and helmet to go with the Rocket Pistol, and the next year they produced a new Buck Rogers gun, the XZ-38 Disintegrator Pistol, as well as a smaller version of the Rocket Pistol, the XZ-35. In 1936 Daisy brought out one of the most colorful Buck Rogers toy guns, the XZ-44 Liquid Helium Water Pistol, finished in bright yellow and red lightning bolts. (It also came in a plainer, but no less striking, copper color.) After World War II, Daisy used the existing tools and dies from the Disintegrator Pistol to create their last Buck Rogers gun. Called the U-235 Atomic Pistol, this gun reflected the then current fascination with atomic energy. Before and after the war, Daisy was not the only company to produce toy ray guns, and other manufacturers flooded the market with Buck Rogers items. No other character, except Mickey Mouse, has ever been associated with more products.

RAY GUNS, CHILDHOOD, AND THE ESCAPE TO SPACE

The phenomenal popularity of the Buck Rogers ray guns was due to more than effective marketing and promotion. Crucial to the success of these toys was a new view of childhood which, together with the developing popular conception of space, joined to make ray guns an important tool in the acting out of modern ideas of fantasy and escape.

By the early years of the twentieth century, American ideas of childhood had experienced a significant change. No longer viewed as small adults, whose primary value was their ability to help support the family economic system, children were treasured instead for their emotional contributions, for the warmth and affection they evoked. In this new romantic view, children were valued for their non-adult qualities, for their representation to adults of an escape from the pressures and concerns of the adult world. Thought to be a unique world set apart from the dull, workaday realm of their parents, the world of children came to be epitomized by J.M. Barrie's beloved children's book, *Peter Pan*. Thus the world of children was understood as a timeless, make-believe fantasy land where boys and girls were unrestrained by the codes which bound their parents and could experience true fun and unending play. Toys became the necessary tools of this playful world of children, and were viewed as an important part of a happy and successful childhood (Cross, 81–120).

The popular view of space first presented by Buck Rogers fit perfectly into this new conception of childhood. Understood as another territory of Never-Never Land, the far reaches of the universe came to be imagined as a magical world where children and adults alike could escape the mundane and everyday. Whether zooming through space in rocket ships, floating above the earth in anti-gravity belts, or zapping green aliens with disintegrator guns, the fantasies of space represented an alternative to life's often harsher realities, especially during the dark days of the Depression.

The fantastic nature of space adventure is wonderfully expressed in the highly imaginative shapes and forms of the toy ray guns that exemplify this alternative world. Included among the countless ray guns produced since the 1930s are sleek silver cap guns with ruby sparking chambers, copper "disintegrator pistols" bristling with flamboyant fins and flashy fluted barrels, and plastic bubble shooters in cartoon colors and outrageous comic book shapes. Abstract aluminum "spinrays" sprout flower-like propellers, splashy yellow blasters are emblazoned with hot lightning-bolt designs, and Japanese tin pistols reveal tiny scenes of starry skies, exploding rockets, and lunar landscapes upon their intricately drawn surfaces. Unconventional in function as well as form, these unlikely armaments shoot smoke rings and colored lights, spurt water, discharge paper streamers, and disarm their targets with soap bubbles and bursts of baking soda.

Such whimsical creations are harmless in nature and innocent in intent. But toy ray guns also evoke darker associations that make them paradoxical as objects of play. Conceived to accompany explorers on their journey into dark unknown regions of the cosmos, they call to mind the aggressive and even hostile actions that have too often characterized our encounters with new frontiers. In fact, the narratives of space adventure mimic the mythic tales of the "discovery" and "settlement" of America's Wild West. Like Buck Rogers, space adventurers have often been modeled on the heroic image of the American cowboy. Similarly, ray guns recall the legendary pearl-handled six-shooter. Like their counterpart in nineteenth century America, these imaginary firearms of the future not only serve to protect or keep the peace, but also evidence our tendency to confront new worlds and alien peoples with distrust and the threat of conquest and aggression.

RAY GUNS AND POST WAR CULTURE

The Second World War changed the popular experience of space technology from an innocent fantasy to the potential of a real-life terror. After German V-2 rockets decimated London and American bombs fell on Japan, the idea of jet propulsion, atomic energy, and space travel could never again be purely benign or fanciful. Perhaps it was, in part, this unease with the dawning space age that contributed to the frequent, disturbing sightings of unidentified flying objects, or UFOs, which began in the United States in the late 1940s.

The advent of television in the 1950s also increased the popular interest in space travel and exploration. Like the Buck Rogers radio dramas of the 1930s, the television "space operas" of the 1950s broadcast tales of space adventures to a wide audience. Television added a dramatic visual dimension to the voices and sound effects of radio, encouraging children to participate even more actively in the fantasies unfolding upon the screen. Space toys became necessary props in these playful reenactments. As in the decades before the war, advertisers were quick to associate their products with the heroes and activities of children's space programs, offering toy premiums like the Space Cadet Membership Kit from Kellogg's Cereal, Captain Video's Electronic Video Goggles from Powerhouse Candy, the set of flying saucer rings from Post Toasties, and the interplanetary coin album from Schwinn Bicycles.

The first TV space series was "Captain Video," which aired in June of 1949. In the 1950s, the small screen was virtually invaded by space heroes like "Rocky Jones, Space Ranger," "Rod Brown of the Rocket Rangers," and "Commando Cody, Sky Marshall of the Universe." Perhaps the most popular space program was "Tom Corbett, Space Cadet." Premiering in 1950, it remained on the air three times a week for five years and appeared on all four commercial TV networks. Tom Corbett was the most heavily merchandised television space show with over 135 products bearing the Space Cadet's famous name. Four toy ray guns identified with Tom Corbett were sold by the Louis Marx Co.: a tin-litho clicker, a flashlight pistol, and two space rifles. Among the other television space shows used to promote ray guns as props for fantastic children's play was "Space Patrol." First broadcast nationally in June of 1951, this program was the inspiration for five space guns, including two smoke ring guns, a flashlight pistol, a rocket dart gun, and the rare Space Patrol Autosonic Rifle.

Fueled by the popularity of television space shows, comic strips, and films like "Forbidden Planet," space toys and ray guns became a toy shop staple in the 1950s and 1960s. Although partially eclipsed by Davy Crockett and the cowboy craze of the mid 1950s, the production and sales of space toys picked up again in 1957 when the launching of the Soviet Union's Sputnik satellite once again refocused the attention of Americans on outer space. After this date, many space toys were advertised to be more "realistic." Modeled on actual space vehicles like satellite launchers and ballistic missiles, they were said to be "scaled from official blueprints." Ray guns, however, continued to be pure invention. Never copied from real firearms or a part of the real space program, toy guns like the Martian Guided Whistle "Bloon" Gun and the Strato Gun (advertised as "earth's only interplanetary cap pistol") continued to reflect the themes of fantasy and escapist adventure that had first inspired the production of space guns in the 1930s.

While perpetuating the escapist fantasy of their predecessors, toy ray guns from the postwar decades were also differentiated by a few important factors. Unlike the earlier guns which were created largely from heavy stamped or die-cast metal, the later ones were more likely to be fabricated of plastic in the United States. Injection molding machines, which force liquid plastic into standardized molds, had appeared as early as the 1930s, but it was not until the 1950s that improvements in plastics technology had begun to revolutionize the American toy industry. Although extraordinary die-cast productions like the ornate Hubley Atomic Disintegrator were still being produced, American ray gun production excelled in the use of plastics technology. In fact, the art of plastic toy making reached new heights with such creations as the powerfully sculpted Smoke Ring Gun by Nu-Age Products, the outlandish Automatic Repeating Bubble Shooting Gun by Arliss, and the beautiful and delicately proportioned Planet Jet by Renwal Manufacturing.

Another element that distinguished postwar ray guns was their more widespread production and distribution. Although before World War II all toy ray guns had been made in the United States for a largely American market, in the decades following the war, many of these toys were produced in Japan for a market that was increasingly international. Tin toys were a specialty of the Japanese. In the late 1950s, as a part of the postwar Japanese economic recovery, Japanese manufacturers began to export significant numbers of lithographed tin ray guns, rockets, and other space toys into the United States and other parts of the world. While thinner and less durable than their American tin counterparts, the Japanese ray guns possessed fanciful surface designs and strikingly beautiful color combinations which were generally more sophisticated and interesting than those on the American guns. With their highly visual and imaginative graphics, Japanese tin guns, like the diminutive Space Control Gun by TN and the whimsical Super Sonic Gun by Daiya, are brilliant examples of the art of tin toy making.

But it was not only the Americans and Japanese who made ray guns. In the two decades following World War II, these toys were produced in numerous other countries. Among some of the most interesting guns from this period are those fabricated in England where, like those made in the United States, such toys were often associated with comic and television space heroes such as Dr. Who and Ace Hart. The most notable of these characters was Dan Dare, the central protagonist in a feature which ran for many years in the boys magazine *Eagle*. A "fearless pilot of the future," Dare did not drink or swear. He fired only in self-defense and always told the truth. Many toy ray guns were produced using Dare's name, including the Dan Dare Cosmic Ray Gun by Palitoy, a striking plastic flashlight gun with dramatically backswept handle and sights.

The late 1950s and 1960s represent the apex of Japanese and European ray gun manufacture as well as the end of the great age of American toy space guns. By the late 1960s and 1970s, high-tech electronic ray guns were being introduced and the fabrication of the majority of toy space guns began moving to Hong Kong, Taiwan, and China. With these developments, a new, and as yet unexplored chapter in the history of toy ray guns began and the "classic" period of toy ray guns came to an end.

Eugene W. Metcalf, Jr.
March 1999
Oxford, Ohio

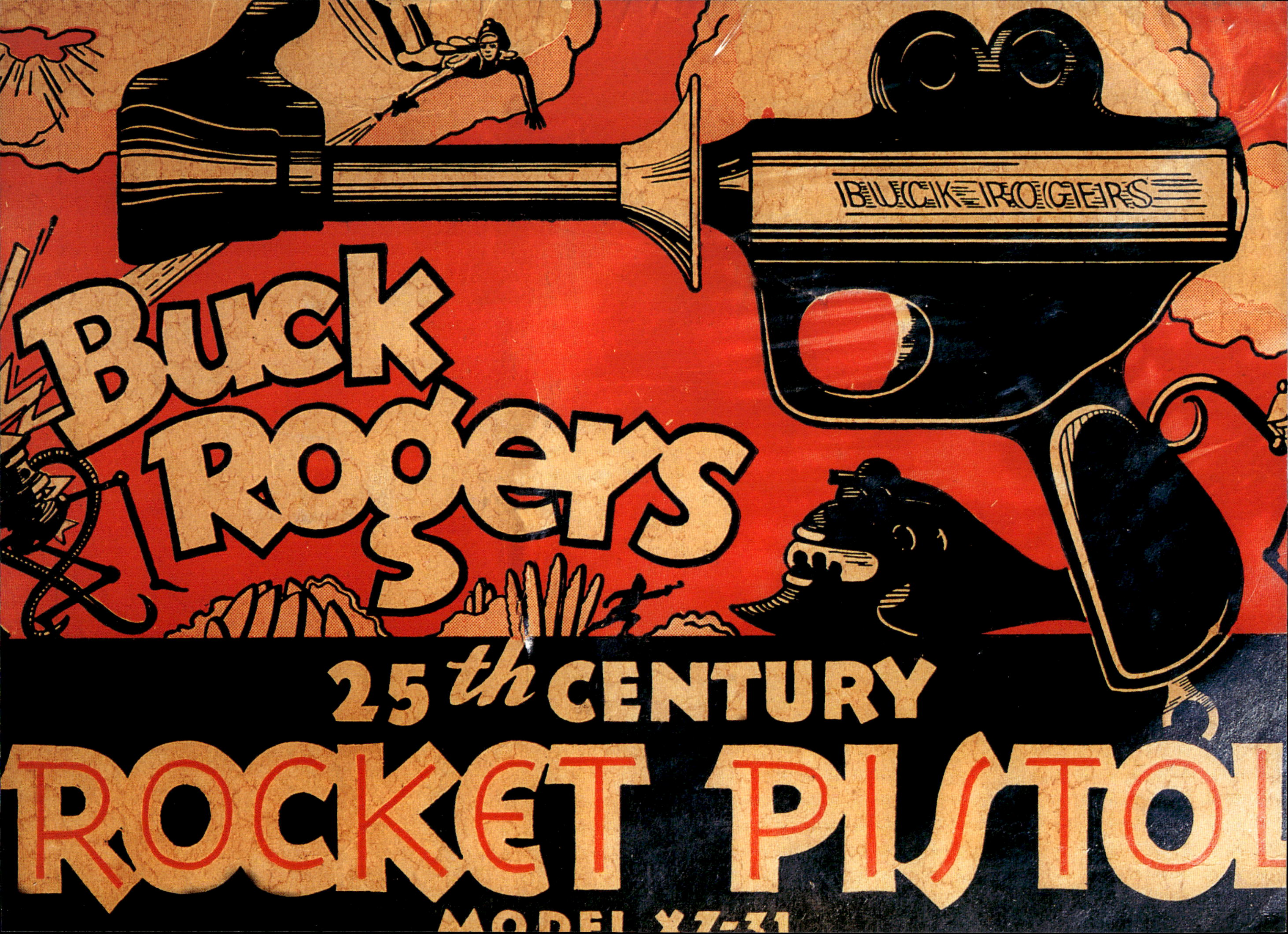
BUCK ROGERS
Buck Rogers
25th CENTURY
ROCKET PISTOL

Buck Rogers Rocket Pistol, XZ-35, pressed steel, 5½ x 7 in., Daisy Manufacturing Co., U.S.A. 1935

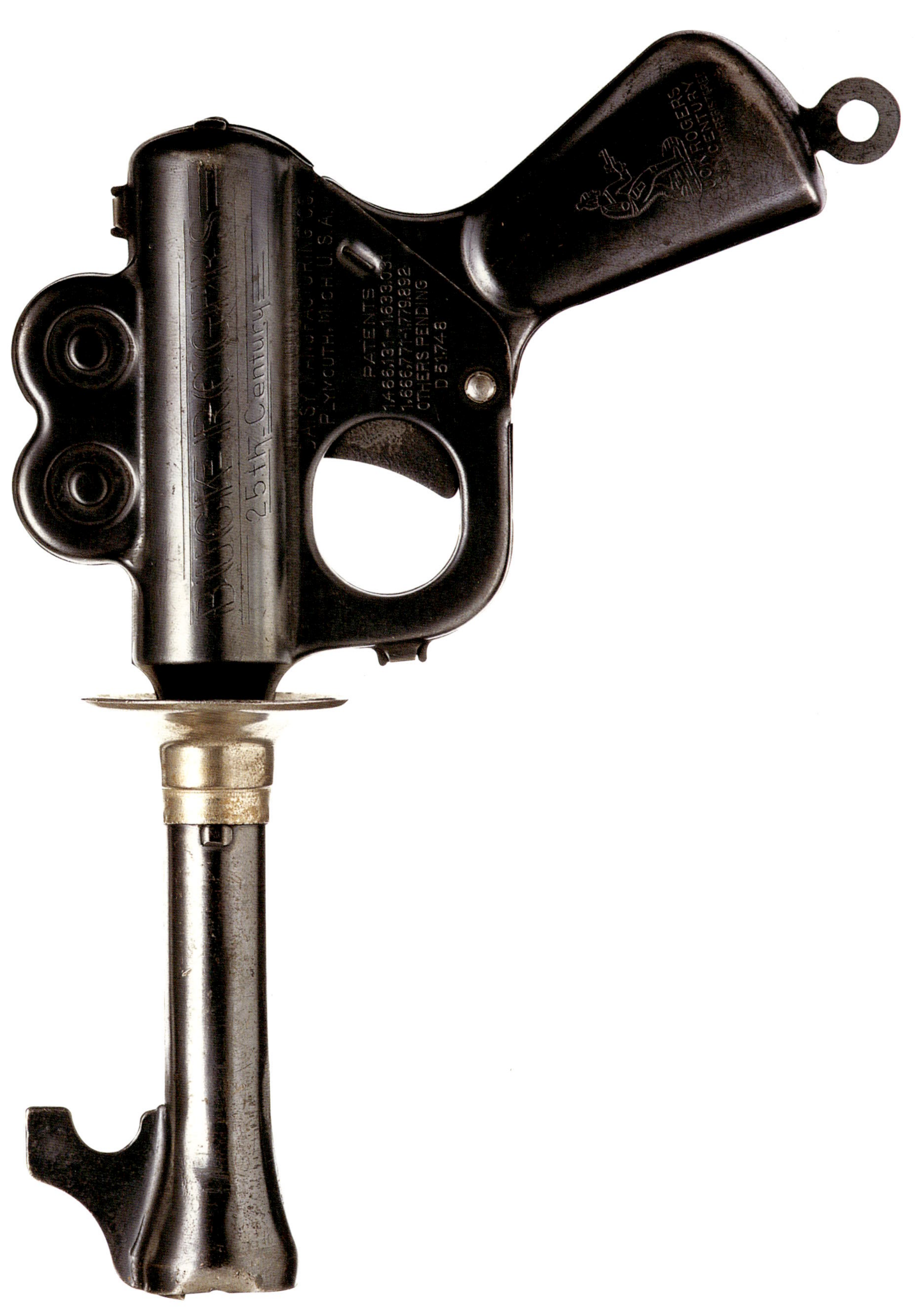

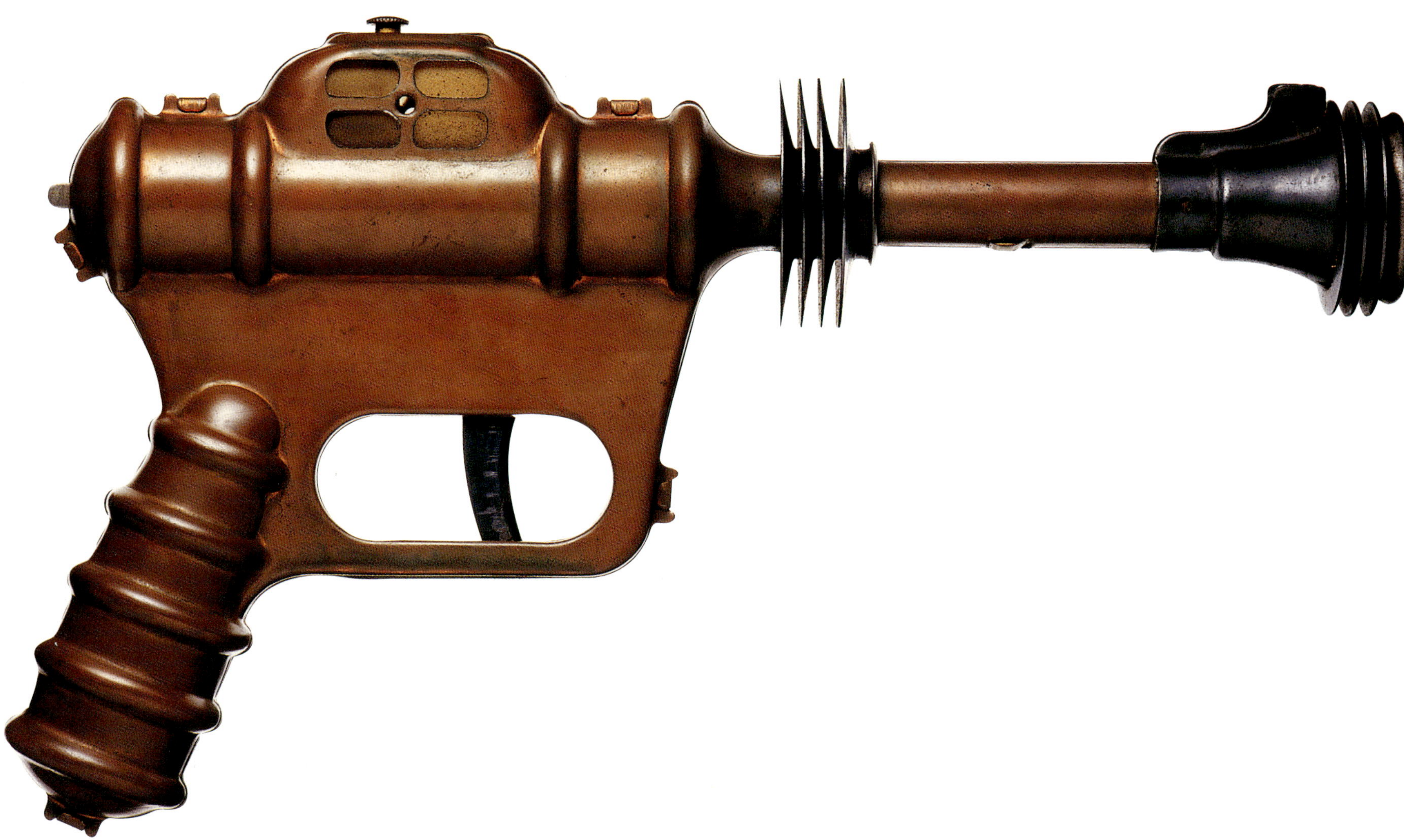

Buck Rogers Disintegrator Pistol, XZ-38, pressed steel with copper finish, 6 x 10 in., Daisy Manufacturing Co., U.S.A. 1936

Nu-Matic Paper Popper, pressed steel, 6 x 6½ in., Langson Manufacturing Co., U.S.A. 1936

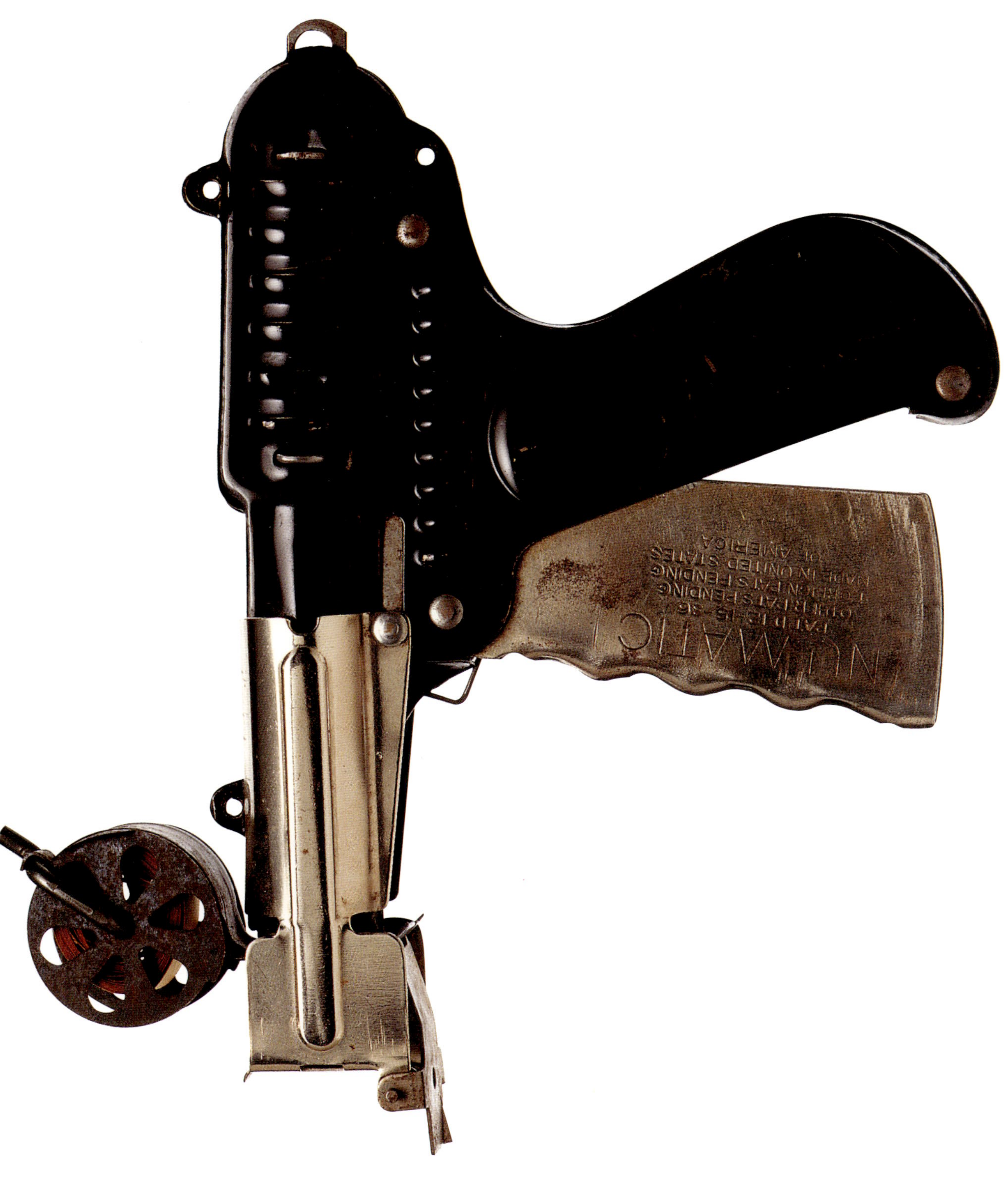

Flash Gordon Radio Repeater, lithographed tin, 4½ x 10 in., Louis Marx Co., U.S.A. mid 1930s

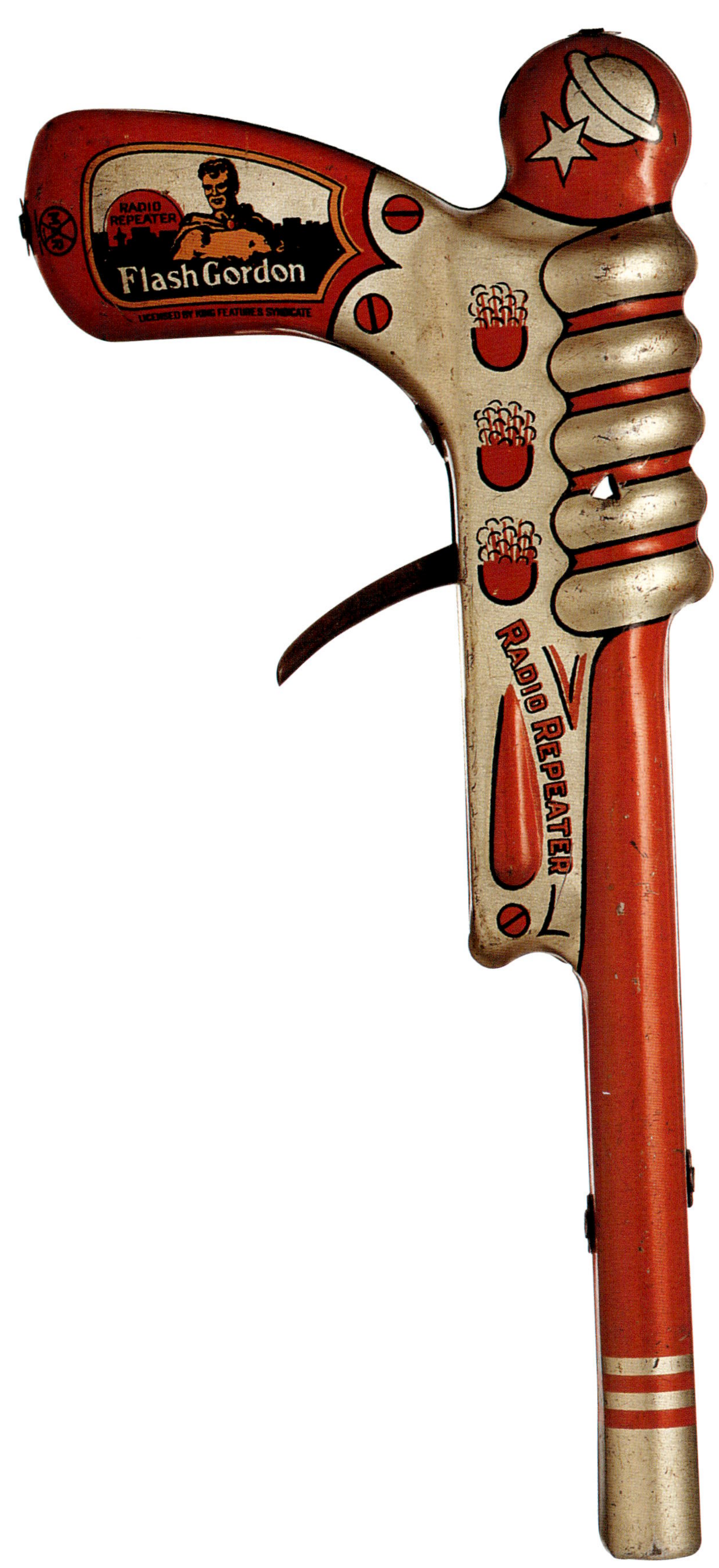

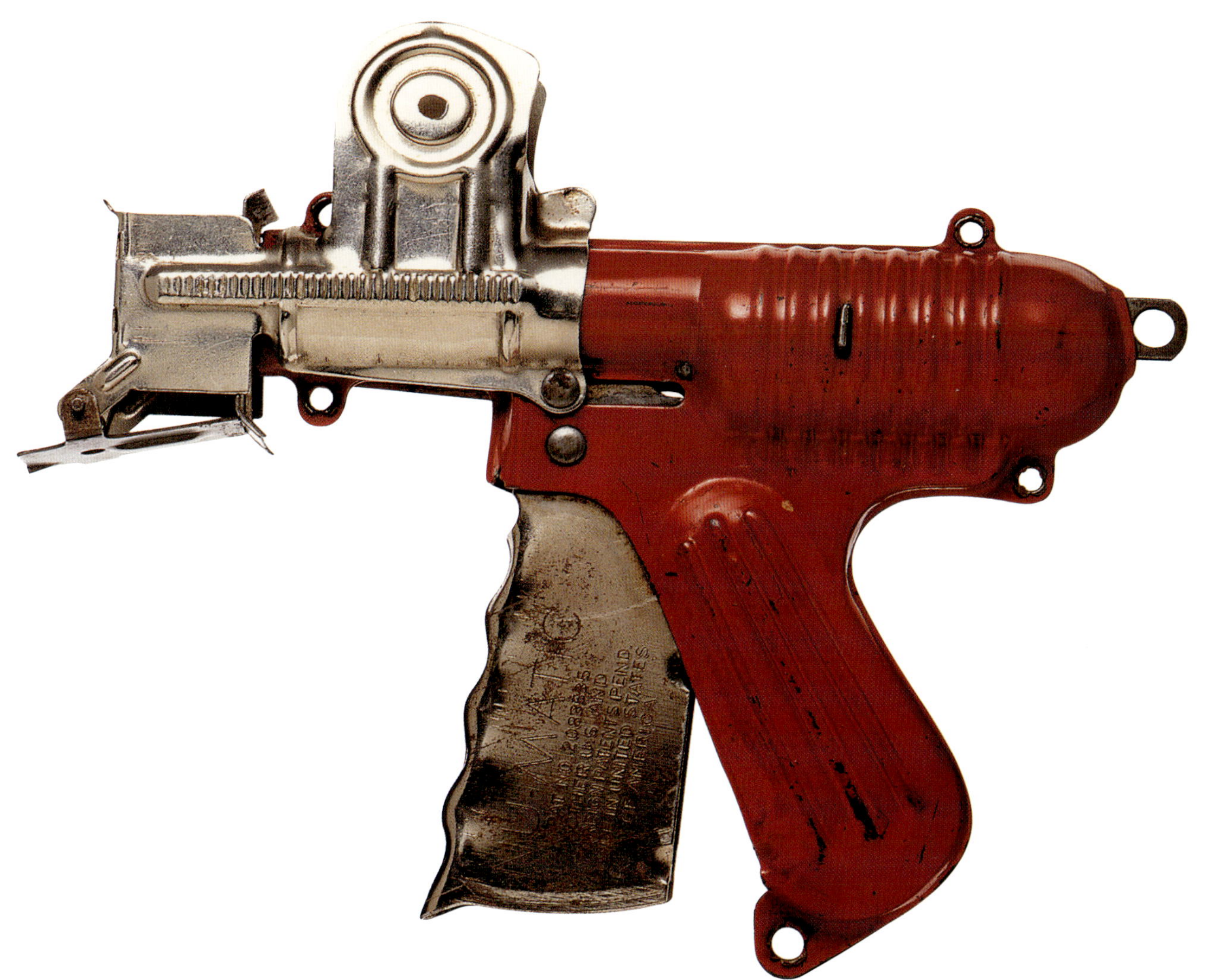

Nu-Matic Paper Popper, pressed steel, 6 x 6½ in., Langson Manufacturing Co., U.S.A. 1930s

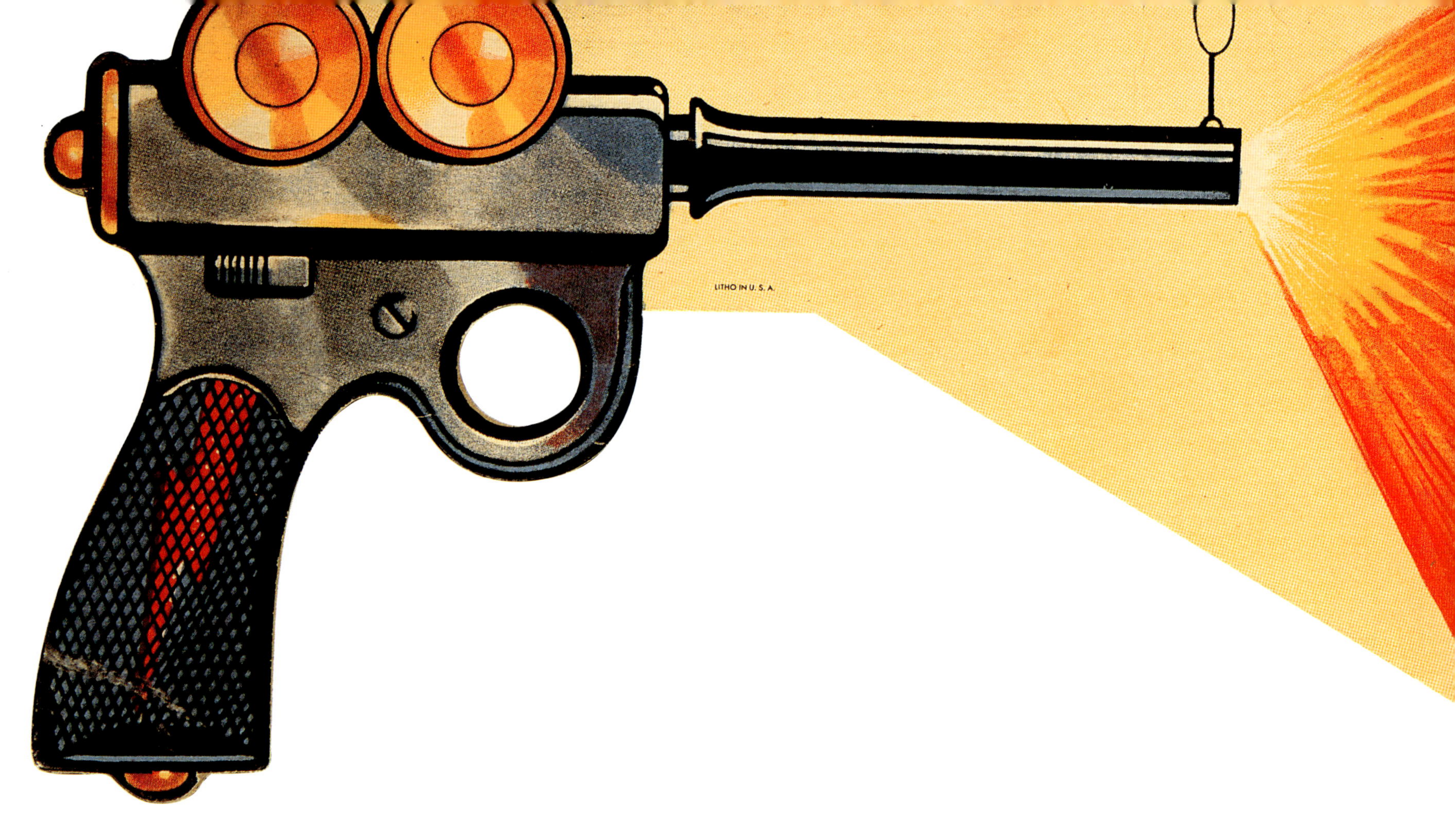

Buck Rogers Pop Gun, cardboard, 5½ x 9½ in., Cocomalt, U.S.A. 1933

Buck Rogers Liquid Helium Water Pistol, XZ-44, pressed steel, 5½ x 7¼ in., Daisy Manufacturing Co., U.S.A. 1936

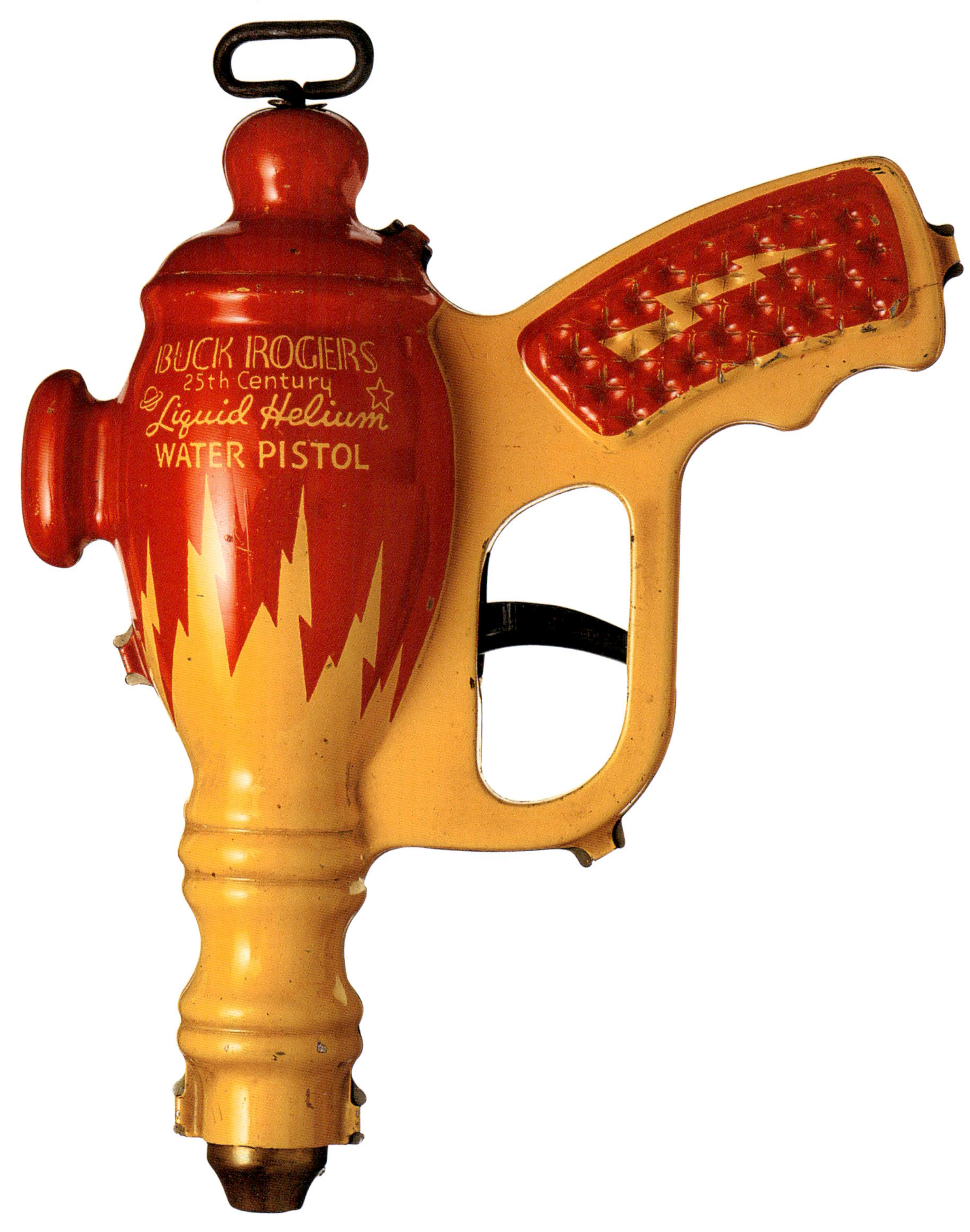

Buck Rogers Holster, 5¼ x 10 in., Daisy Manufacturing Co., U.S.A. 1936, with Disintegrator Pistol

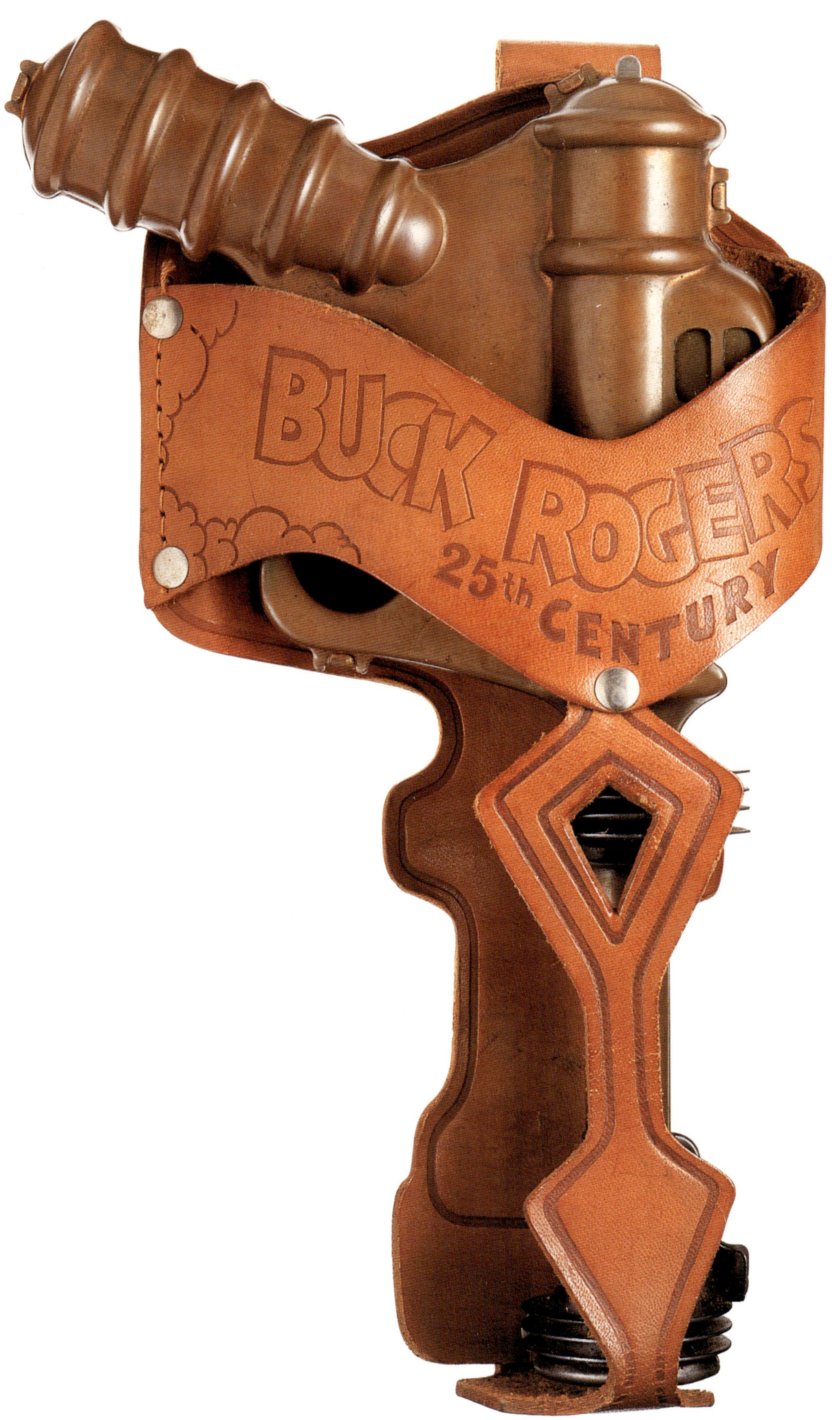

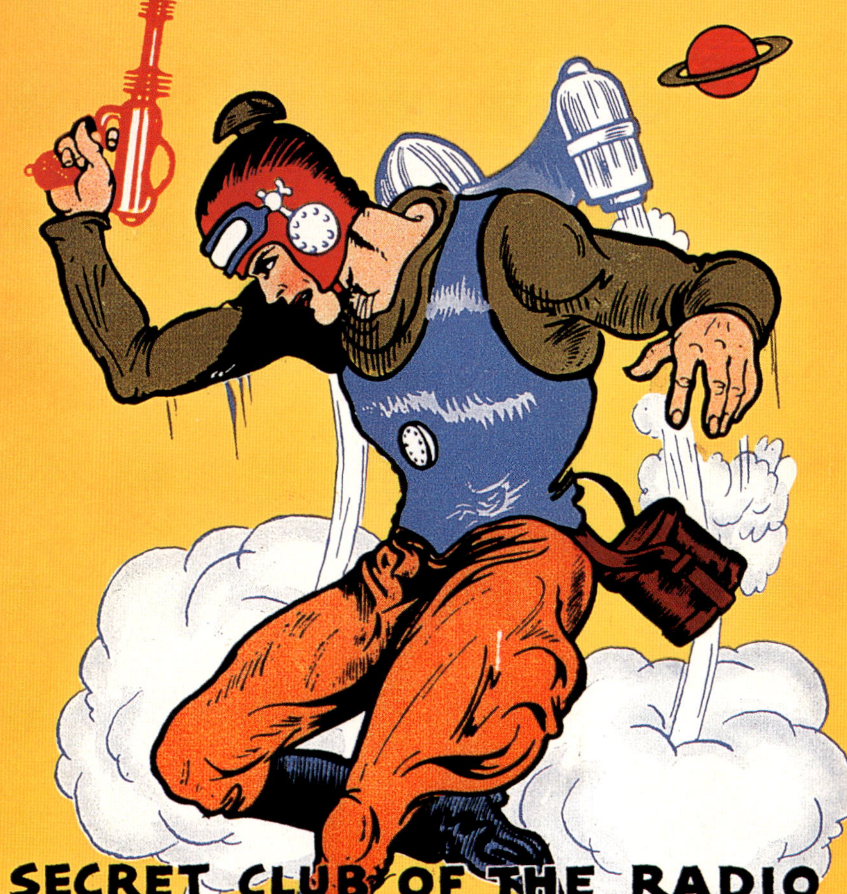

Buck Rogers "Solar Scouts" Radio Club, manual, 5 x 7½ in., Cream of Wheat, U.S.A. 1936

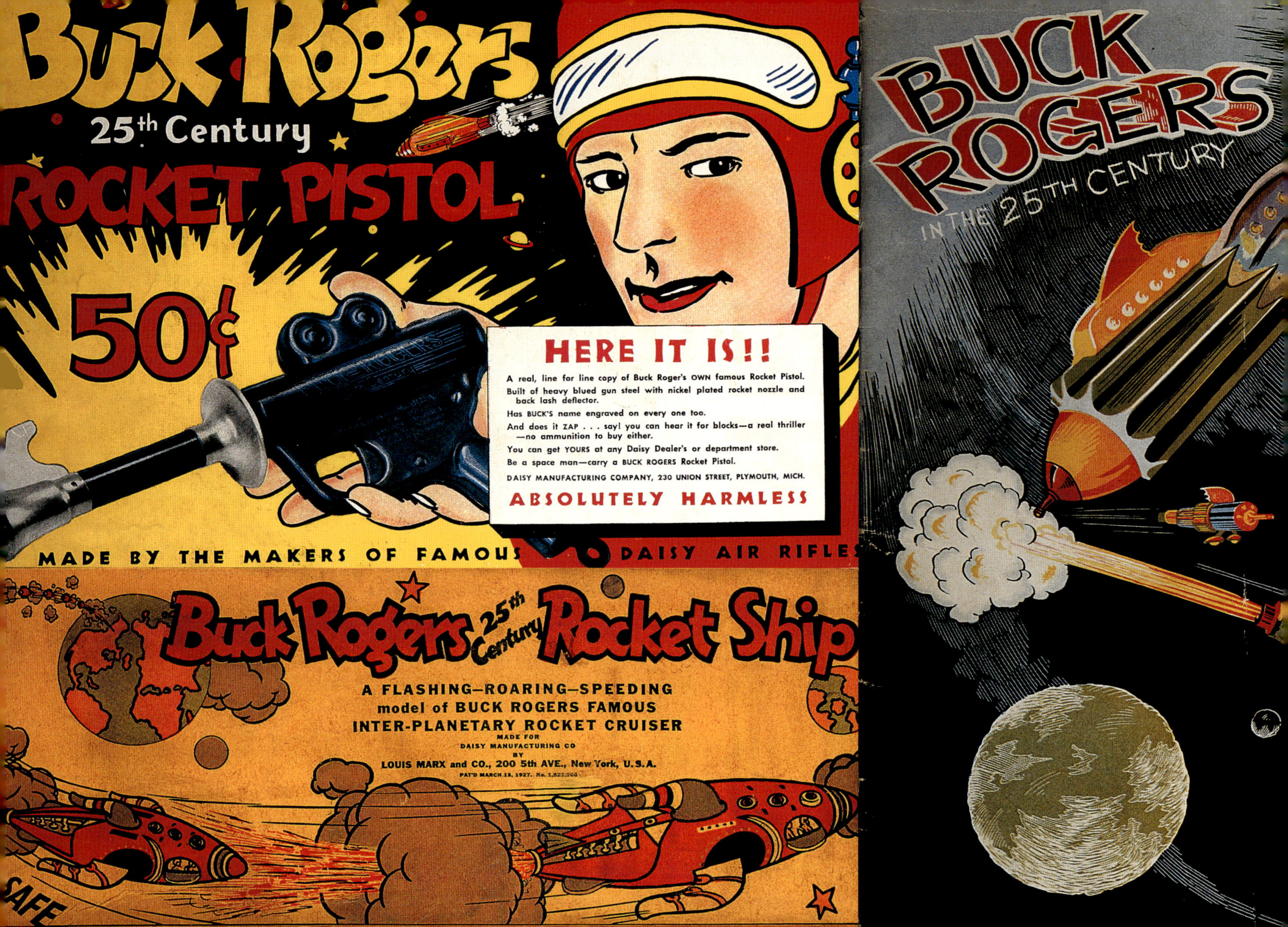

Buck Rogers
25th Century
ROCKET PISTOL
50¢
HERE IT IS!!
A real, line for line copy of Buck Roger's OWN famous Rocket Pistol.
Built of heavy blued gun steel with nickel plated rocket nozzle and back lash deflector.
Has BUCK'S name engraved on every one too.
And does it ZAP . . . say! you can hear it for blocks—a real thriller —no ammunition to buy either.
You can get YOURS at any Daisy Dealer's or department store.
Be a space man—carry a BUCK ROGERS Rocket Pistol.
DAISY MANUFACTURING COMPANY, 230 UNION STREET, PLYMOUTH, MICH.
ABSOLUTELY HARMLESS
MADE BY THE MAKERS OF FAMOUS DAISY AIR RIFLES
Buck Rogers 25th Century Rocket Ship
A FLASHING—ROARING—SPEEDING
model of BUCK ROGERS FAMOUS
INTER-PLANETARY ROCKET CRUISER
MADE FOR
DAISY MANUFACTURING CO
BY
LOUIS MARX and CO., 200 5th AVE., New York, U.S.A.
PAT'D MARCH 15, 1927.
SAFE
BUCK ROGERS
IN THE 25TH CENTURY

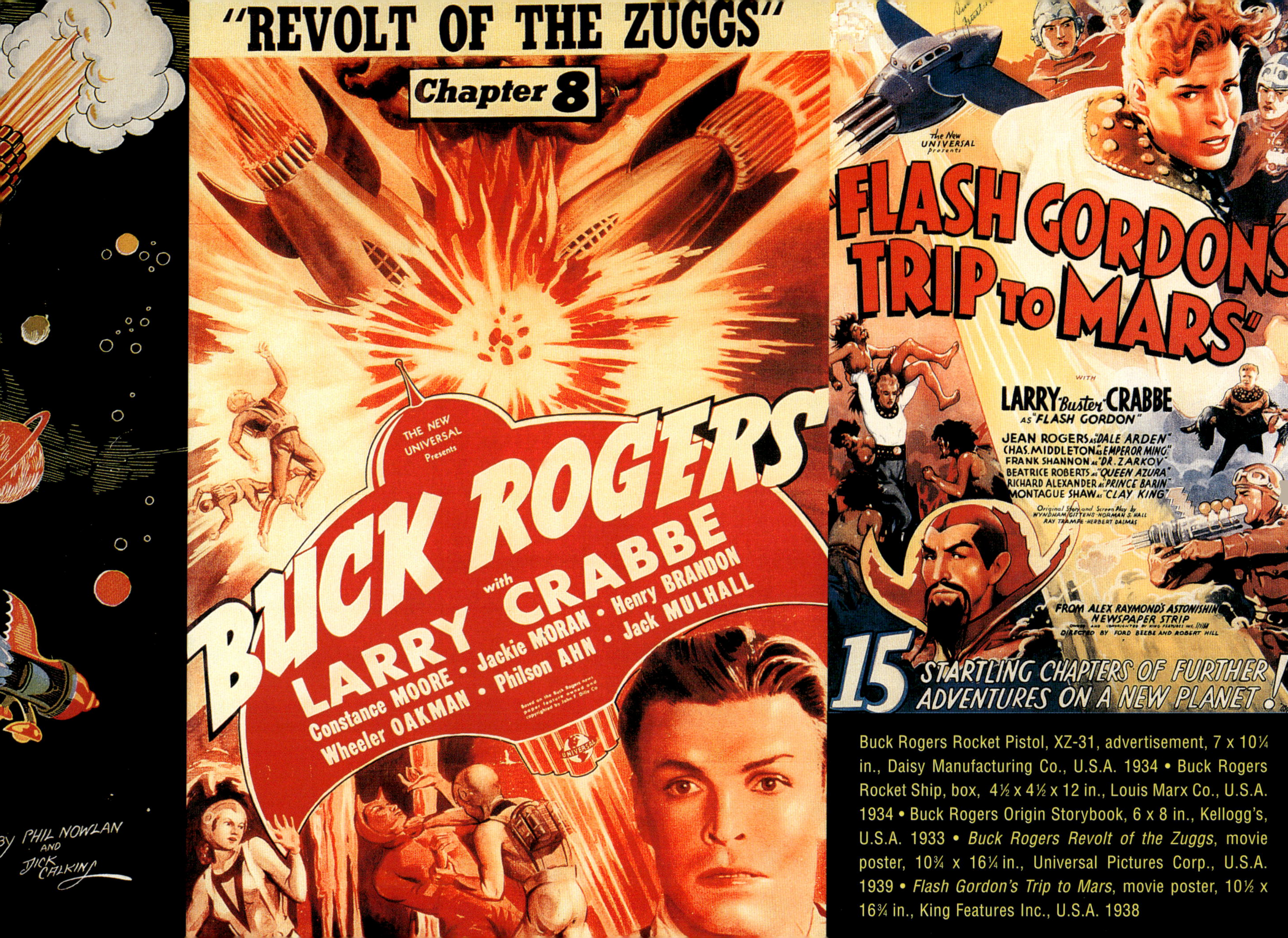

Buck Rogers Rocket Pistol, XZ-31, advertisement, 7 x 10¼ in., Daisy Manufacturing Co., U.S.A. 1934 • Buck Rogers Rocket Ship, box, 4½ x 4½ x 12 in., Louis Marx Co., U.S.A. 1934 • Buck Rogers Origin Storybook, 6 x 8 in., Kellogg's, U.S.A. 1933 • *Buck Rogers Revolt of the Zuggs*, movie poster, 10¾ x 16¼ in., Universal Pictures Corp., U.S.A. 1939 • *Flash Gordon's Trip to Mars*, movie poster, 10½ x 16¾ in., King Features Inc., U.S.A. 1938

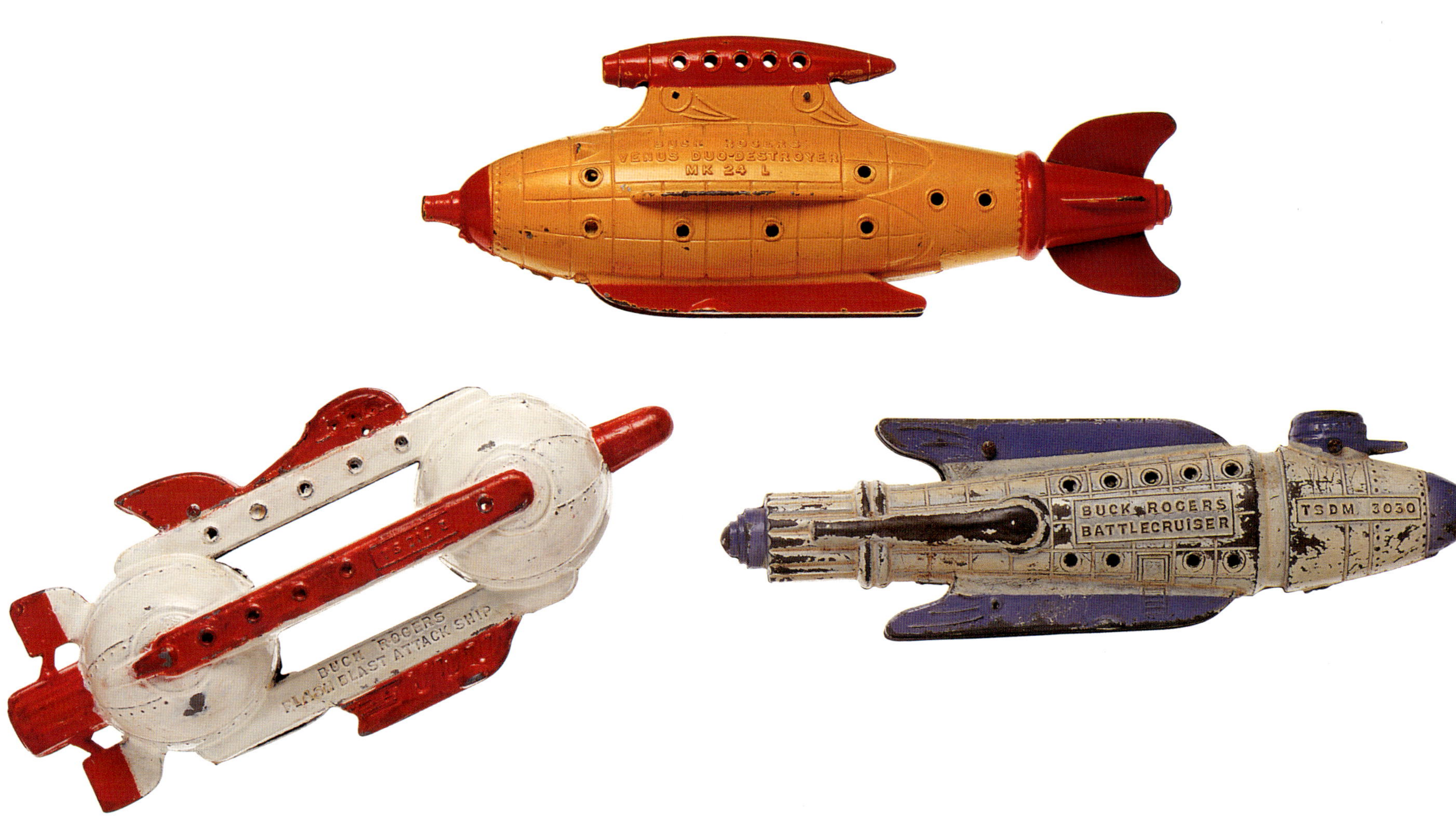

Buck Rogers Tootsie Toy Rocket Ships: Flash Blast Attack Ship (1¾ x 5 in.), Venus Duo-Destroyer (1½ x 4¾ in.), and Battle Cruiser (2 x 4½ in.), Dowst Manufacturing Co., U.S.A. 1937

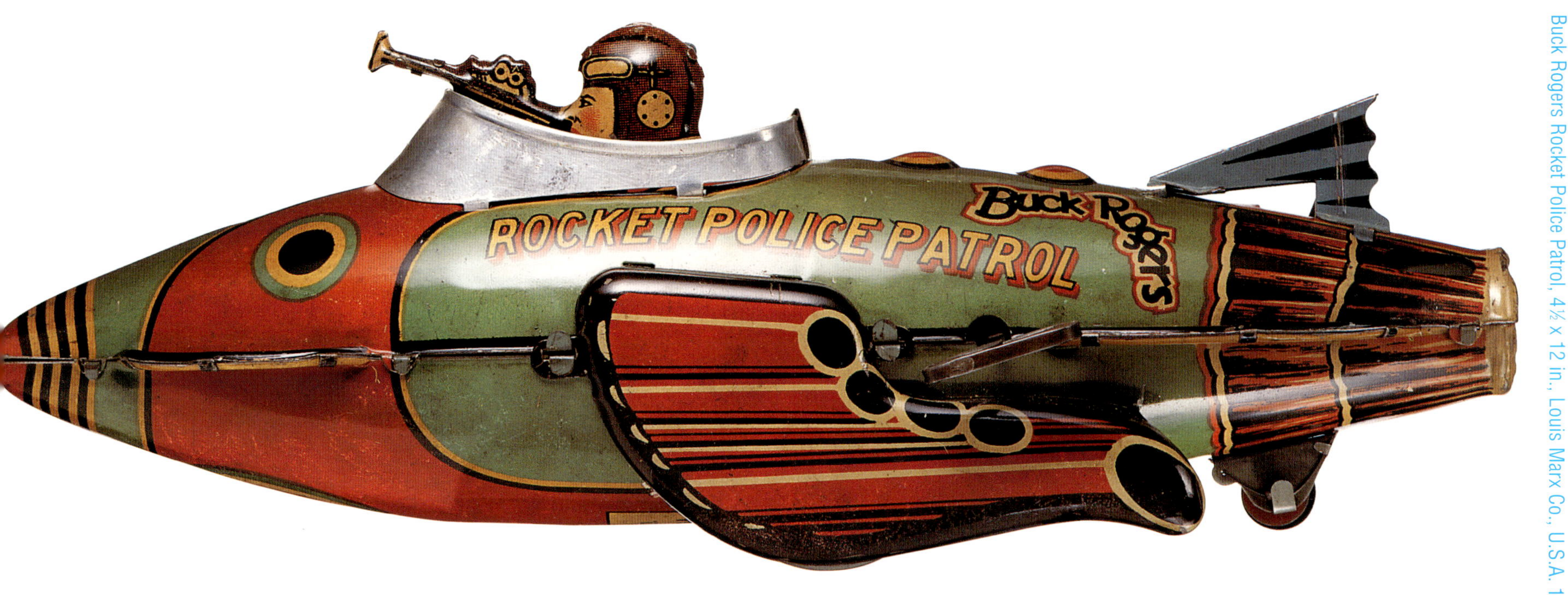

Buck Rogers Rocket Police Patrol, 4½ x 12 in., Louis Marx Co., U.S.A. 1939

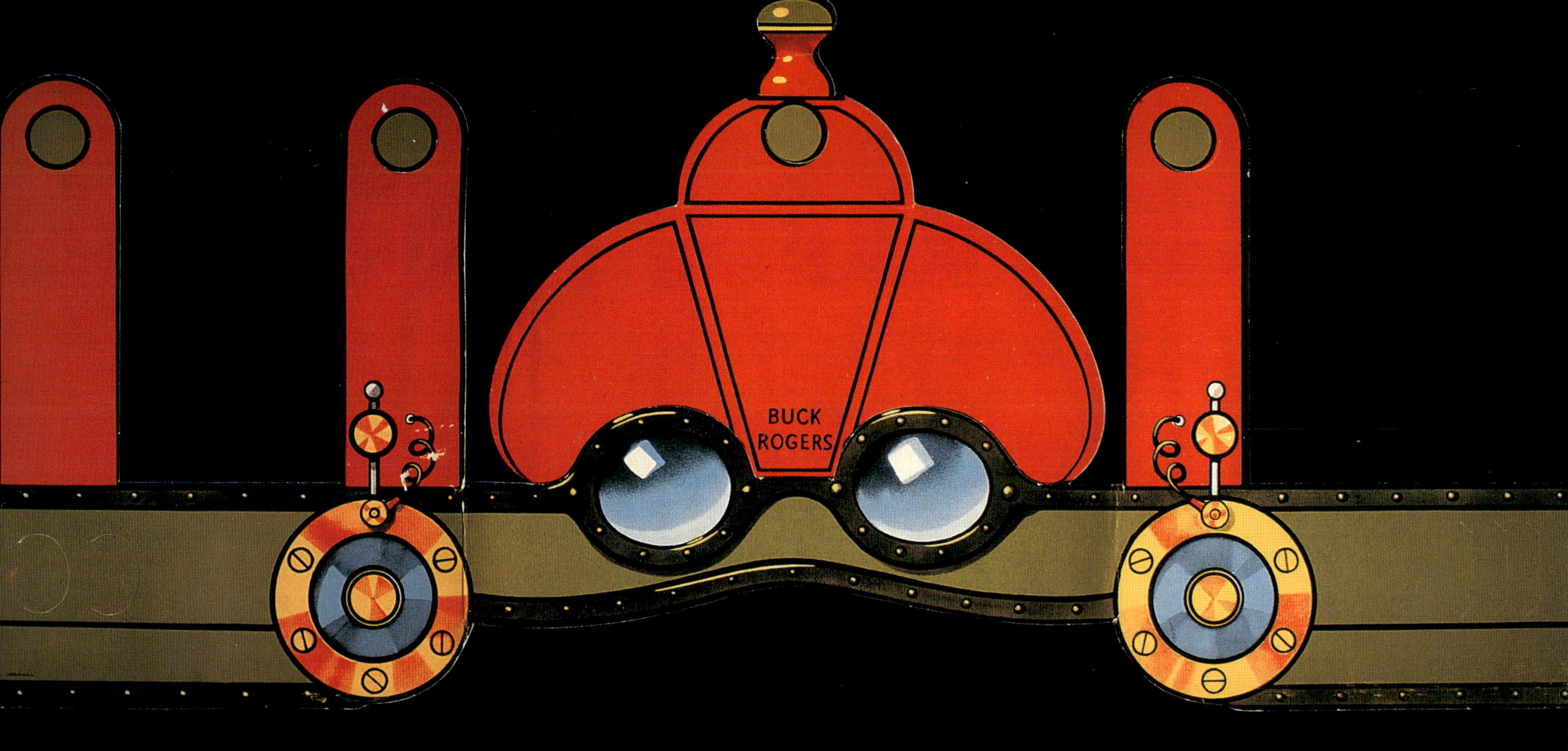

Buck Rogers Helmet, 11 x 24 in., Cocomalt, U.S.A. 1933

Buck Rogers Rocket Ship, 4½ x 12 in., Louis Marx Co., U.S.A. 1934

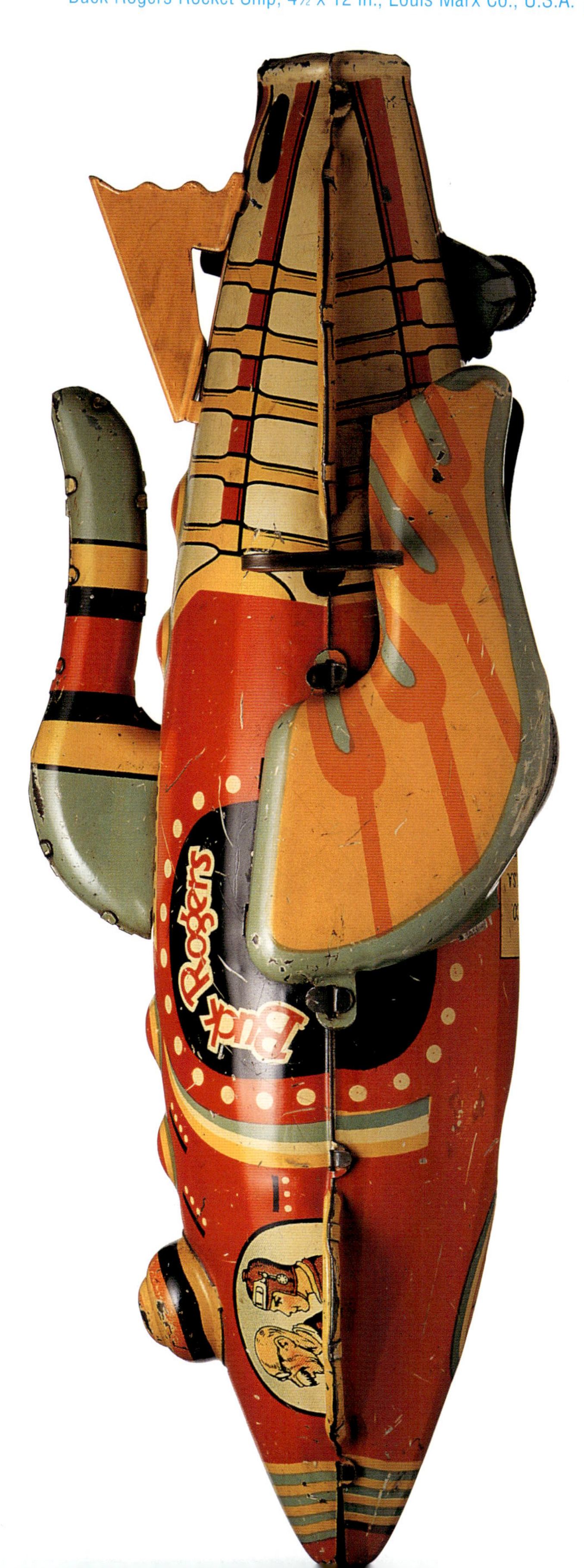

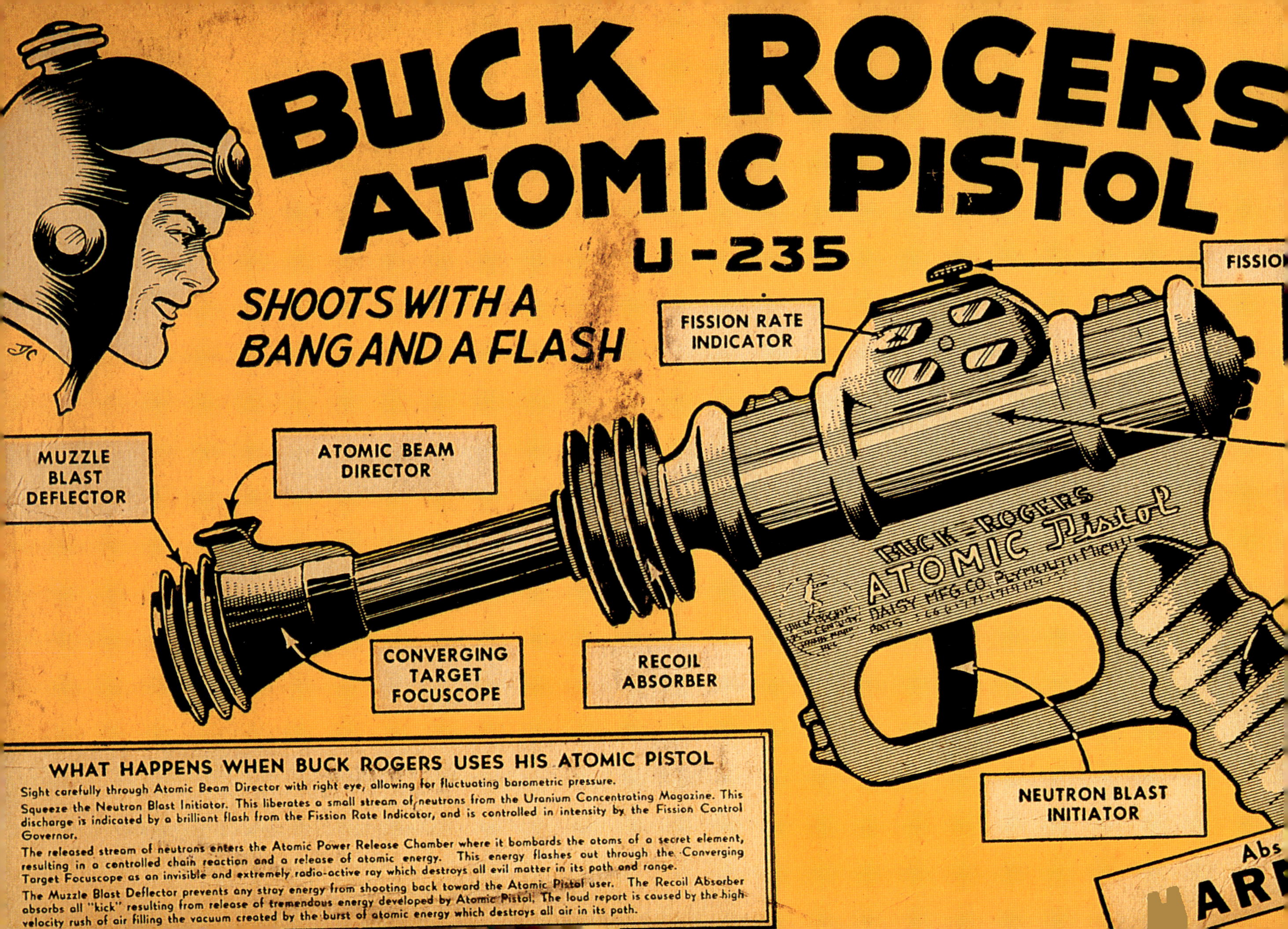
BUCK ROGERS
ATOMIC PISTOL
U-235
SHOOTS WITH A
BANG AND A FLASH
FISSION RATE
INDICATOR
MUZZLE
BLAST
DEFLECTOR
ATOMIC BEAM
DIRECTOR
BUCK-ROGERS
ATOMIC Pistol
DAISY MFG. CO.
CONVERGING
TARGET
FOCUSCOPE
RECOIL
ABSORBER
NEUTRON BLAST
INITIATOR
WHAT HAPPENS WHEN BUCK ROGERS USES HIS ATOMIC PISTOL
Sight carefully through Atomic Beam Director with right eye, allowing for fluctuating barometric pressure.
Squeeze the Neutron Blast Initiator. This liberates a small stream of neutrons from the Uranium Concentrating Magazine. This
discharge is indicated by a brilliant flash from the Fission Rate Indicator, and is controlled in intensity by the Fission Control
Governor.
The released stream of neutrons enters the Atomic Power Release Chamber where it bombards the atoms of a secret element,
resulting in a controlled chain reaction and a release of atomic energy. This energy flashes out through the Converging
Target Focuscope as an invisible and extremely radio-active ray which destroys all evil matter in its path and range.
The Muzzle Blast Deflector prevents any stray energy from shooting back toward the Atomic Pistol user. The Recoil Absorber
absorbs all "kick" resulting from release of tremendous energy developed by Atomic Pistol. The loud report is caused by the high
velocity rush of air filling the vacuum created by the burst of atomic energy which destroys all air in its path.

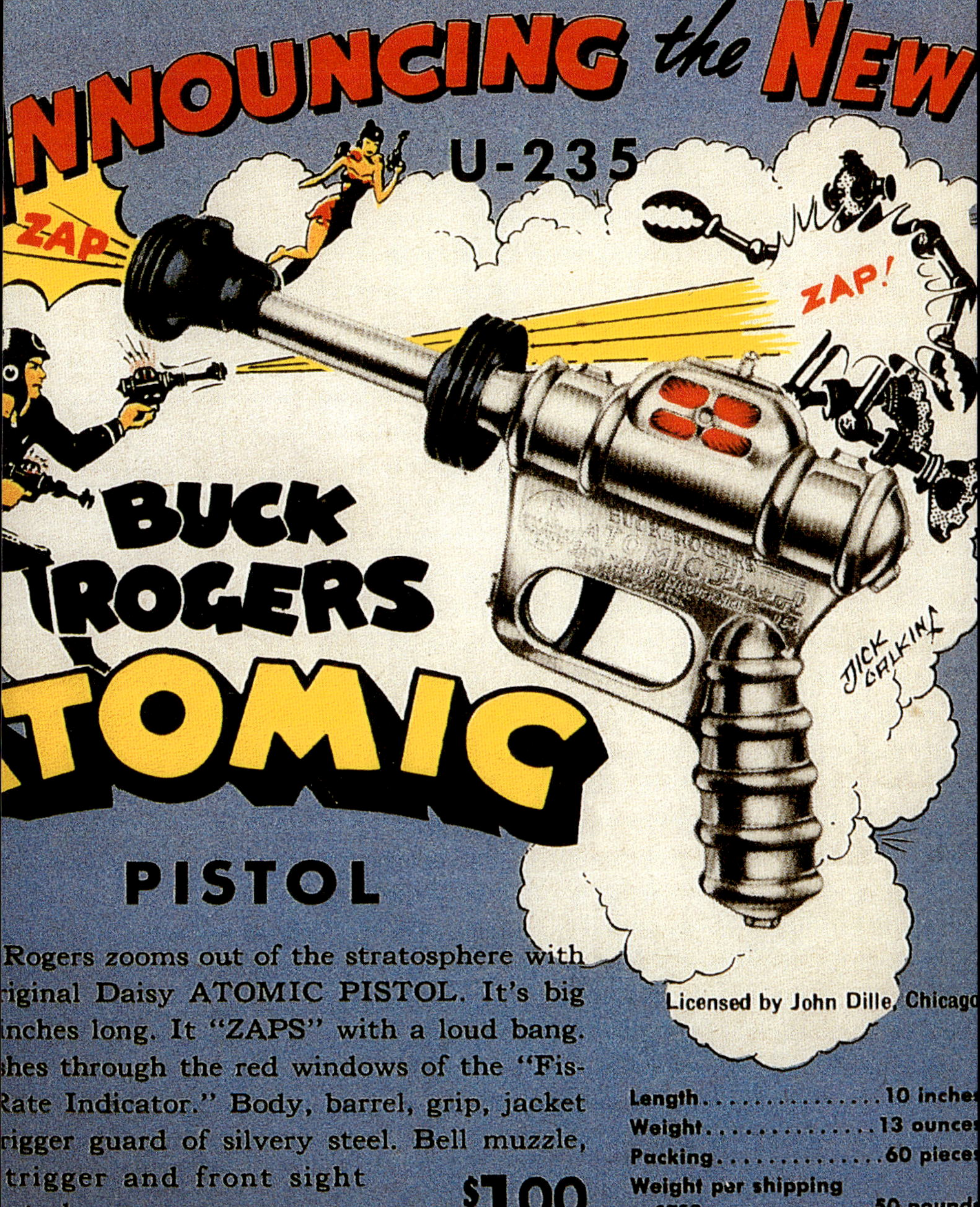

Buck Rogers Atomic Pistol, U-235, box (back panel), 1¾ x 6 x 9¾ in., Daisy Manufacturing Co., U.S.A. 1947 • Buck Rogers Atomic Pistol, U-235, advertisement, 7¾ x 9¼ in., Daisy Manufacturing Co., U.S.A. 1947

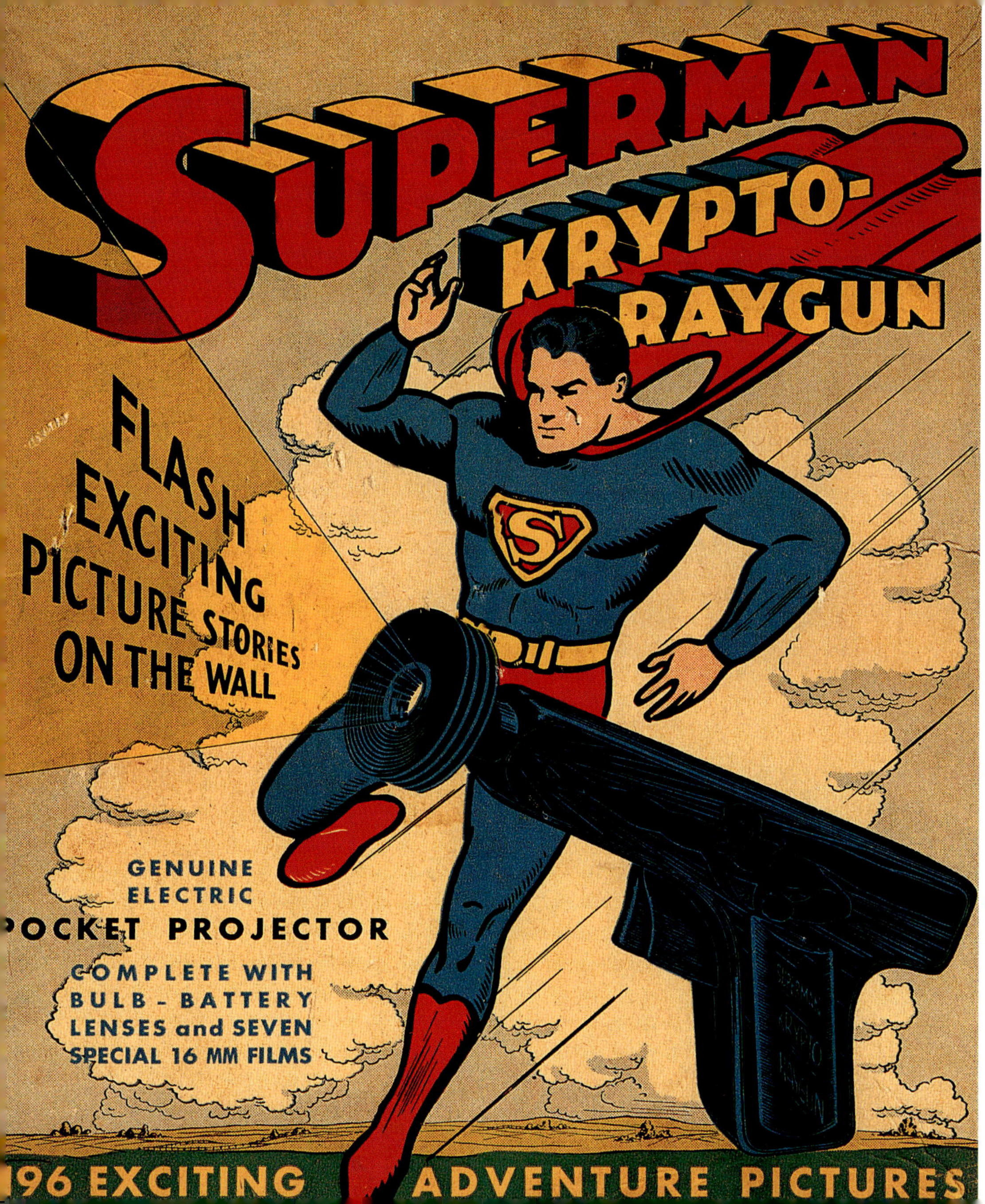

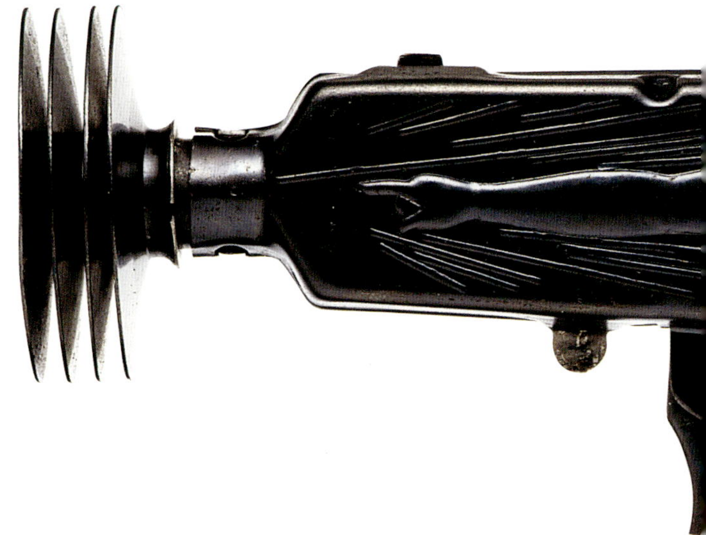

Superman Krypto-Ray Gun Projector Pistol, box, 1¾ x 8¼ x 10¼ in., Daisy Manufacturing Co., U.S.A. 1940

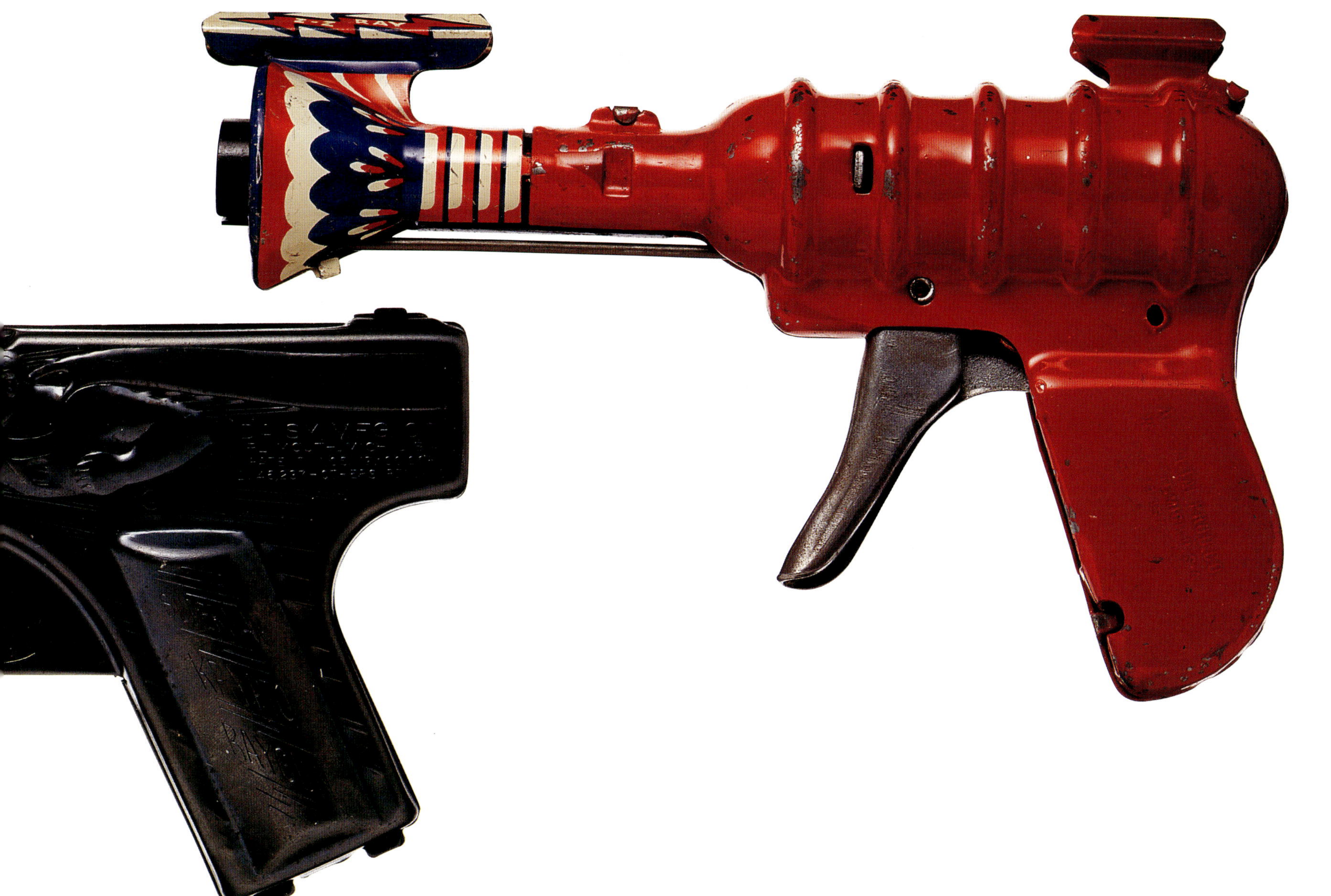

ZZ Pop Ray Gun, pressed steel, 4½ x 7 in., Wyandotte (All Metal Products) Co., U.S.A. early 1940s

Superman Krypto-Ray Gun Projector Pistol, pressed steel, 4 x 7 in., Daisy Manufacturing Co., U.S.A. 1940

Space Gun, die-cast metal with rubber bulb handle, 3 x 7½ in., maker unknown, U.S.A. late 1940s

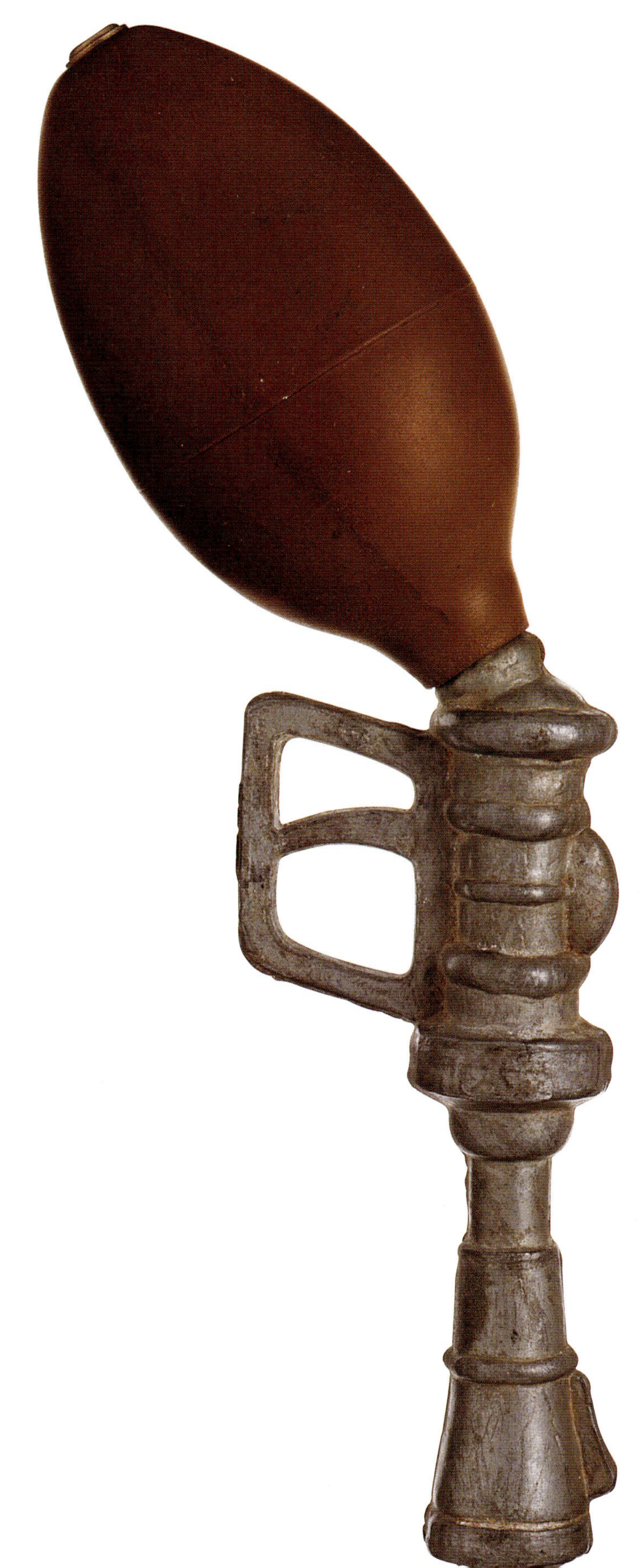

Atom Bubble and Water Gun, die-cast metal, 3½ x 7¼ in., Flyrite Products Inc., U.S.A. late 1940s

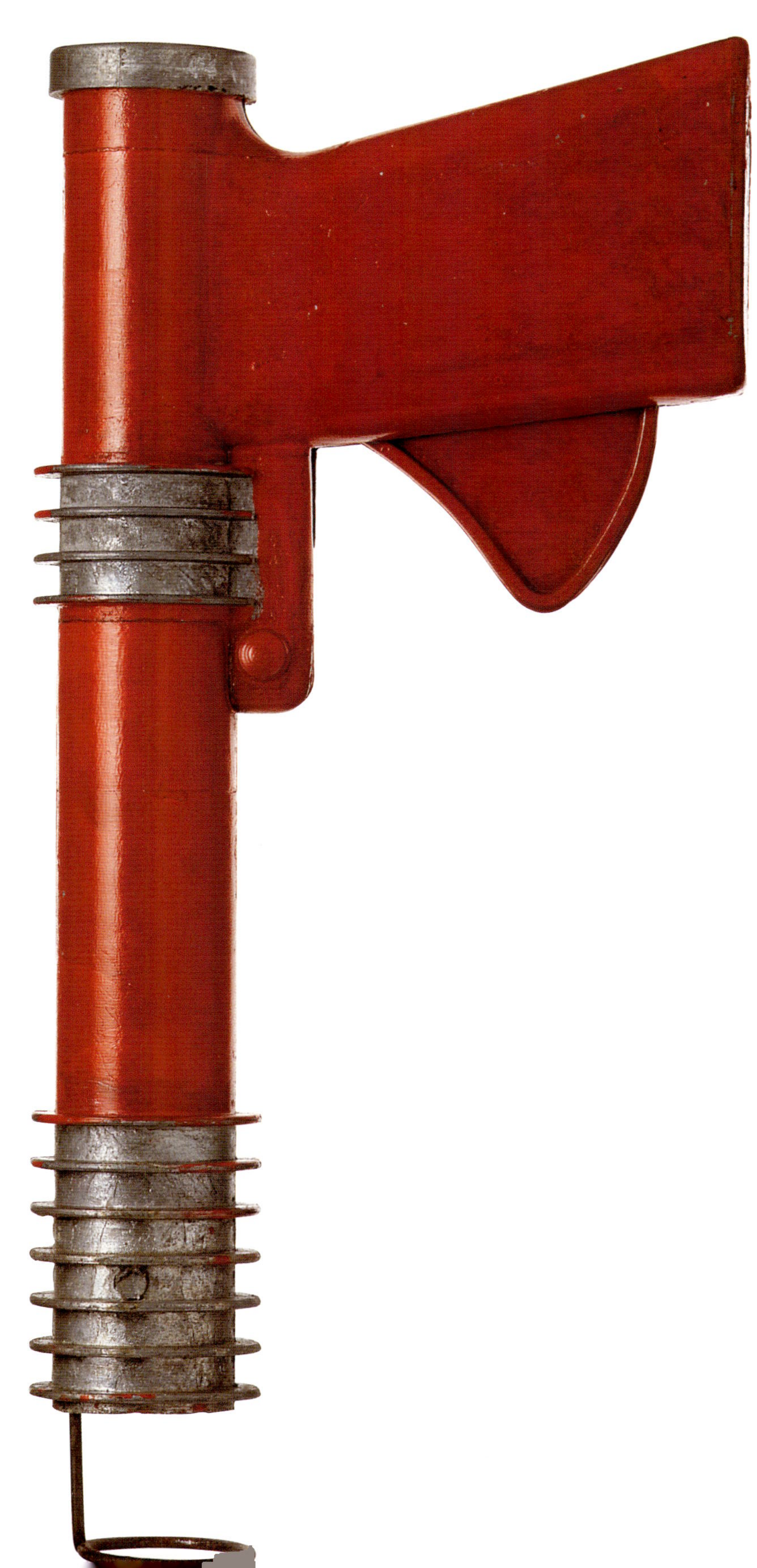

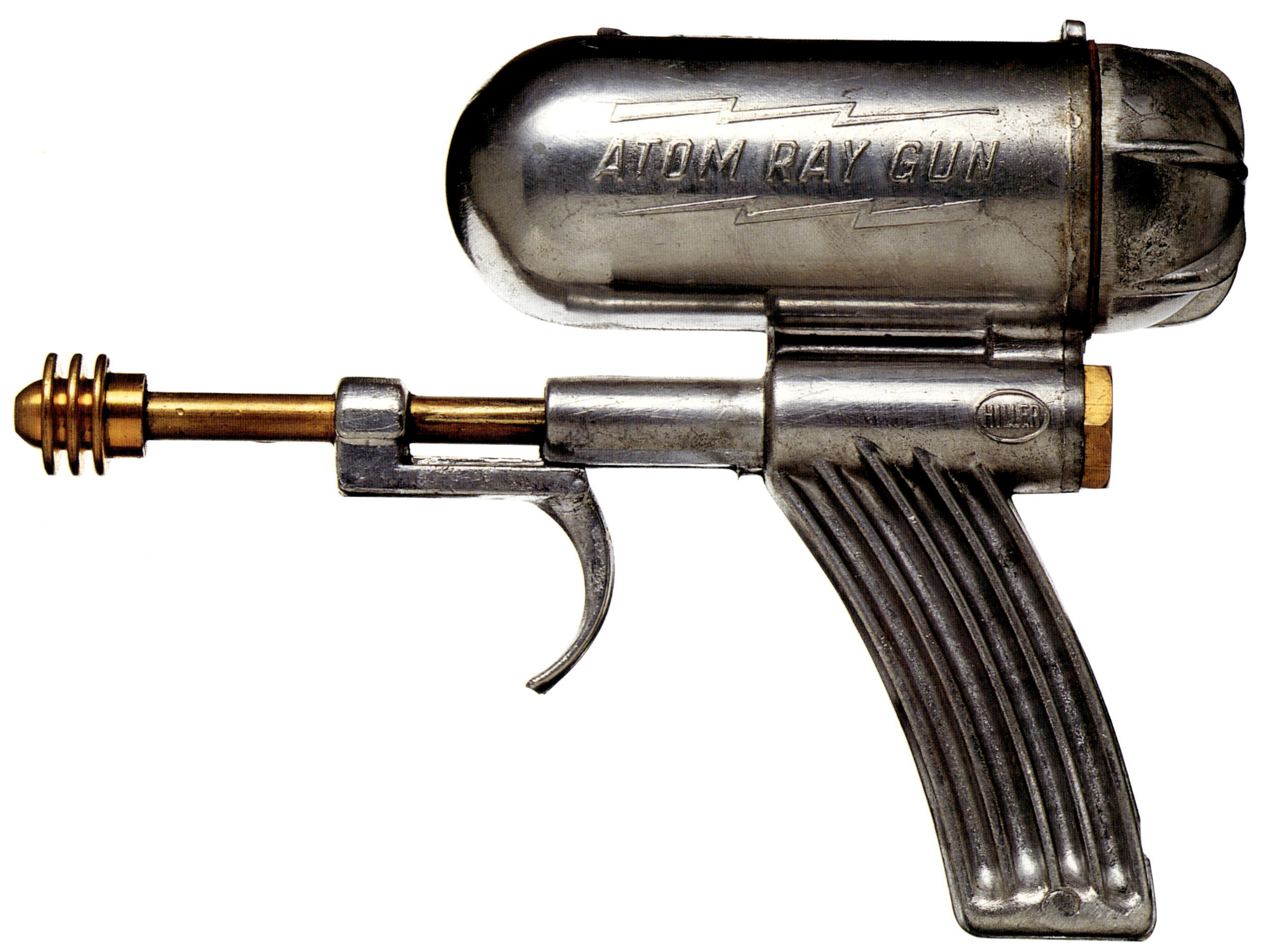
ATOM RAY GUN
HILLER

Spinray Blast Pistol, cast aluminum with tin propeller, 4¾ x 6½ in., Armstrong and Brewer, U.S.A. late 1940s

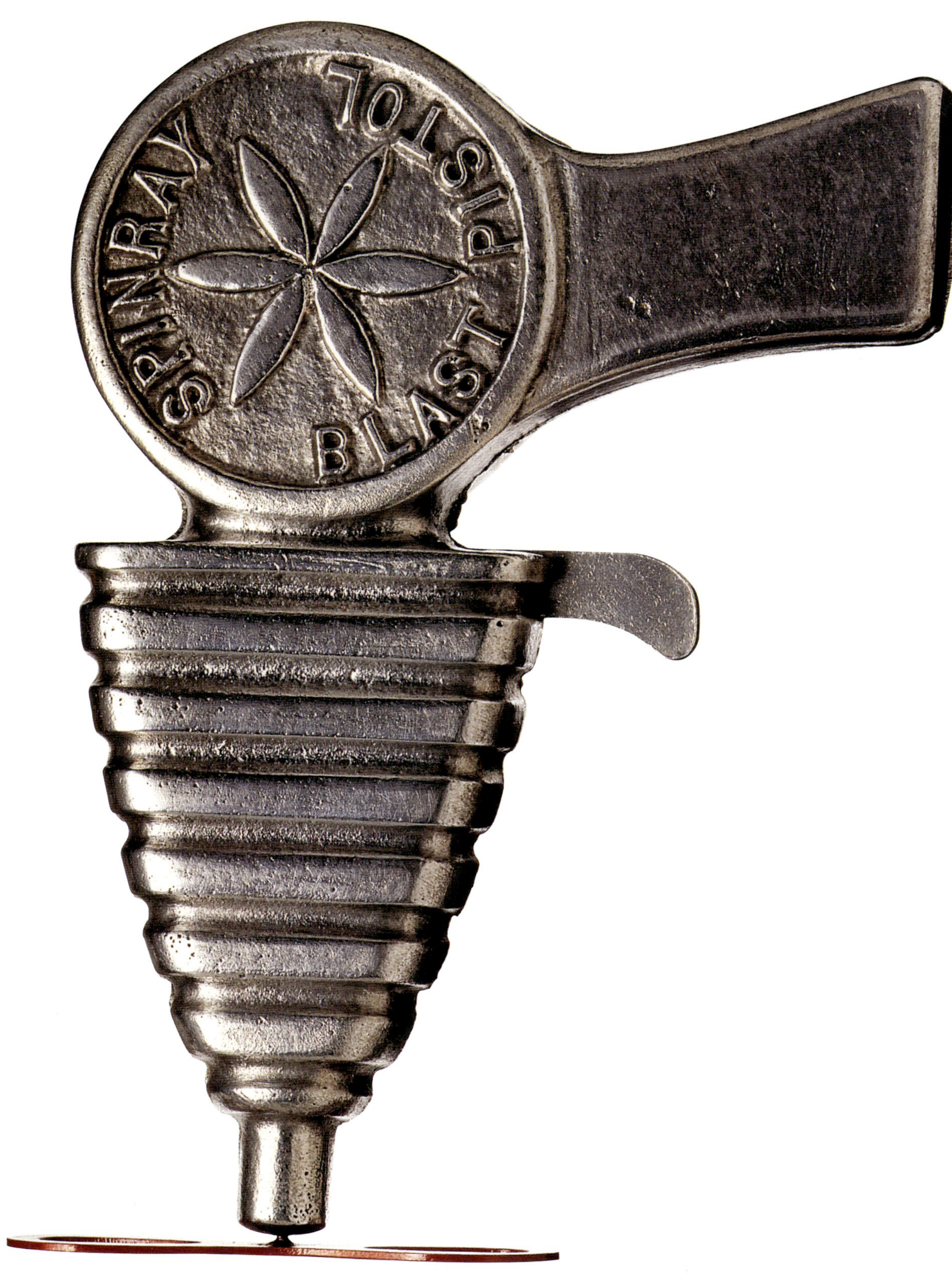

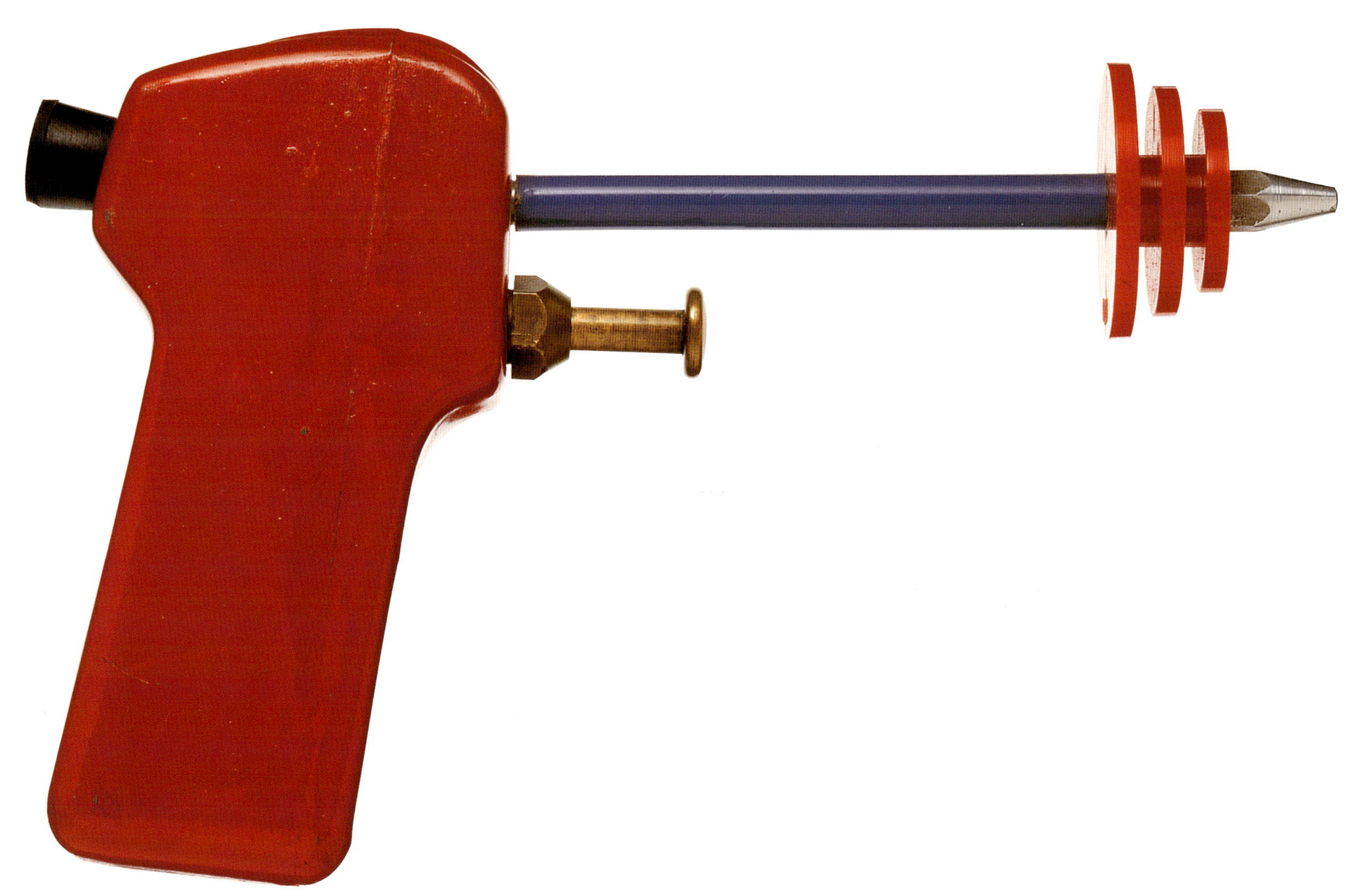

Atom-Matic Water Rocket Gun, cast aluminum, brass, and plastic, 4½ x 7 in., The Playcraft Co., U.S.A. late 1940s

Prototype Model #1022, plastic, 6 x 10 in., Louis Marx Co., Erie Factory, U.S.A. 1949

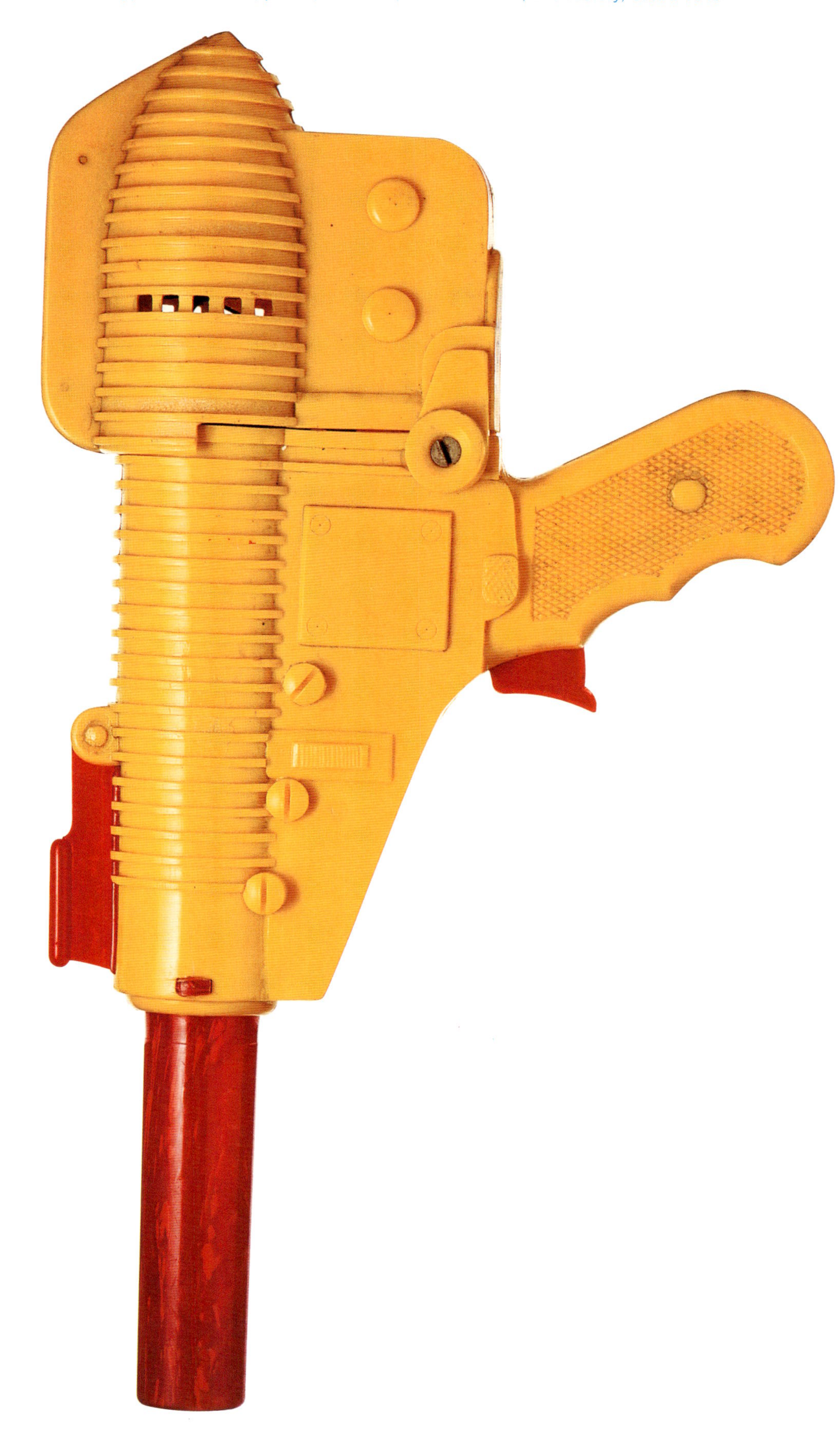

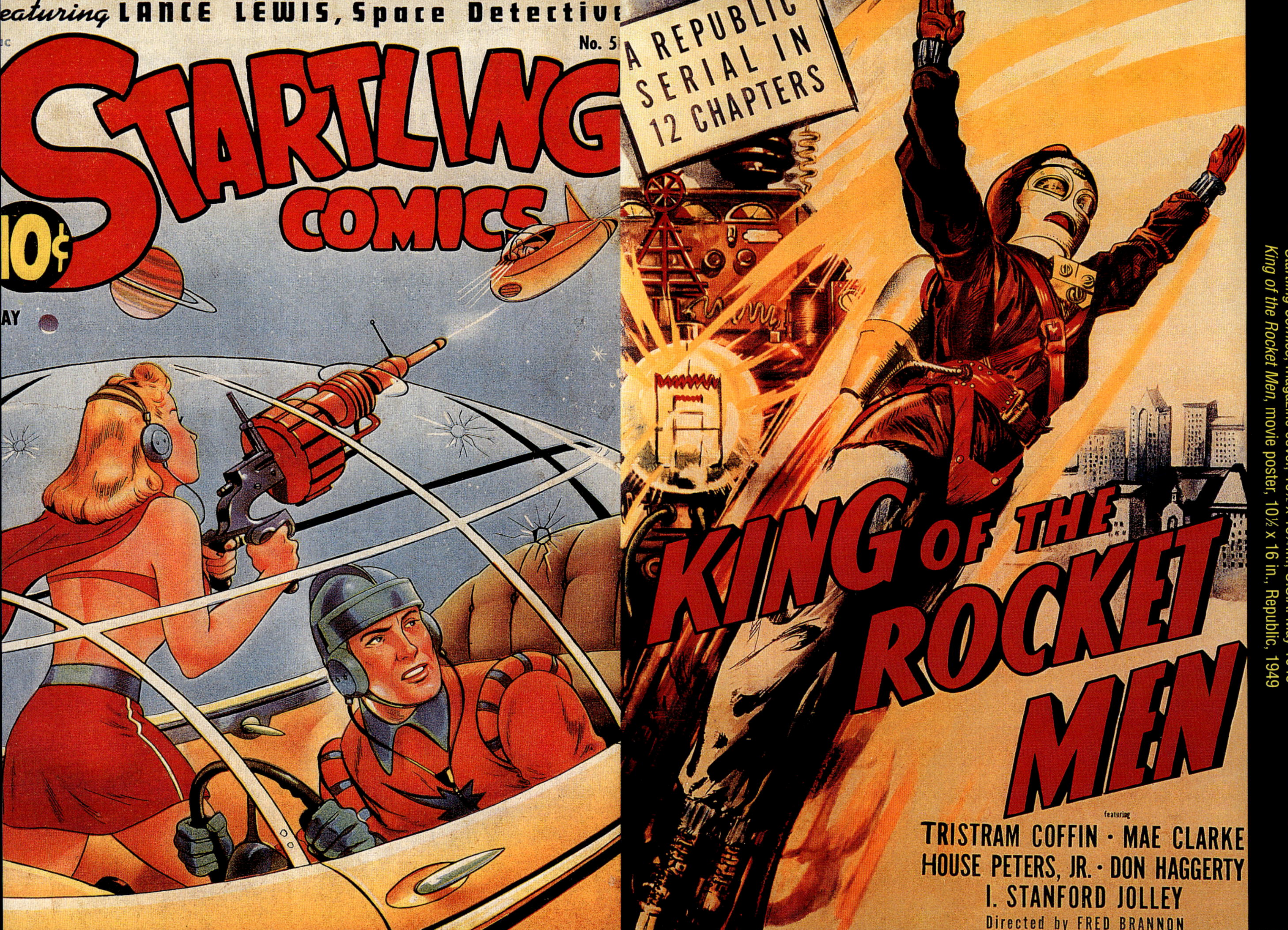

King of the Rocket Men, movie poster, 10½ x 16 in., Republic, 1949

Buck Rogers, badges and buttons (diameters from ¾ to 2¼ in.), U.S.A. 1930s through 1950s

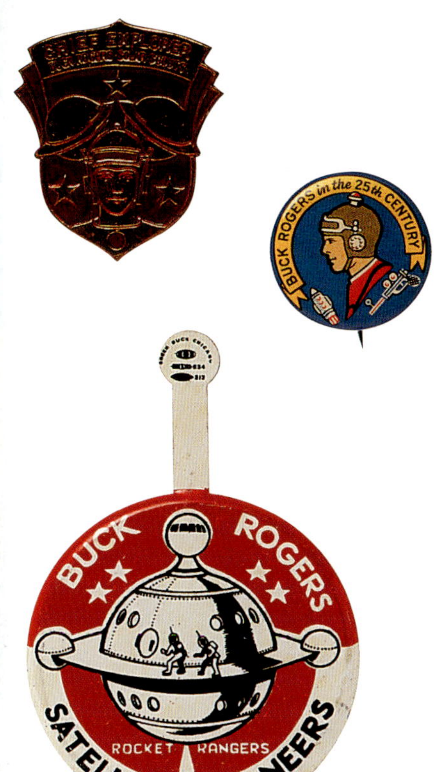

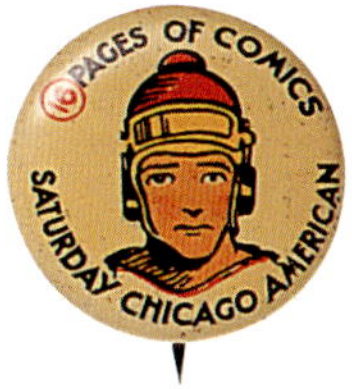

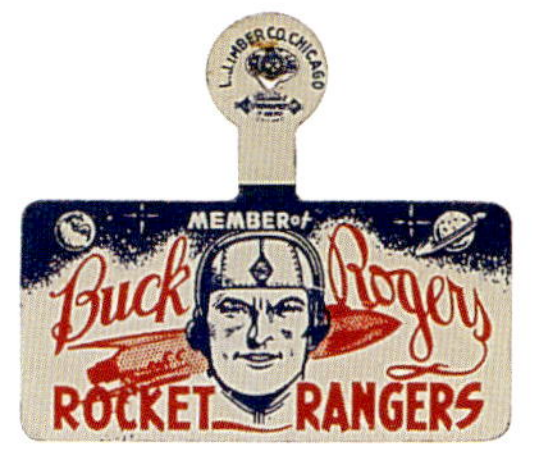

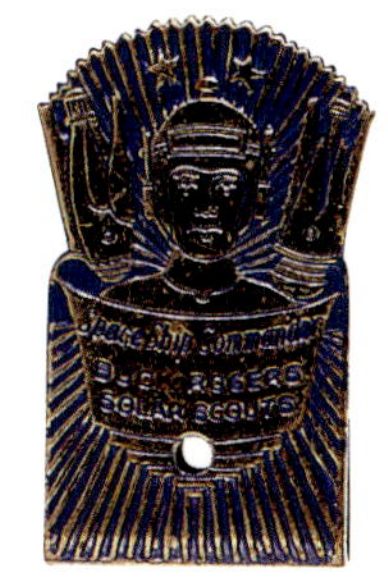

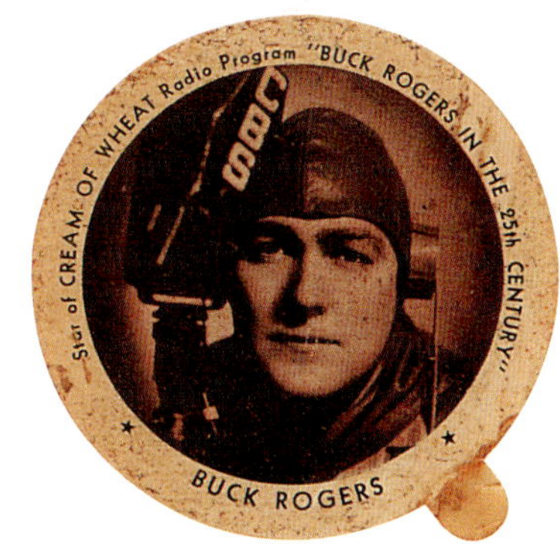

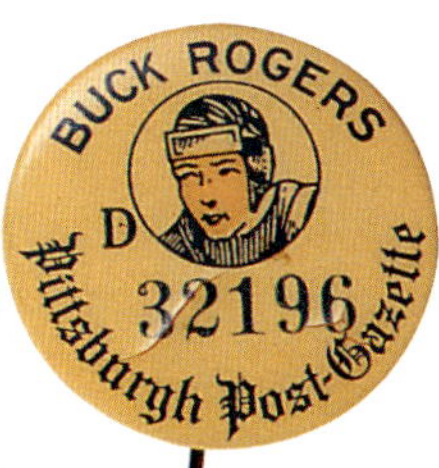

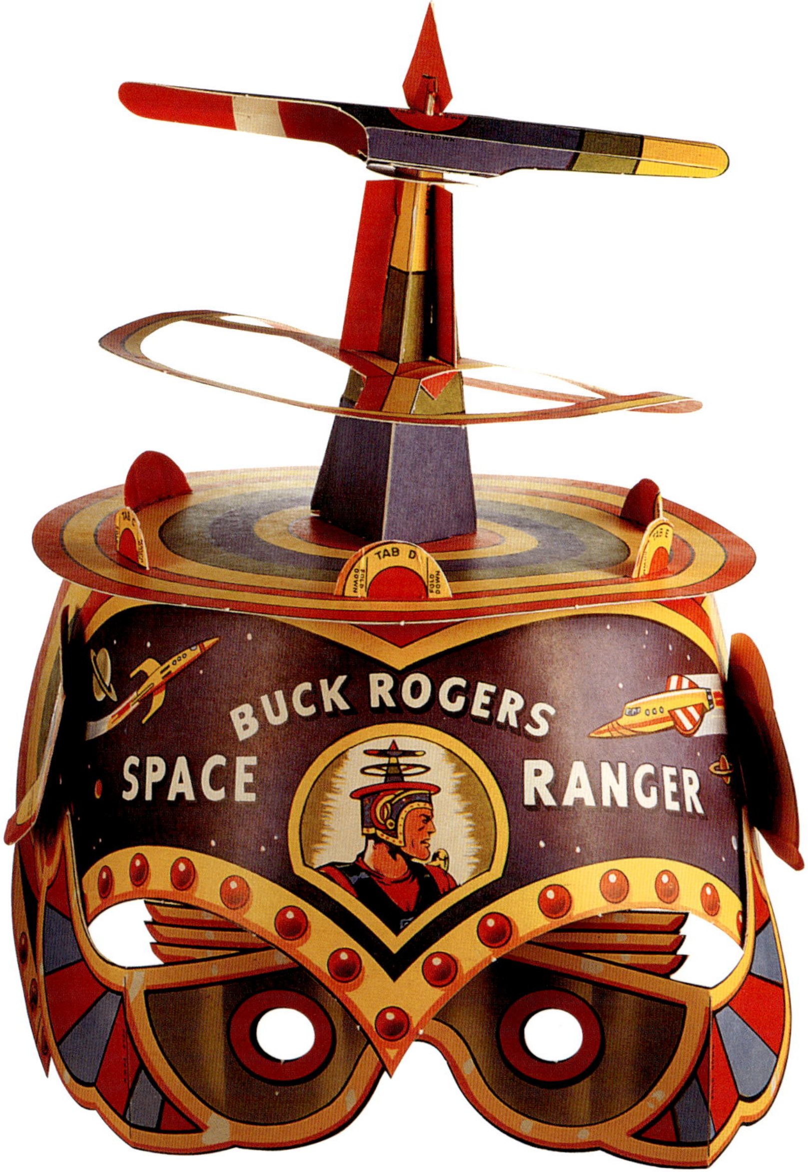

Buck Rogers Space Ranger Helmet, circumference 7½ x 11 in., Sylvania Electric Products, U.S.A. 1952

Buck Rogers Space Ranger Gun, cardboard, 5 x 8 in., Sylvania Electric Products, U.S.A. 1952

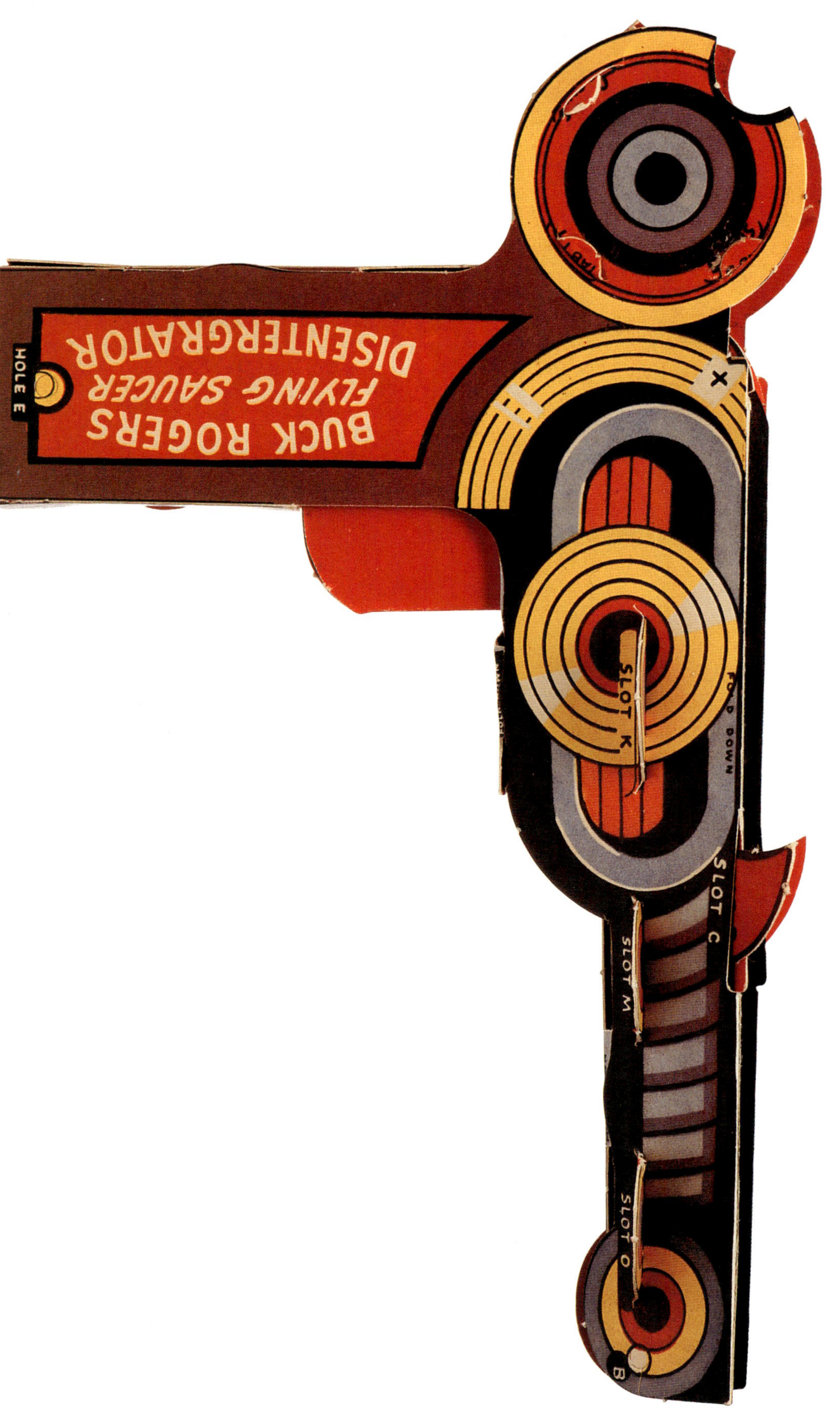

Buck Rogers Super Sonic Ray Gun, plastic, 4¾ x 7¾ in., Norton-Honer Mfg. Co., U.S.A. late 1950s

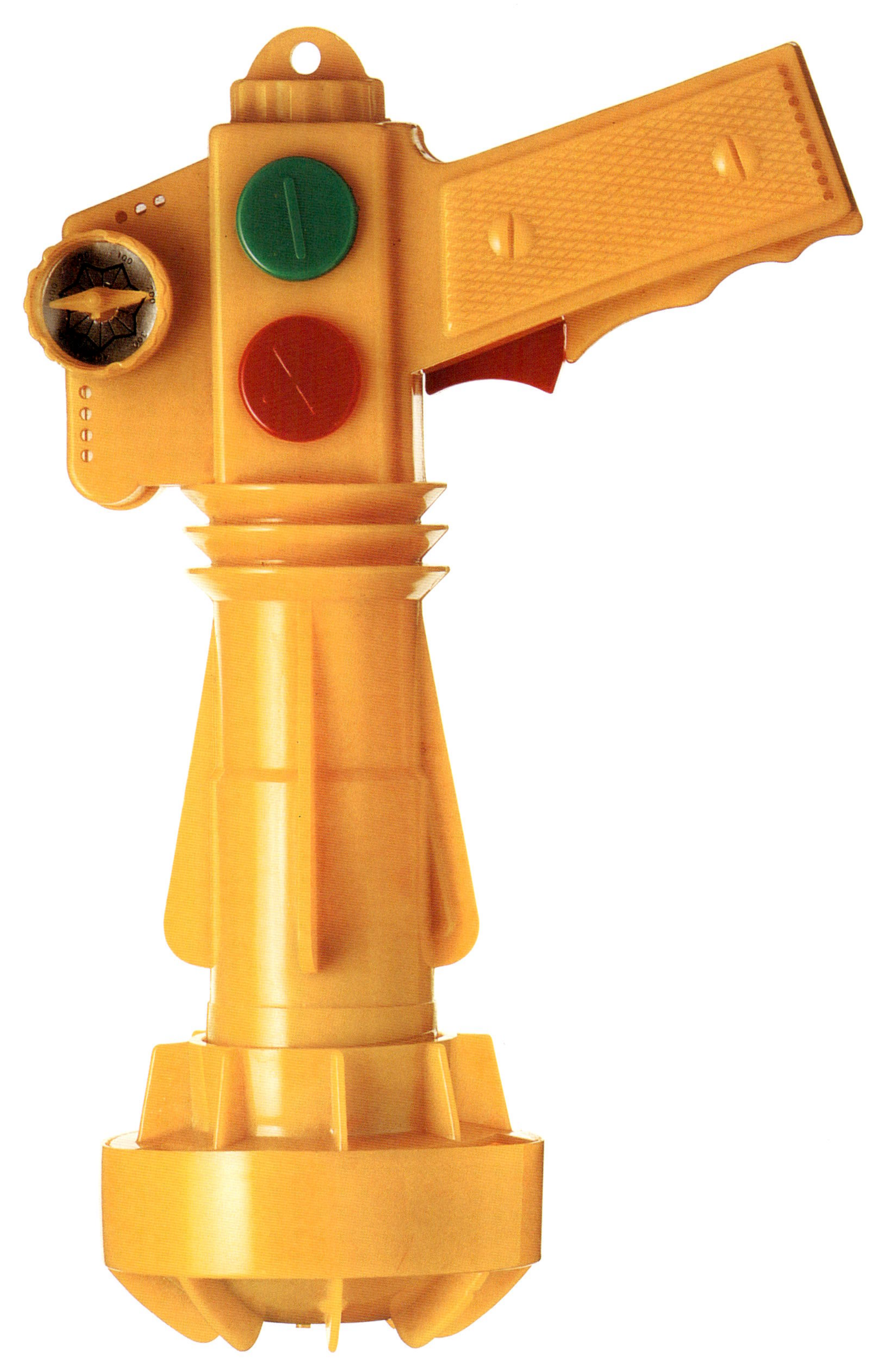

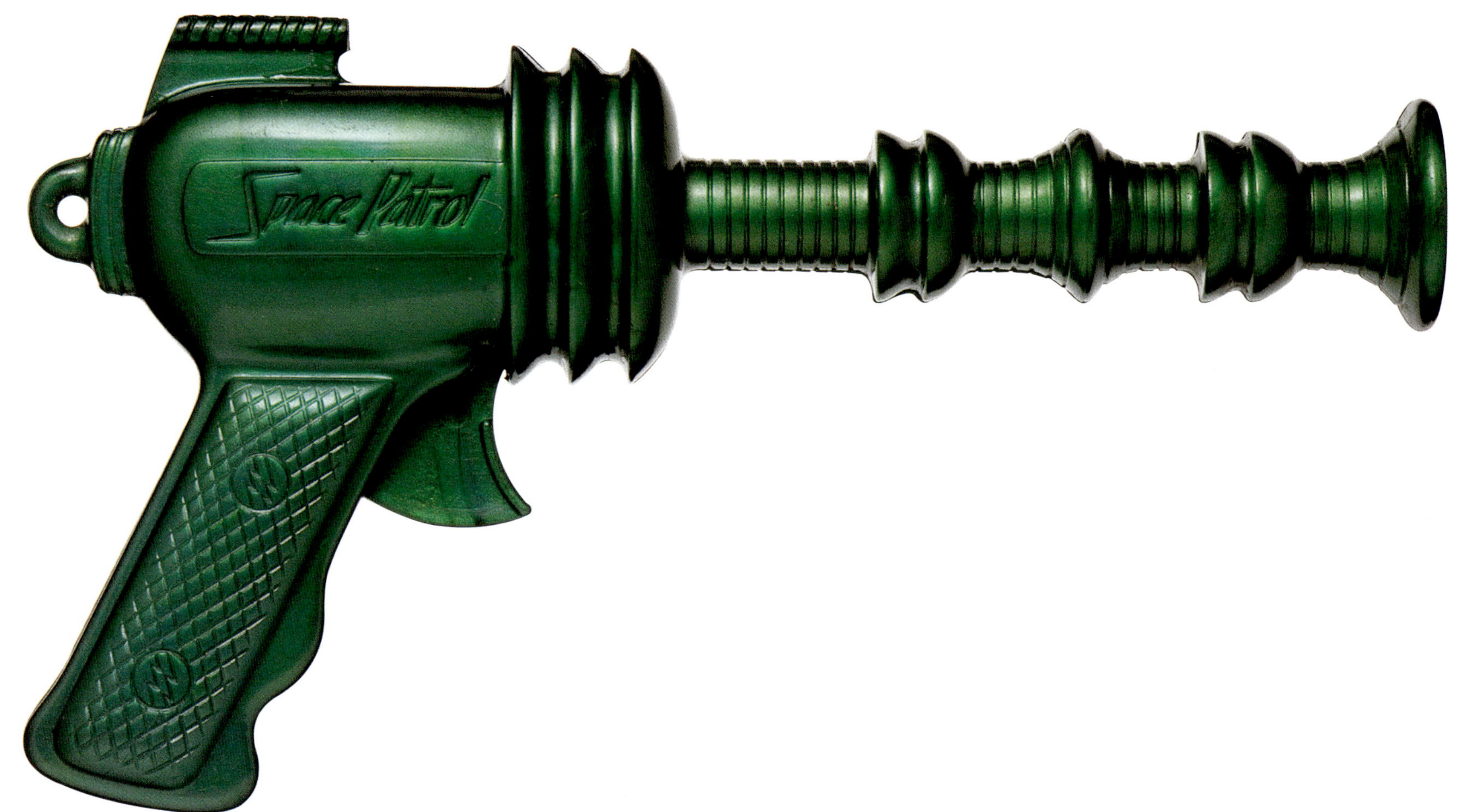

Space Patrol Smoke Gun, plastic, 3½ x 6 in., U.S. Plastics Corp., U.S.A. mid 1950s

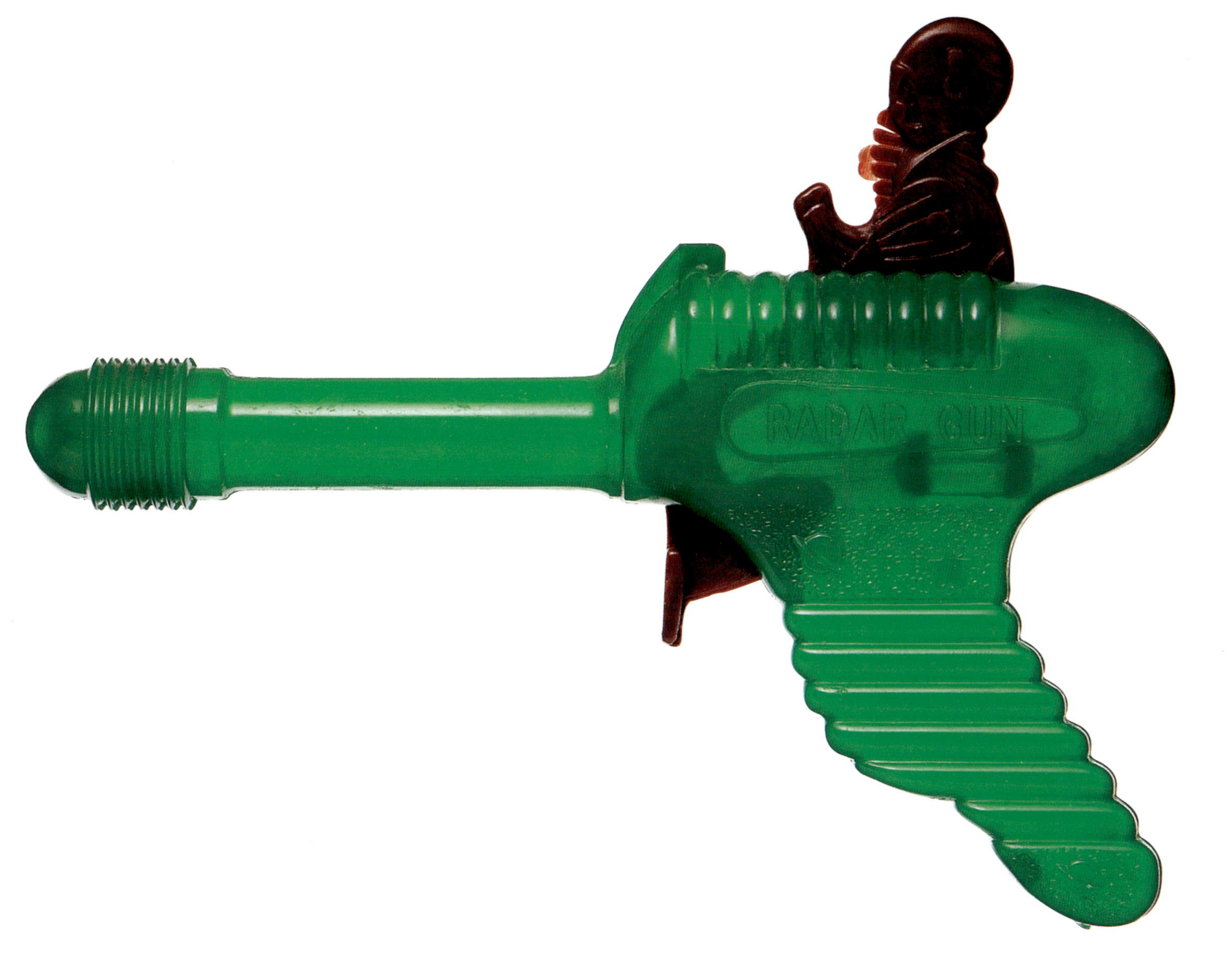

Radar Gun, plastic, 4¾ x 6¼ in., maker unknown, U.S.A. 1950s

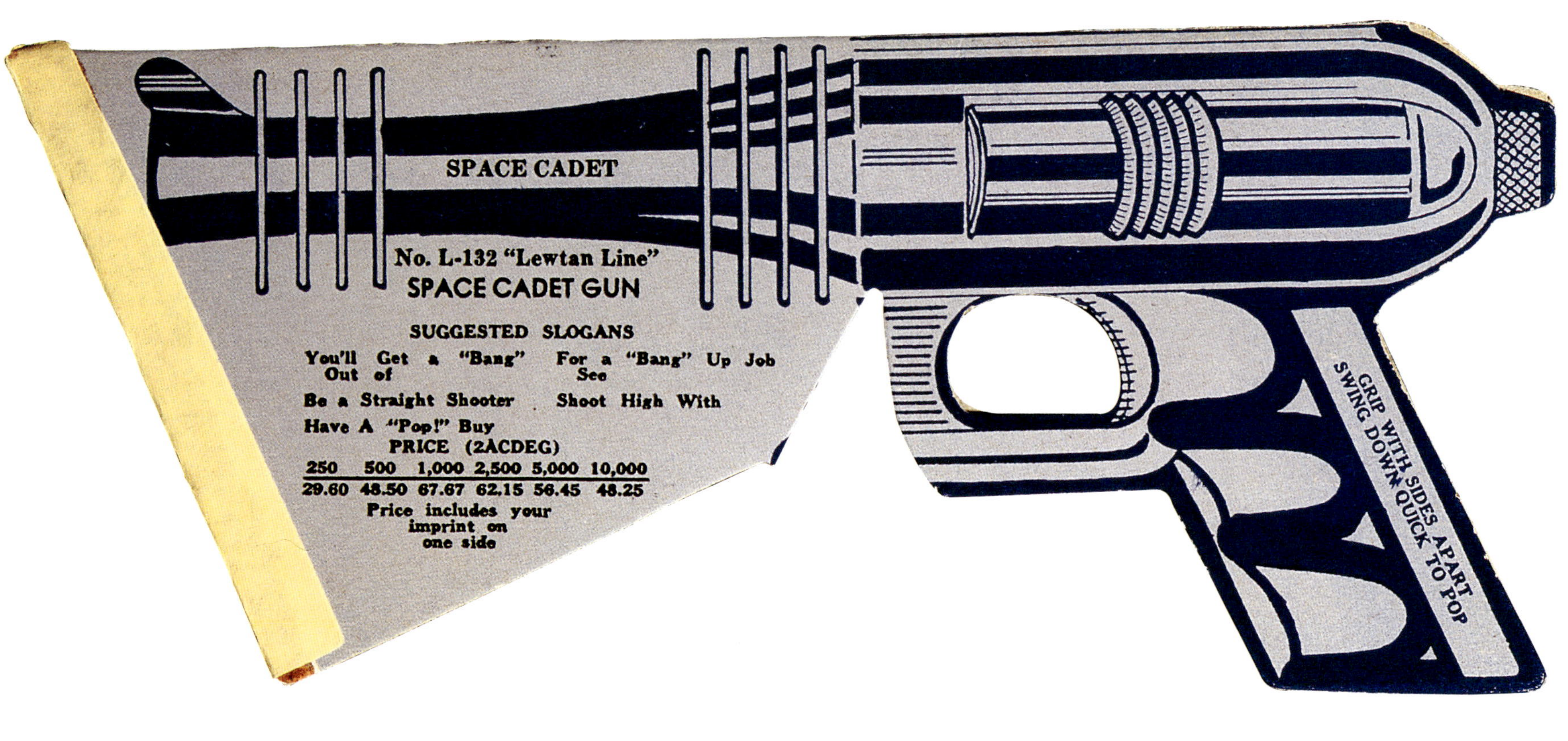
SPACE CADET
No. L-132 "Lewtan Line"
SPACE CADET GUN
SUGGESTED SLOGANS
You'll Get a "Bang" Out of
For a "Bang" Up Job See
Be a Straight Shooter
Shoot High With
Have A "Pop!" Buy
PRICE (2ACDEG)
250 500 1,000 2,500 5,000 10,000
29.60 48.50 67.67 62.15 56.45 48.25
Price includes your imprint on one side
GRIP WITH SIDES APART
SWING DOWN QUICK TO POP

Automatic Repeating Bubble Shooting Gun, plastic, 5½ x 8 in., Arliss Co., Inc., U.S.A. 1950s

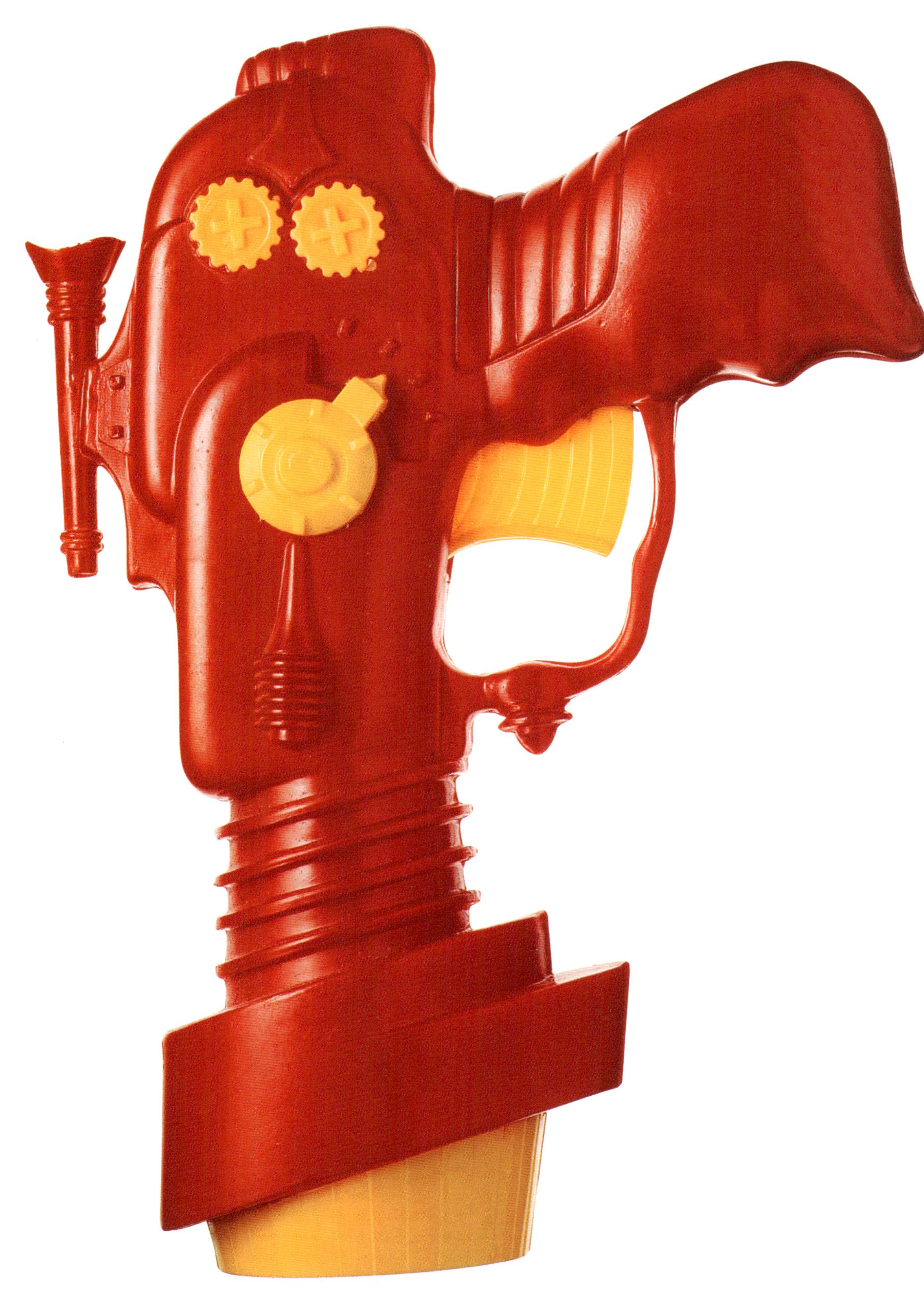

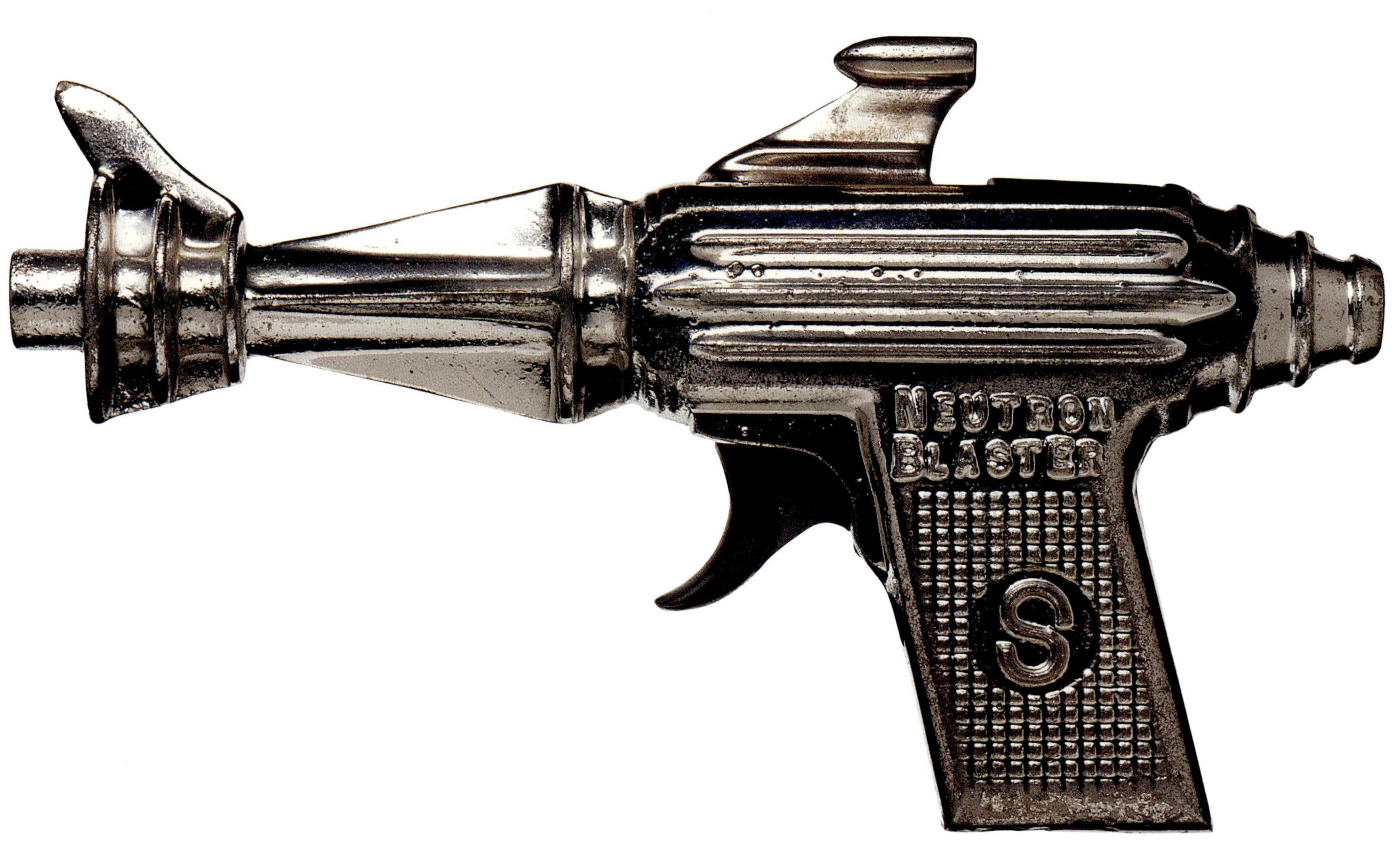
NEUTRON
BLASTER
S

Strato Gun, die-cast metal, 4½ x 9¼ in., Futuristic Products Co., U.S.A. mid 1950s

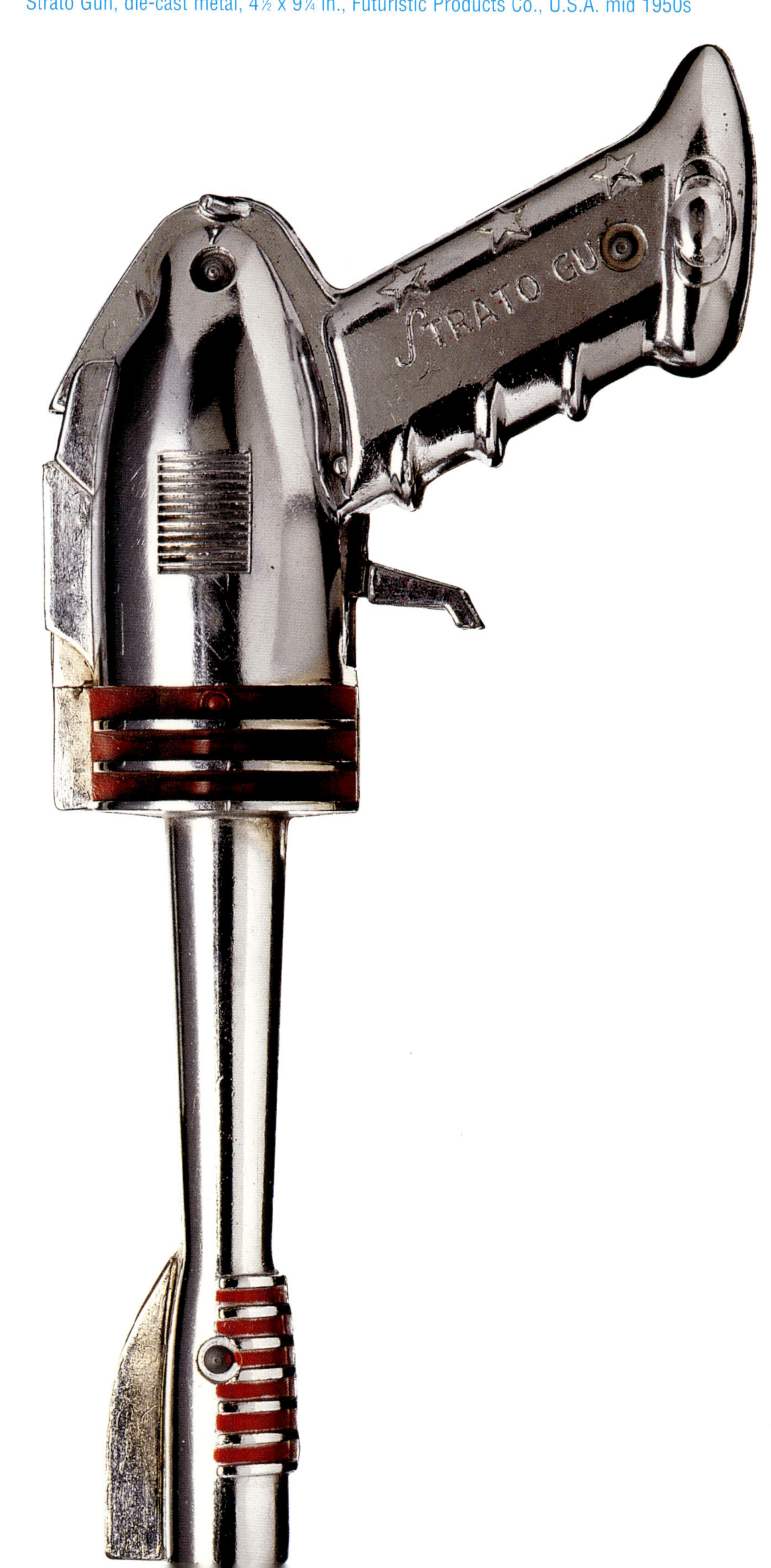

Rocket Dart Pistol, pressed steel, 5½ x 7 in., Daisy Manufacturing Co., U.S.A. early 1950s

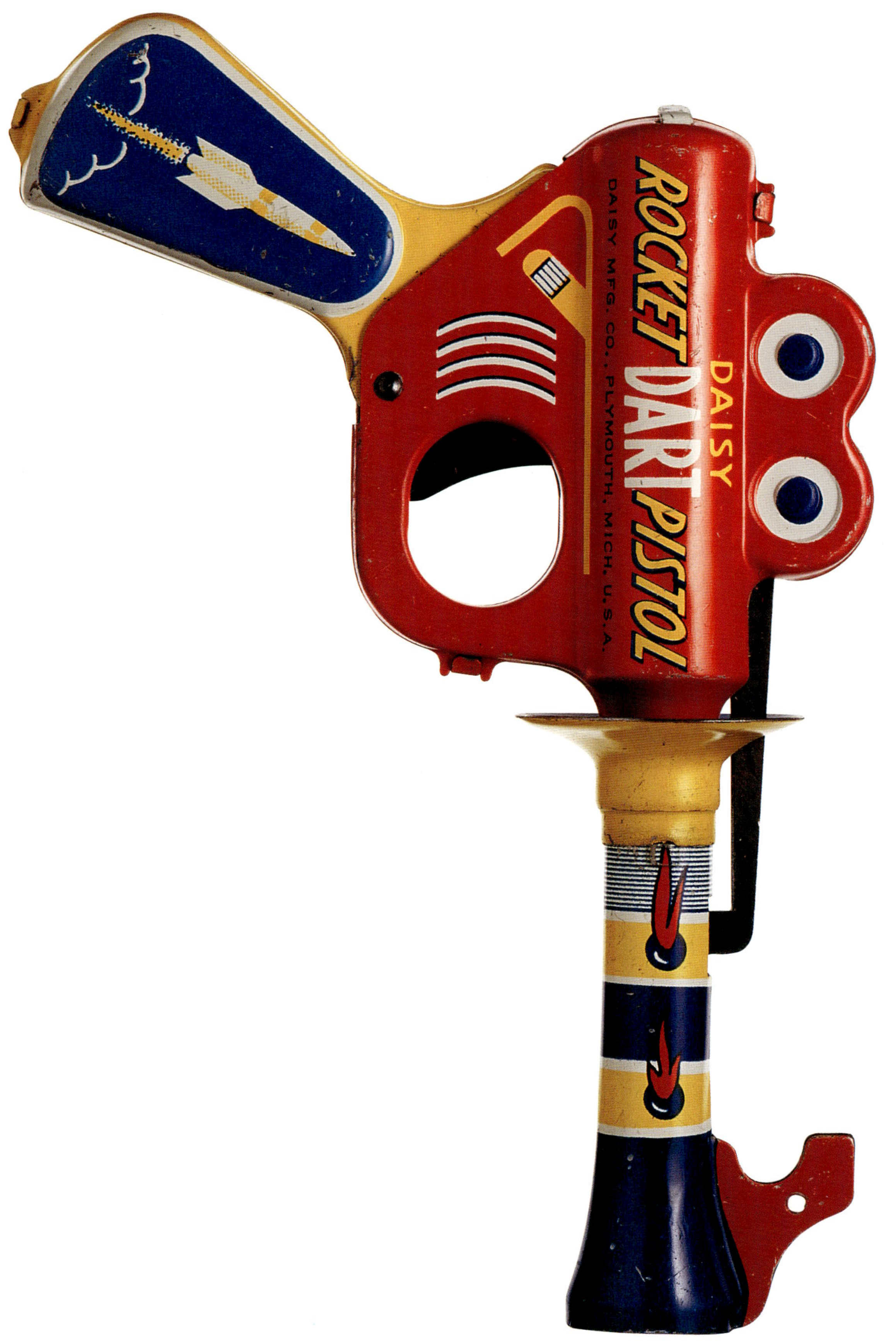

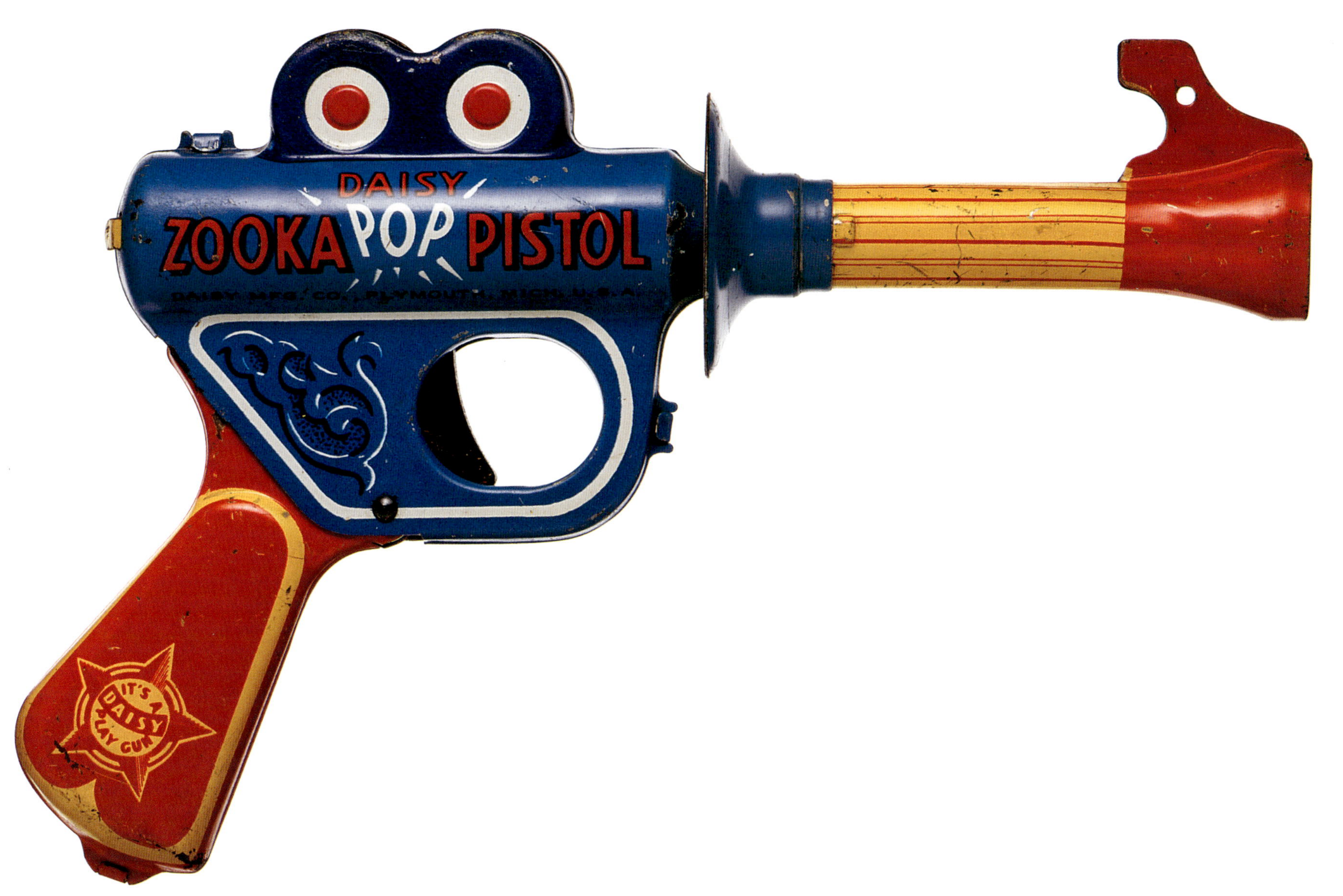
DAISY
ZOOKA POP PISTOL
DAISY MFG. CO., PLYMOUTH, MICH. U.S.A.
IT'S A DAISY PLAY GUN

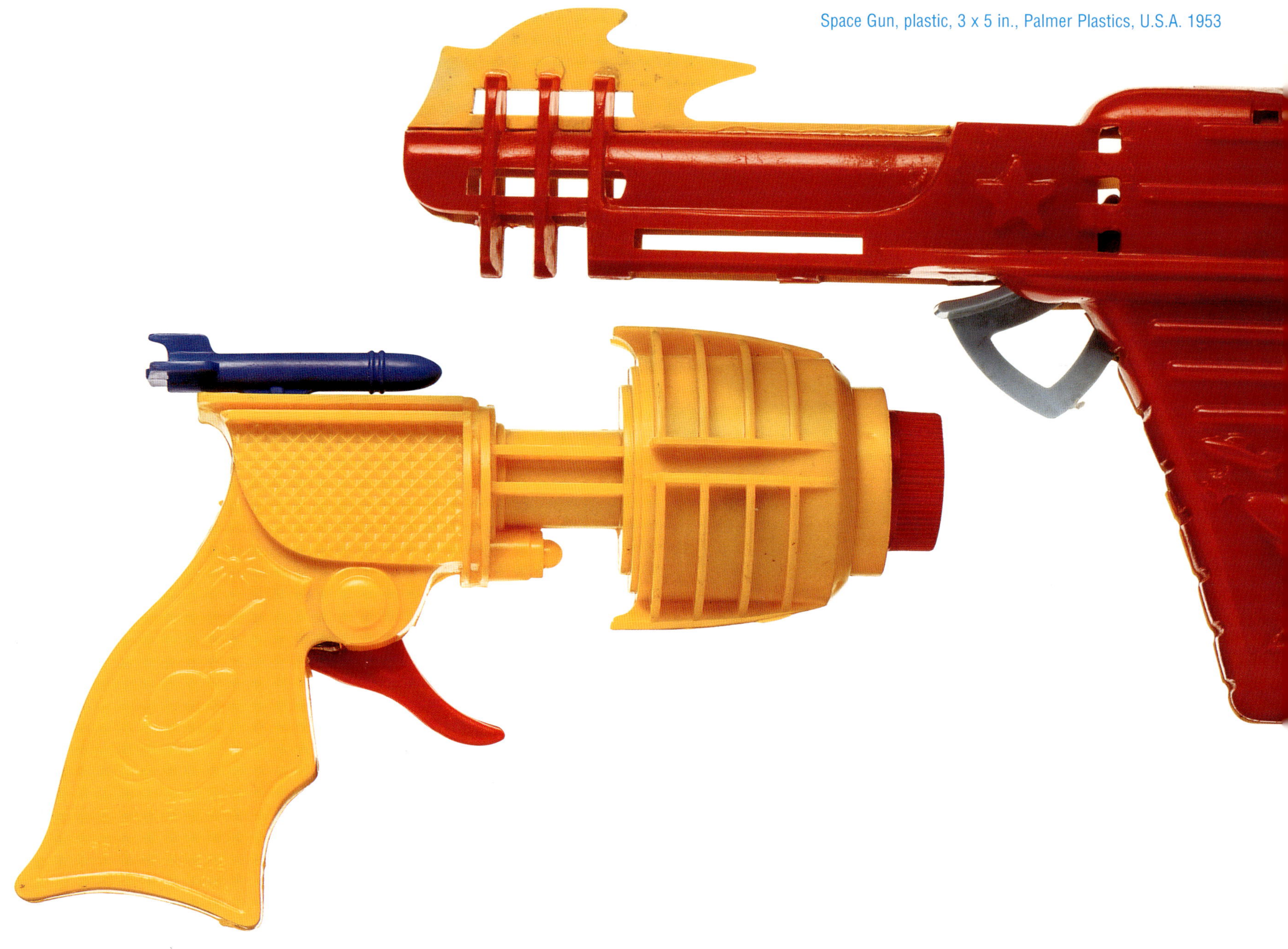

Space Gun, plastic, 3 x 5 in., Palmer Plastics, U.S.A. 1953

Planet Jet, plastic, 3¾ x 5¾ in., Renwal Manufacturing Co., U.S.A. mid 1950s

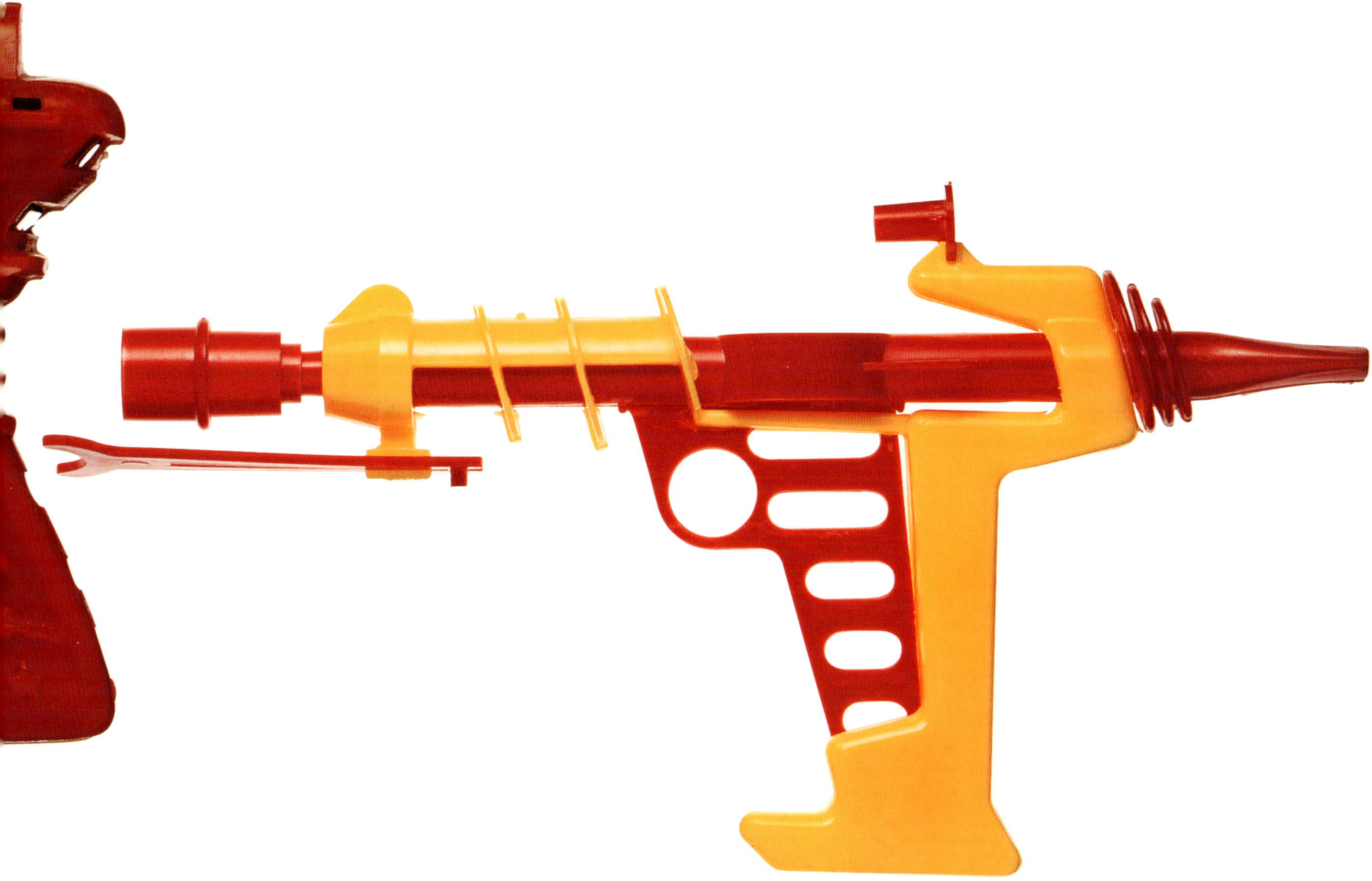

Martian "Guided Whistle" Bloon-Rocket with Jet-Blast Bloon-Gun, plastic, 5 x 9½ in., Mercury Plastics Corporation, U.S.A. 1950s

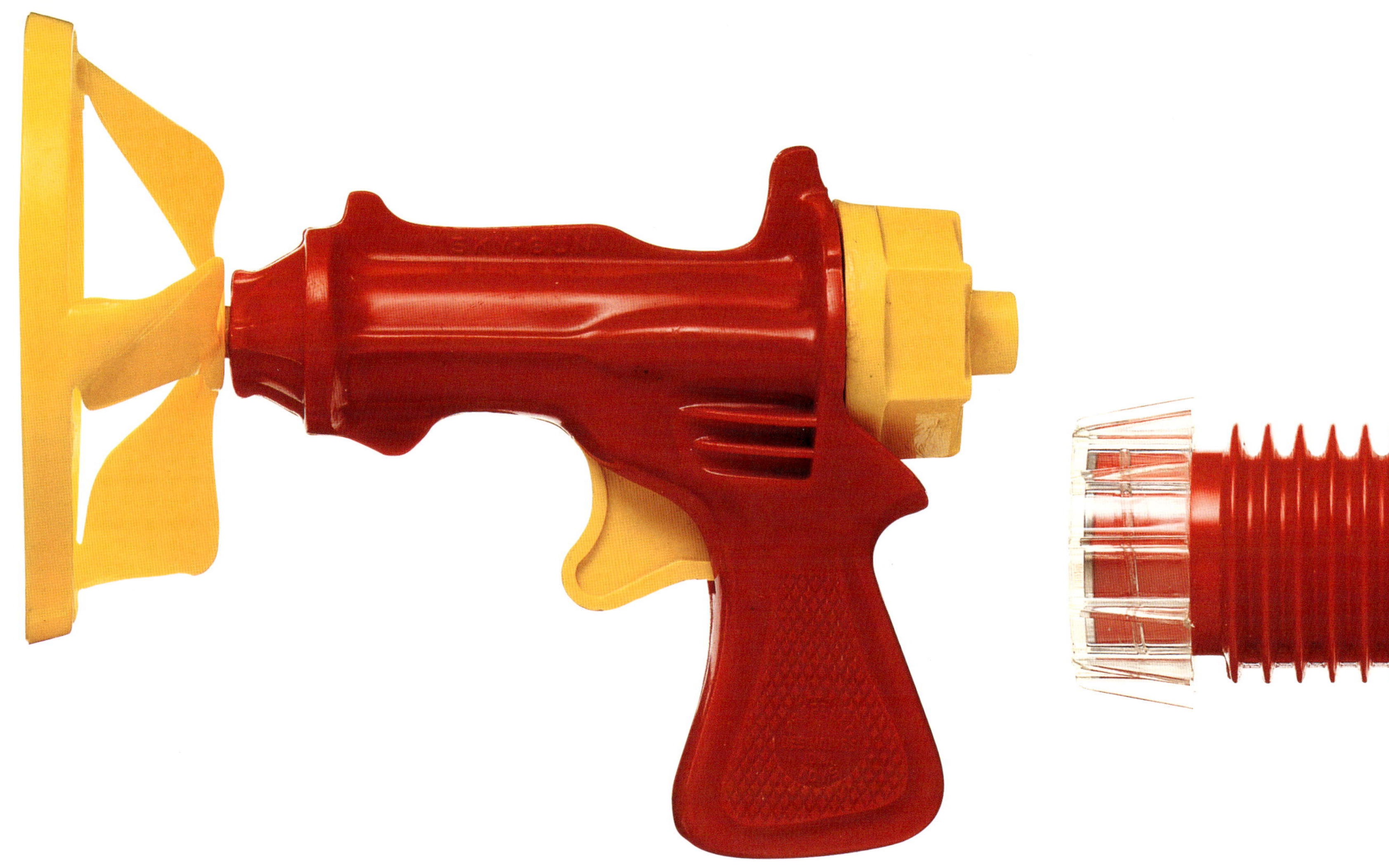

Sky Gun, plastic, 4 x 5 in., Propello Toys, U.S.A. 1950s

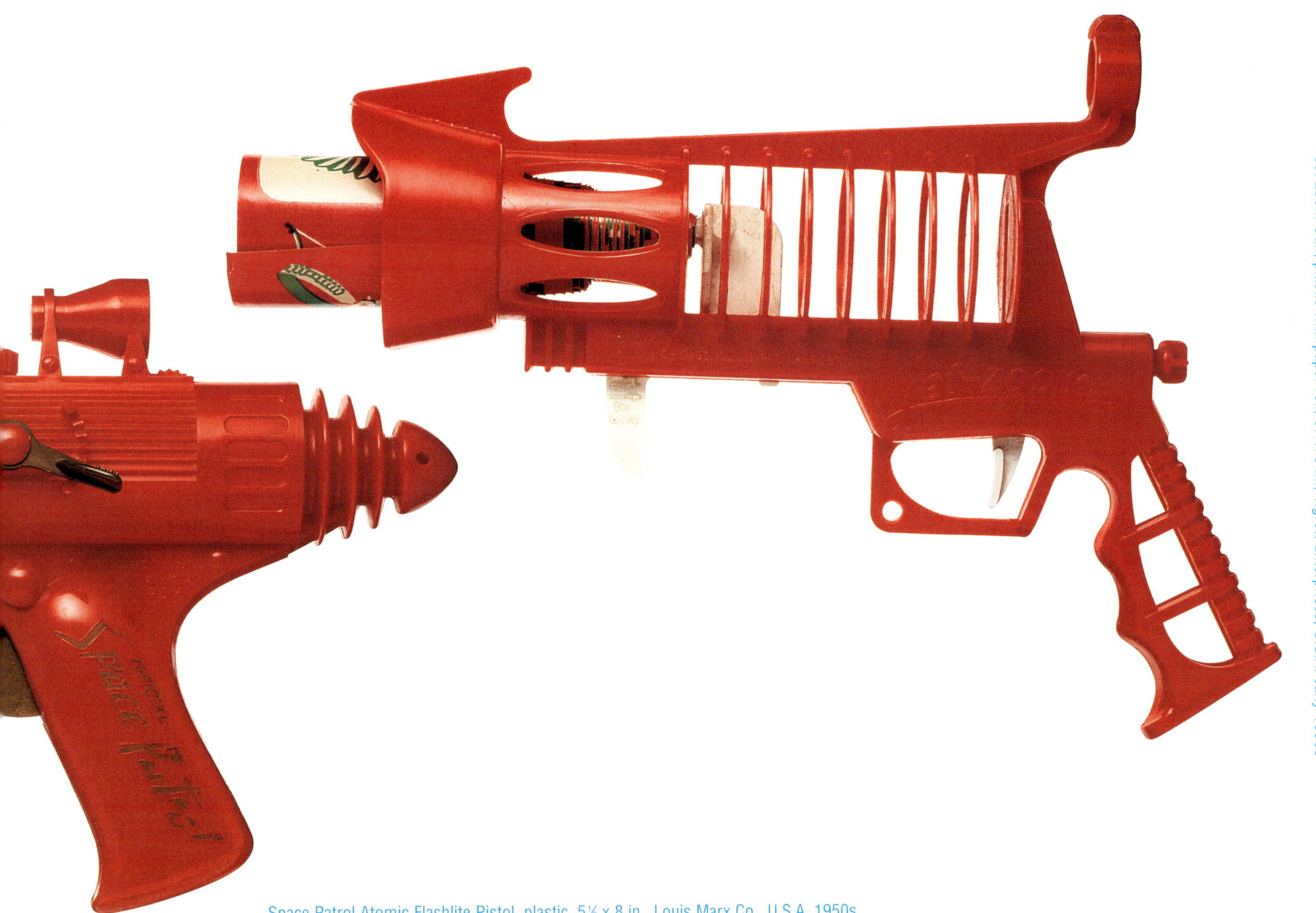

Jet Zoom Gun, plastic with paper roll, 6¾ x 9 in., Tigrett Enterprises, U.S.A. early 1950s

Space Patrol Atomic Flashlite Pistol, plastic, 5½ x 8 in., Louis Marx Co., U.S.A. 1950s

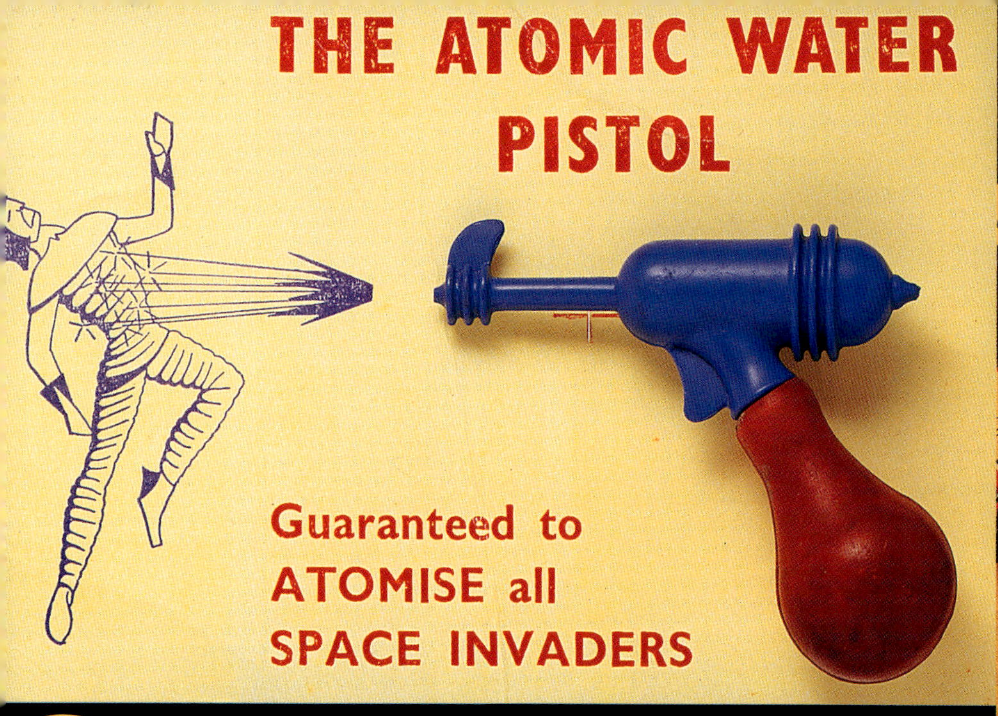
THE ATOMIC WATER
PISTOL
Guaranteed to
ATOMISE all
SPACE INVADERS

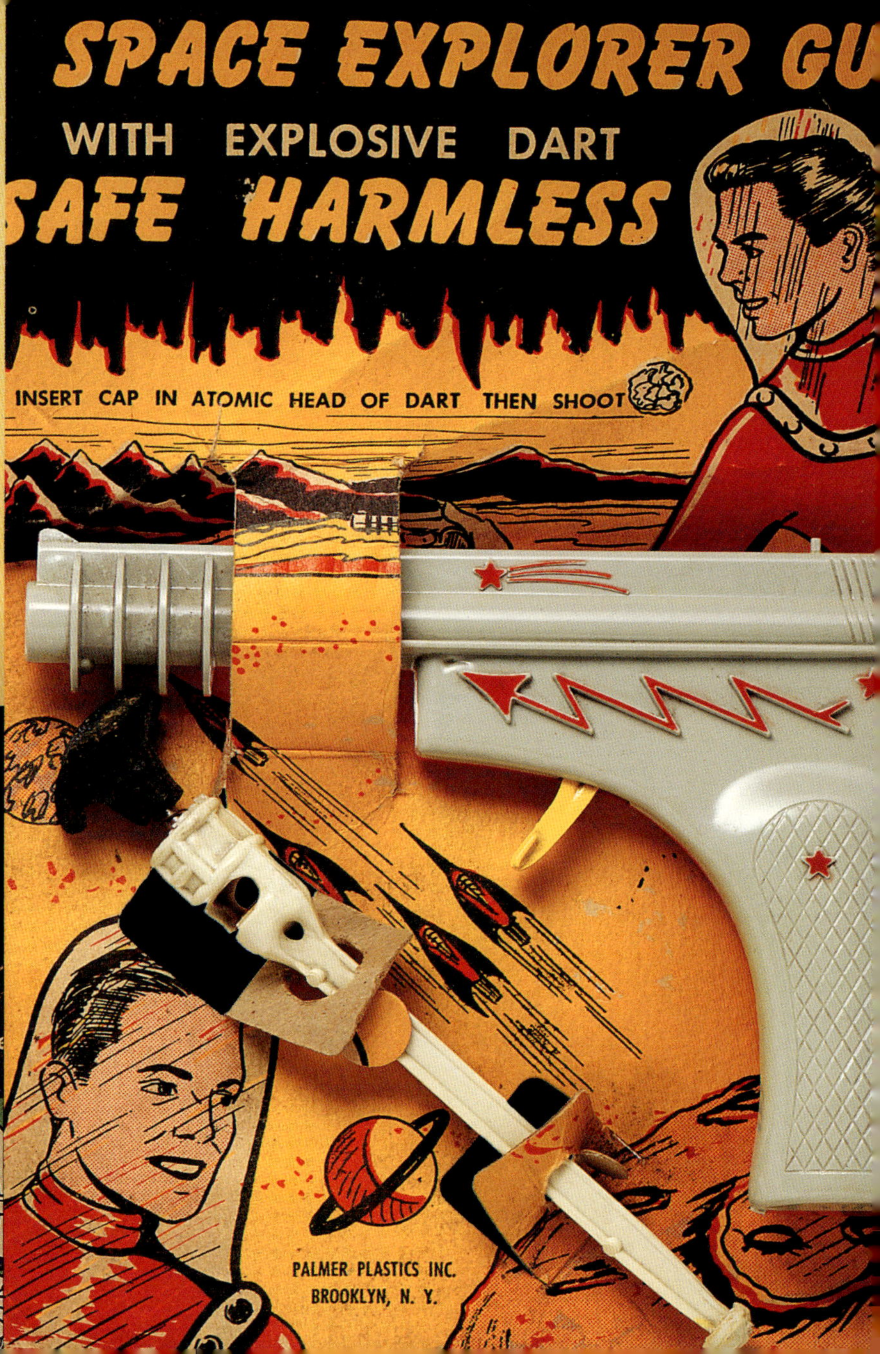

SPACE EXPLORER GU
WITH EXPLOSIVE DART
SAFE HARMLESS
INSERT CAP IN ATOMIC HEAD OF DART THEN SHOOT
PALMER PLASTICS INC.
BROOKLYN, N. Y.

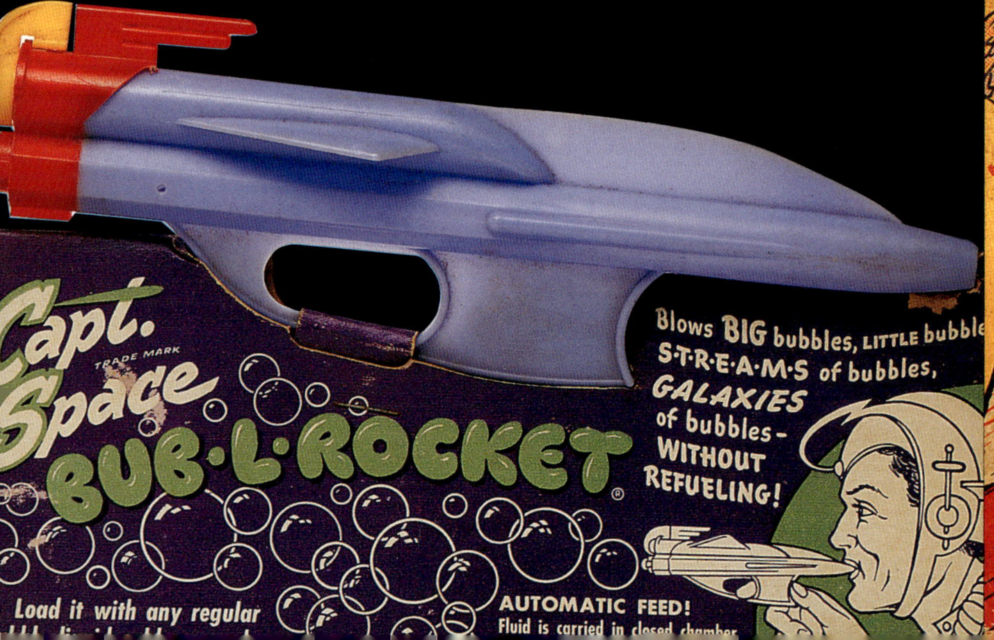
Capt. Space
TRADE MARK
BUB·L·ROCKET
Blows BIG bubbles, LITTLE bubble
S·T·R·E·A·M·S of bubbles,
GALAXIES
of bubbles-
WITHOUT
REFUELING!
AUTOMATIC FEED!
Load it with any regular

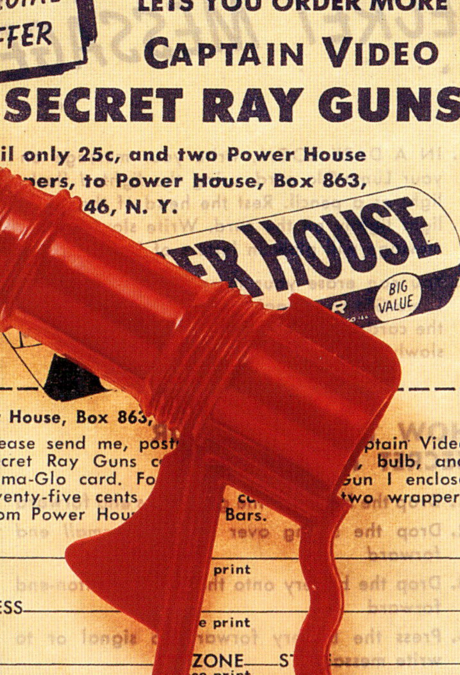

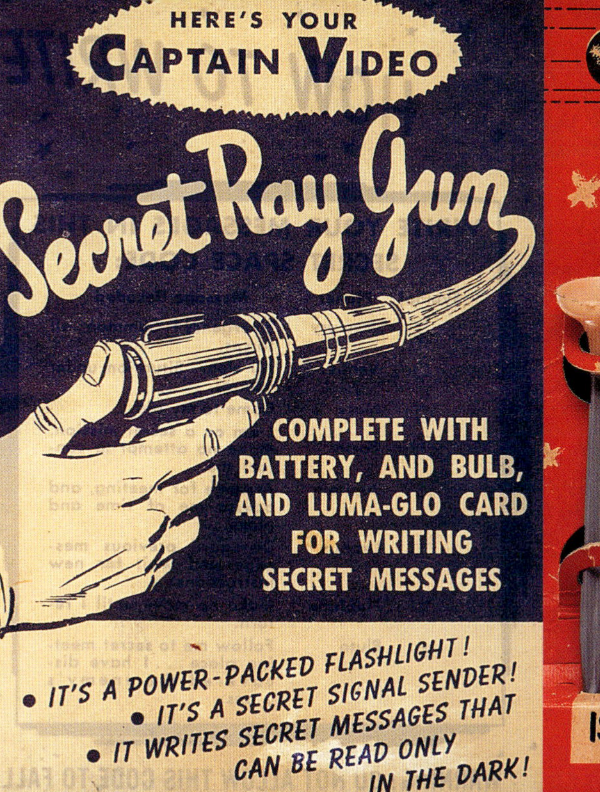

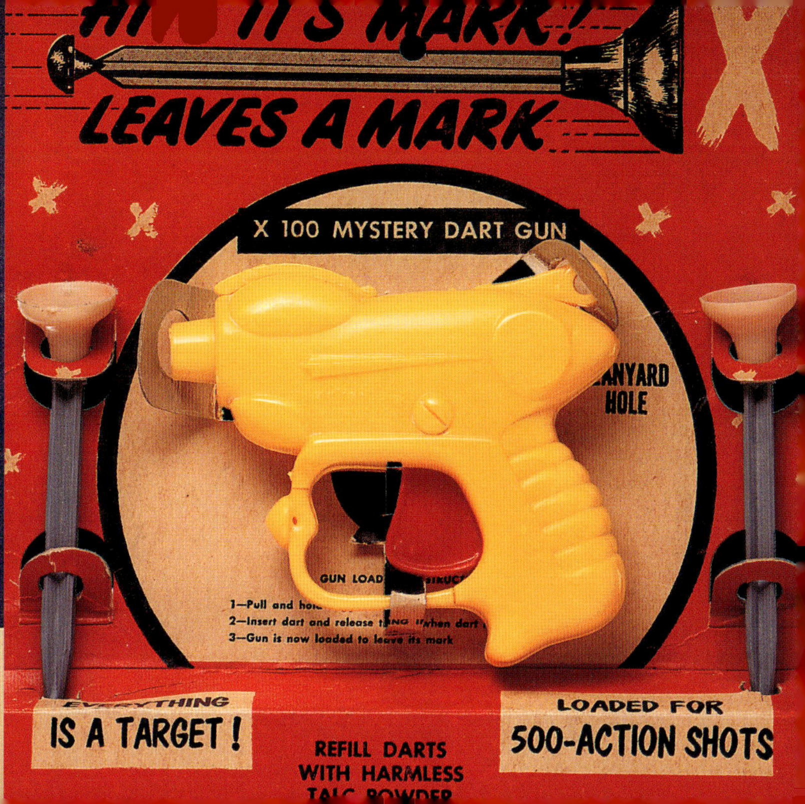

LEAVES A MARK
X 100 MYSTERY DART GUN
LANYARD HOLE
IS A TARGET!
REFILL DARTS
WITH HARMLESS
LOADED FOR
500-ACTION SHOTS

Smoke Ring Gun, plastic, 6 x 9 in., Nu-Age Products Inc., U.S.A. early 1950s

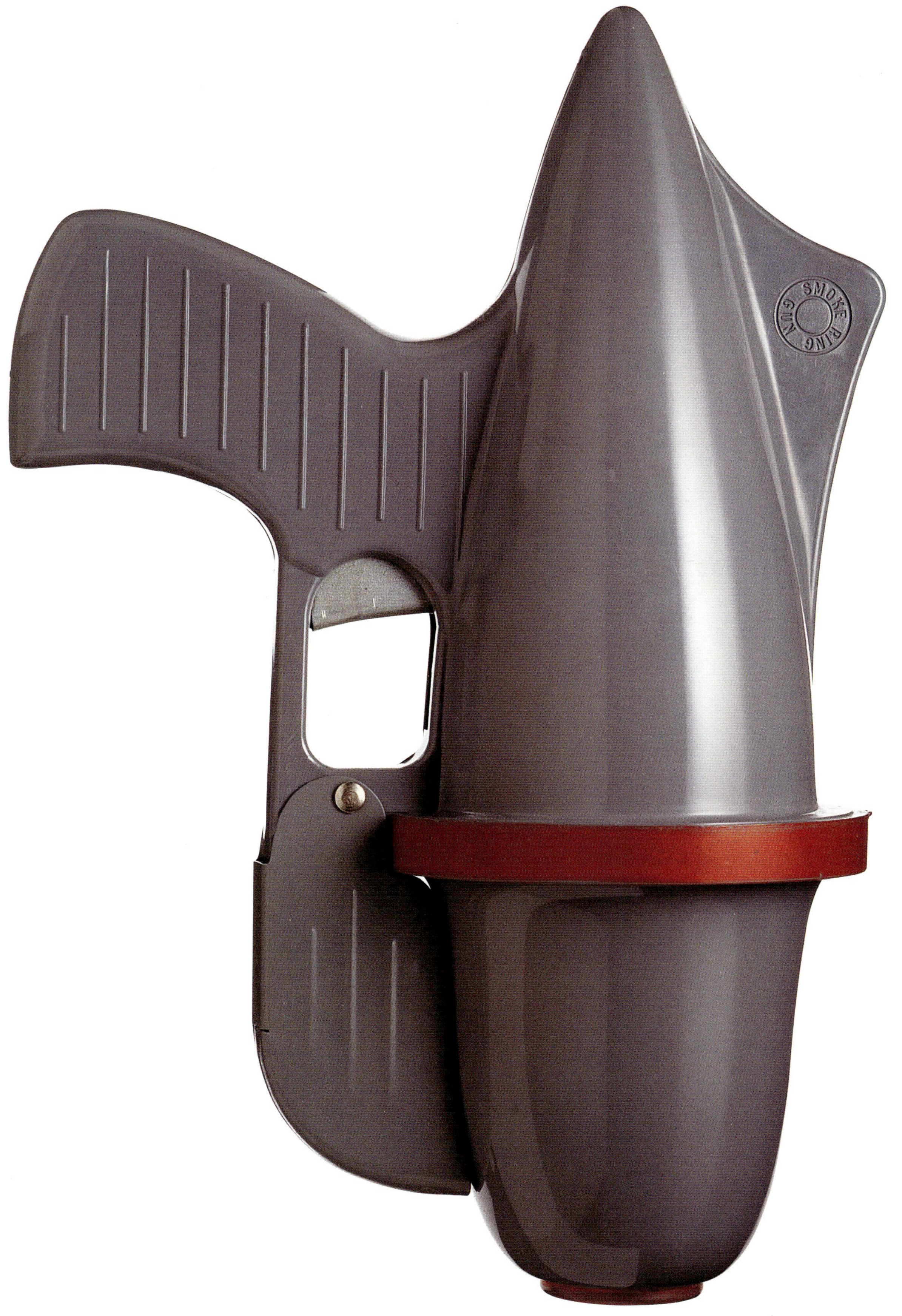

Whistle Gun, plastic, 2¾ x 4¾ in., maker unknown, U.S.A. 1950s

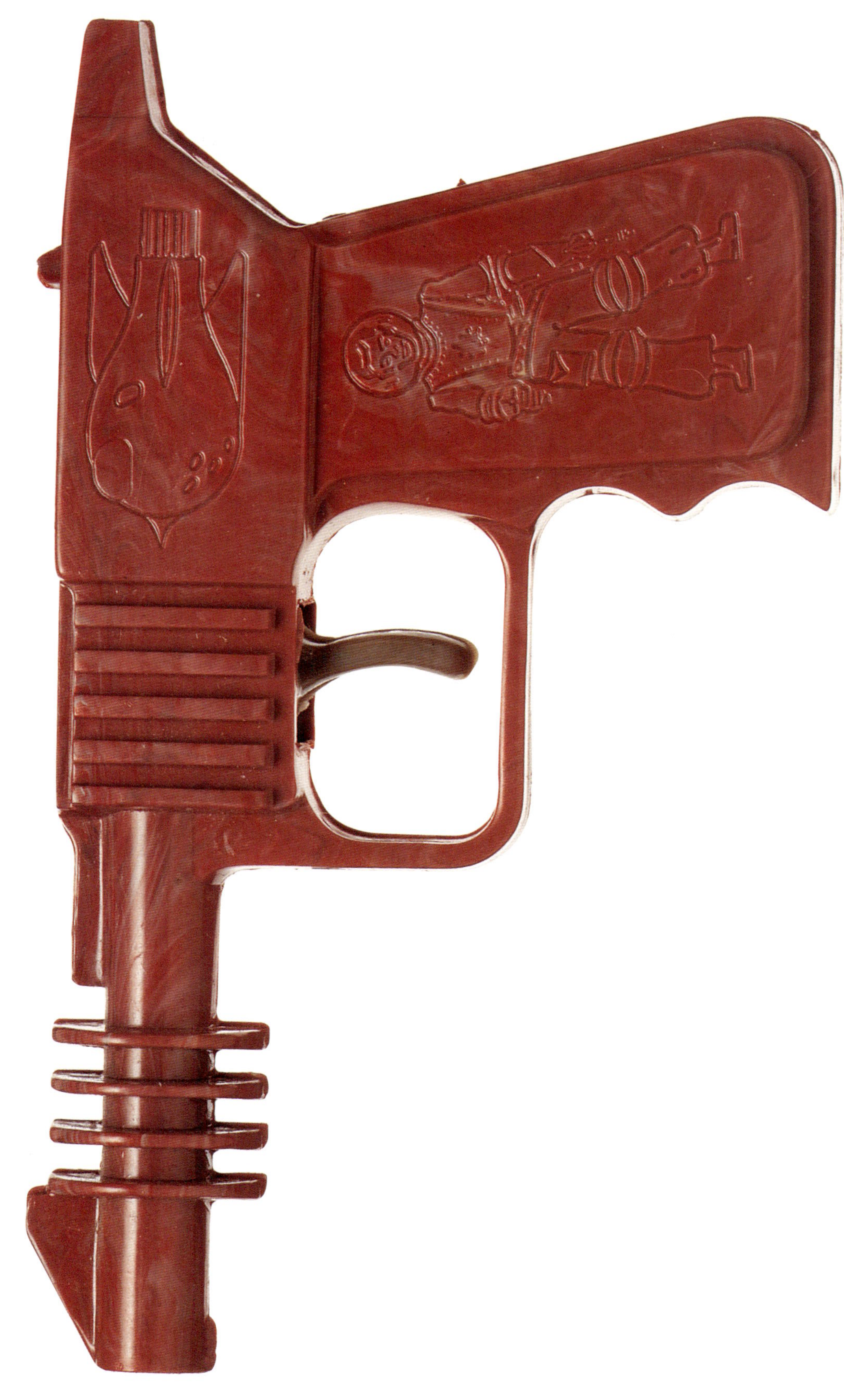

Space Gun, plastic, 2 x 4½ in., Thomas Co., U.S.A. 1950s

Space Patrol Rocket Dart Gun, plastic, 5¼ x 9¾ in., U.S. Plastics Co., U.S.A. 1954

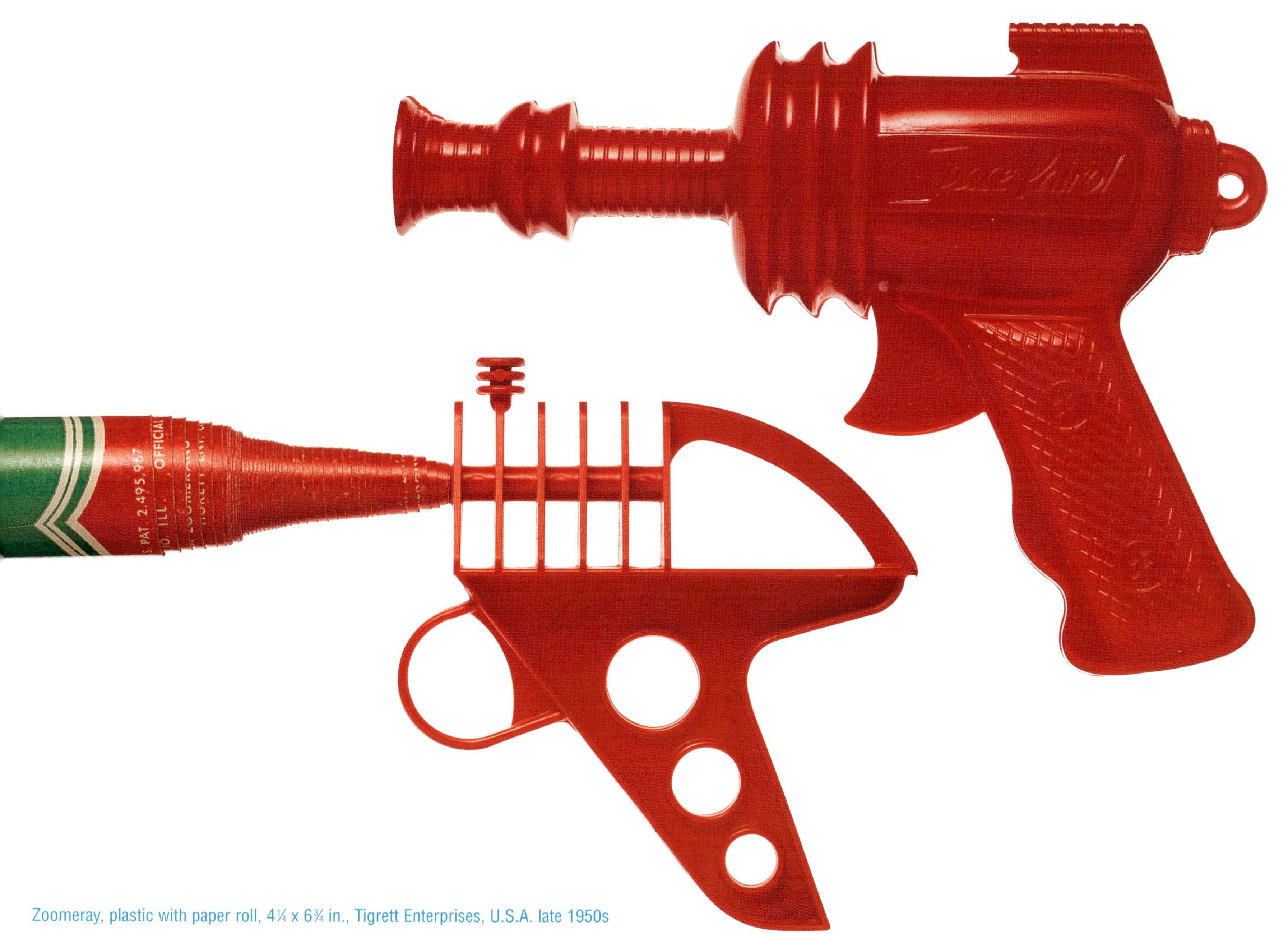

Space Patrol Cosmic Smoke Gun, plastic, 3½ x 4½ in., U.S. Plastics Co., U.S.A. 1952

Zoomeray, plastic with paper roll, 4¼ x 6¾ in., Tigrett Enterprises, U.S.A. late 1950s

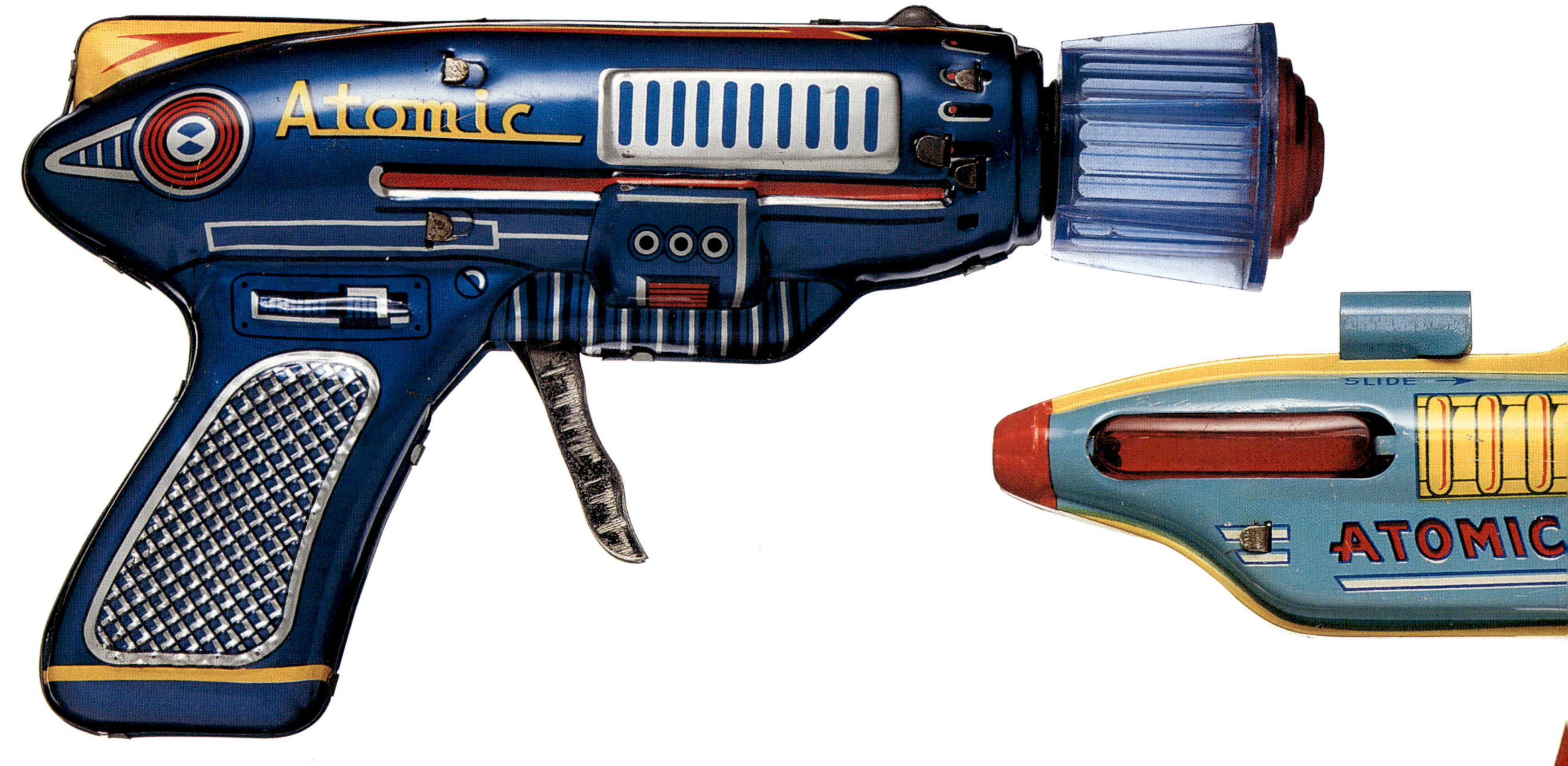

Atomic Pistol, tin and plastic, 4¼ x 7½ in., T.N., Japan late 1950s

Atomic Flash Gun, pressed steel, 5 x 7½ in., J Chein & Co., U.S.A. mid 1950s

Space Pistol, lithographed tin with plastic propeller, 5 x 7¾ in., T.N., Japan late 1950s

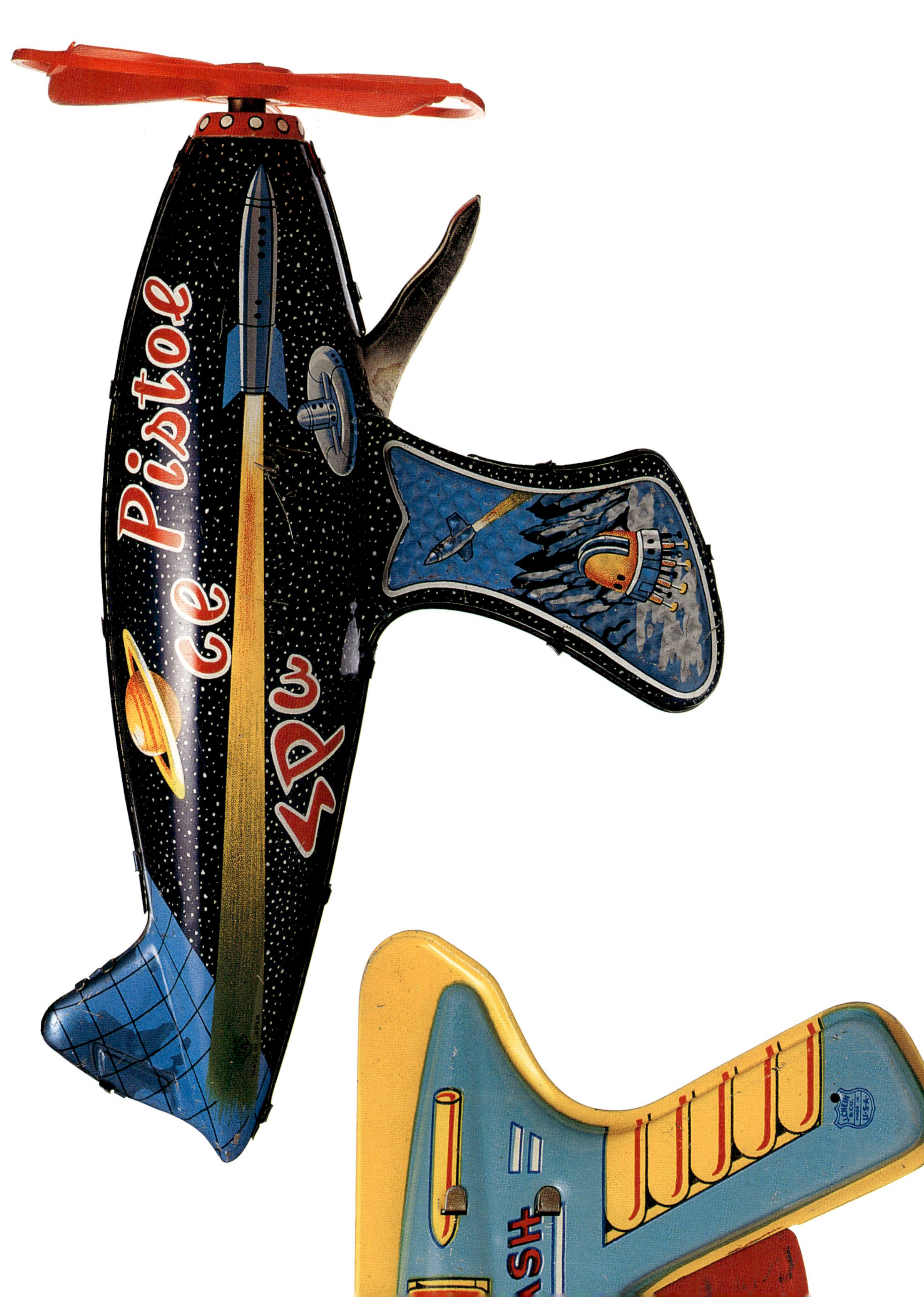

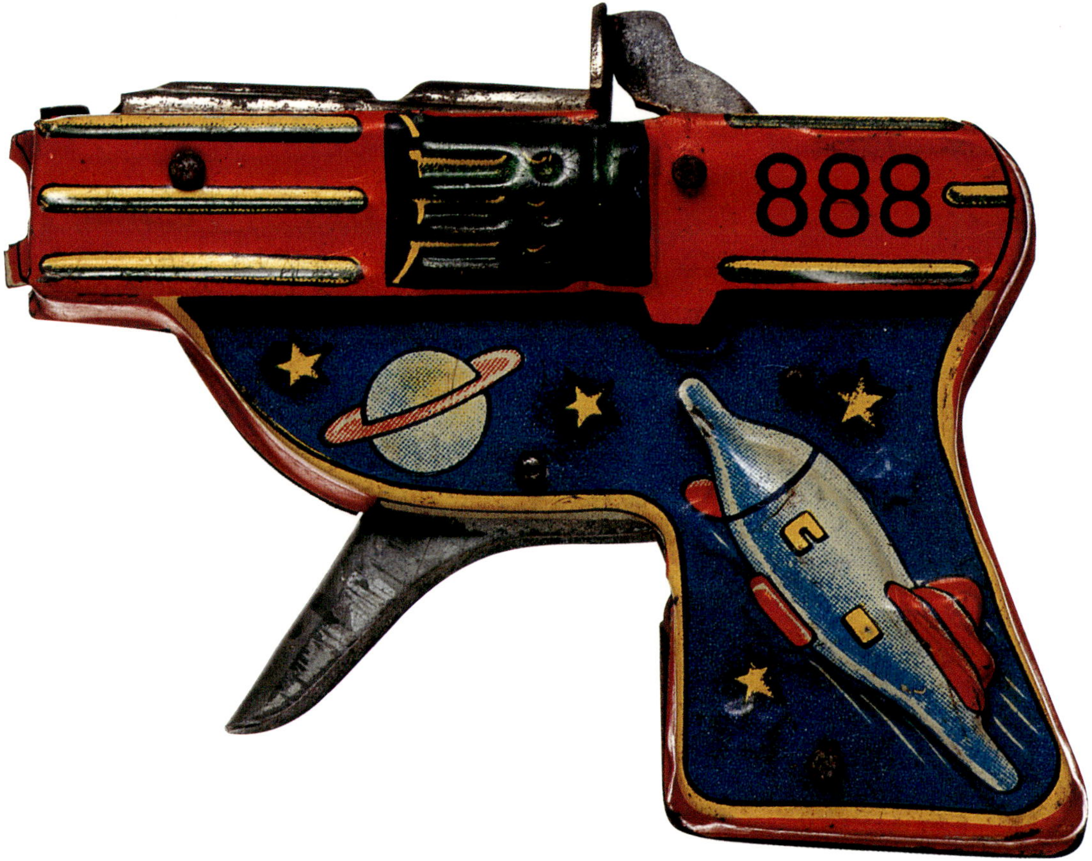

888 Space Gun, lithographed tin, 2½ x 3 in., maker unknown, Japan 1950s

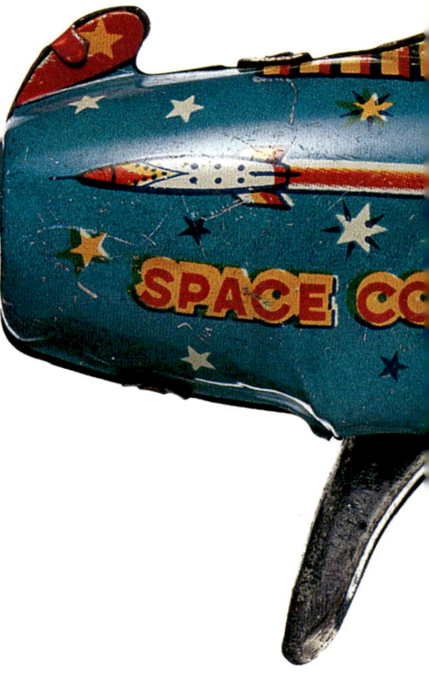

Space Control Gun, lithographed tin, 3 x 3¾ in., T.N., Japan 1950s

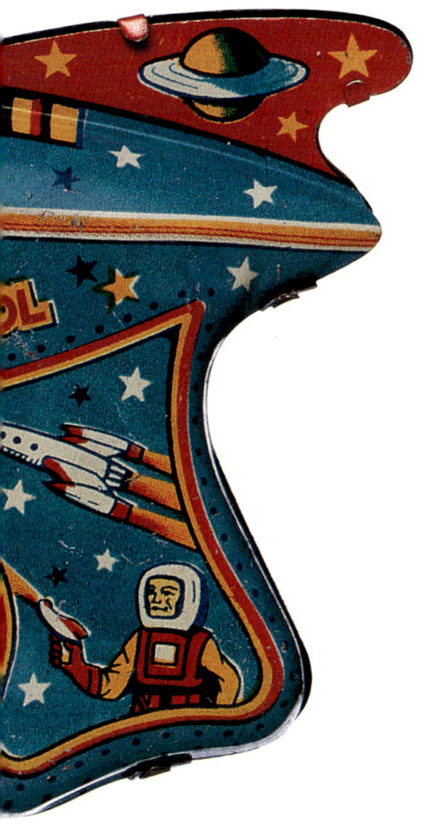

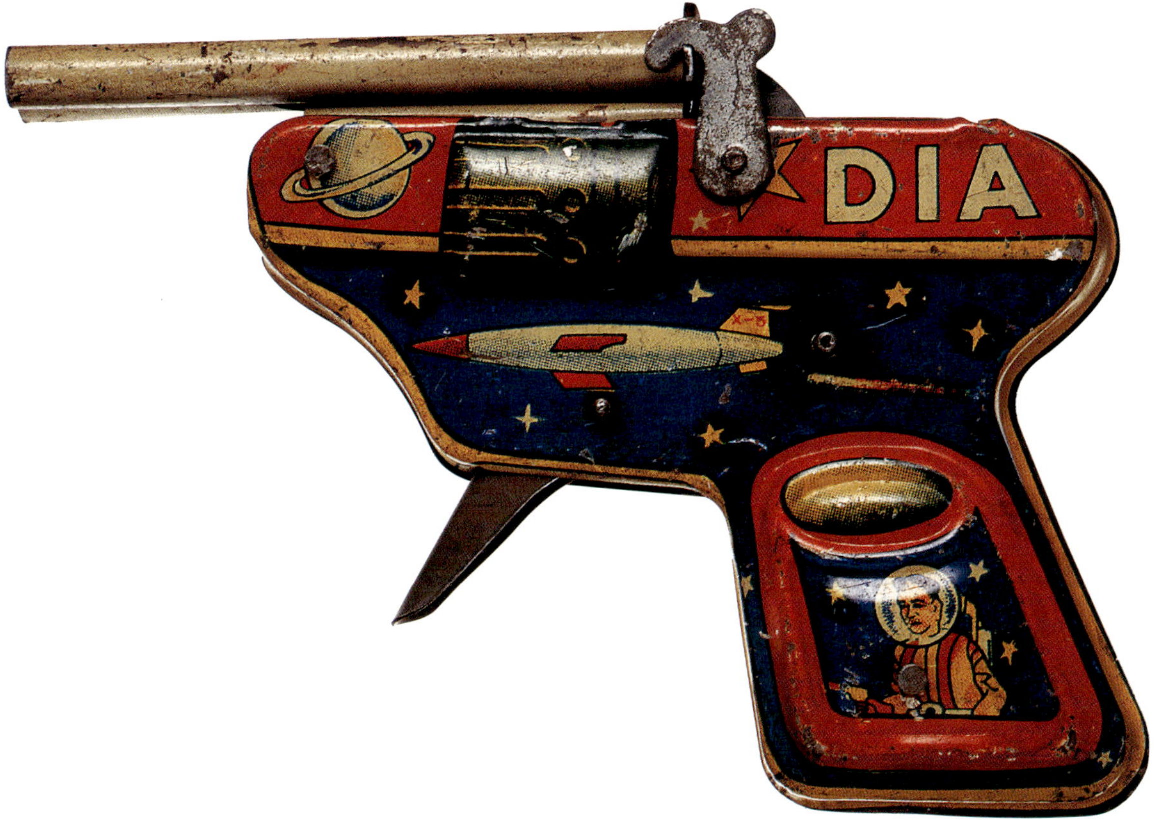

DIA Space Gun, lithographed tin, 3 x 4 in., maker unknown, Japan 1950s

Atomic Jet-Gun, cast aluminum, 4 x 6 in., Crescent Toys, England 1950s

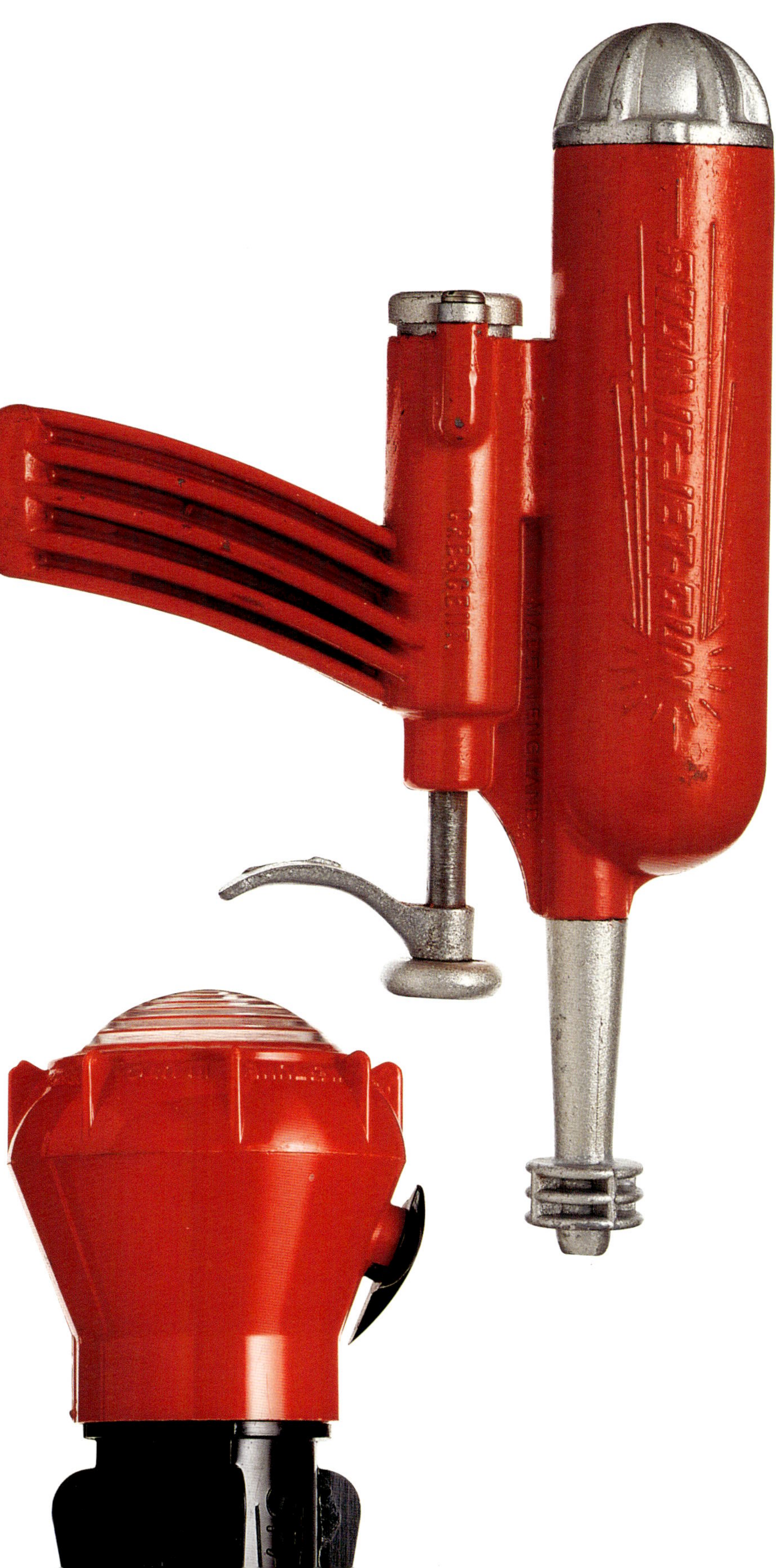

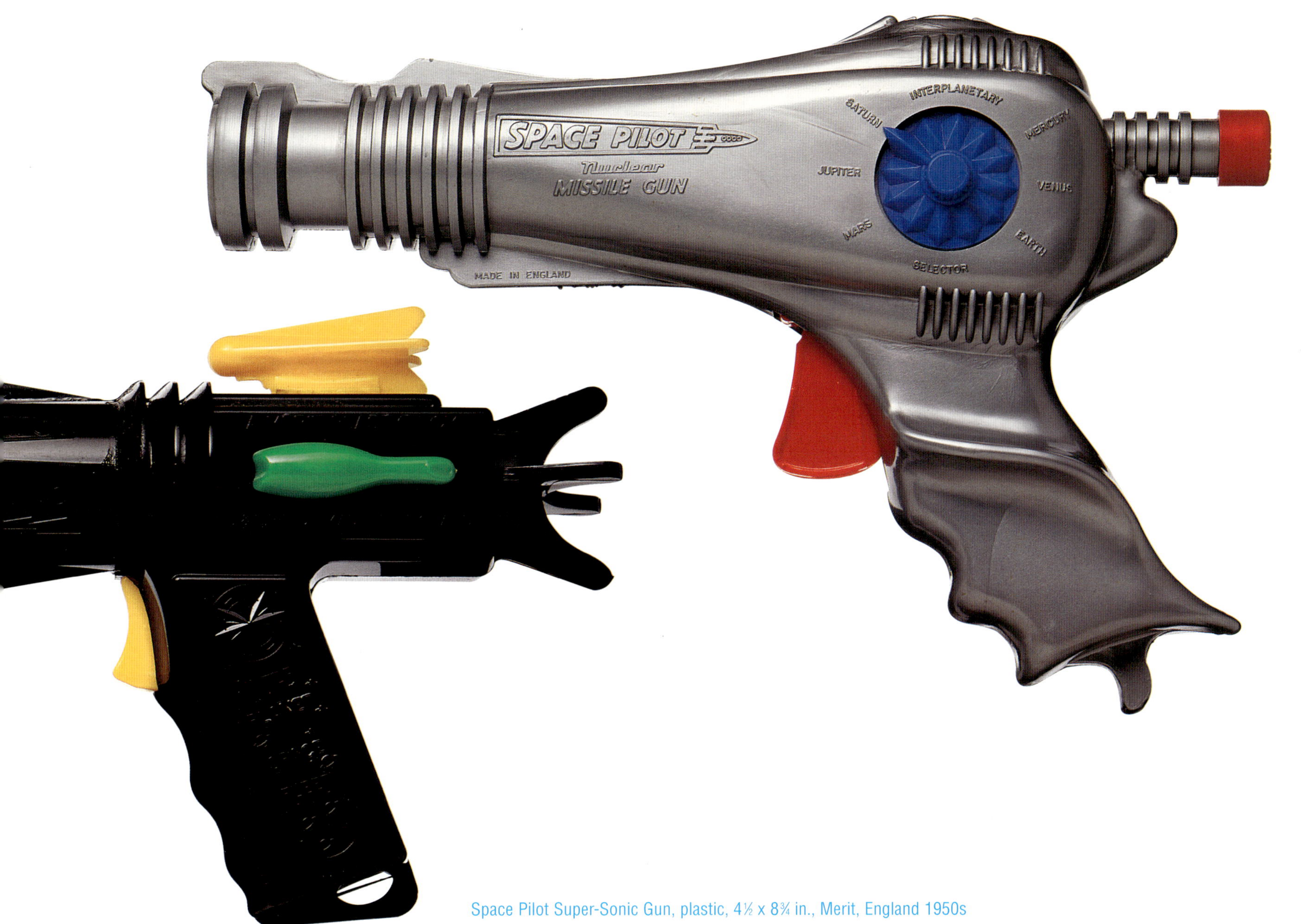

Space Pilot Missile Gun, plastic, 6 x 9 in., Merit, England 1950s

Space Pilot Super-Sonic Gun, plastic, 4½ x 8¾ in., Merit, England 1950s

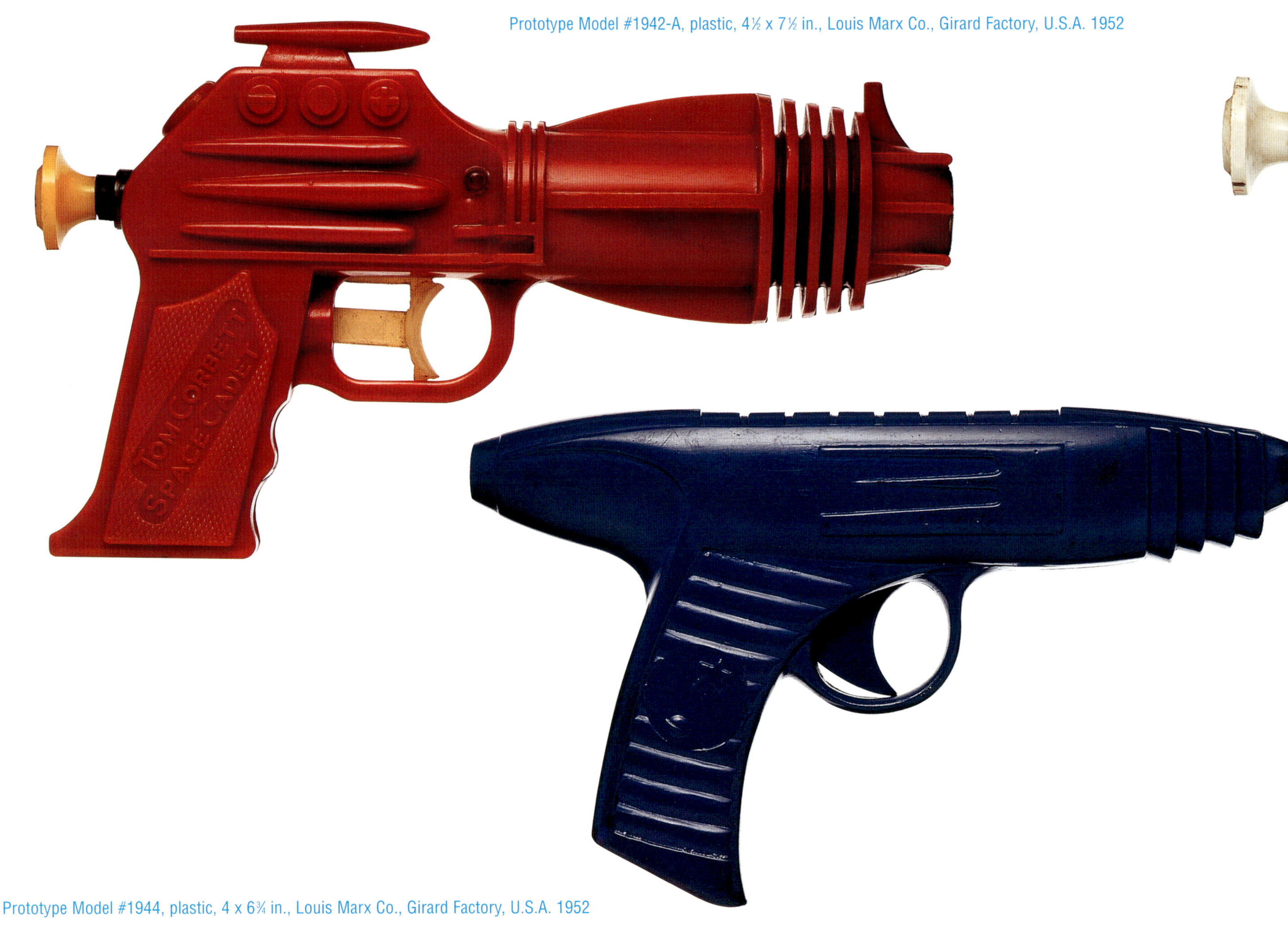

Prototype Model #1942-A, plastic, 4½ x 7½ in., Louis Marx Co., Girard Factory, U.S.A. 1952

Prototype Model #1944, plastic, 4 x 6¾ in., Louis Marx Co., Girard Factory, U.S.A. 1952

Prototype Model #1843, plastic, 4¼ x 7 in., Louis Marx Co., Girard Factory, U.S.A. 1952

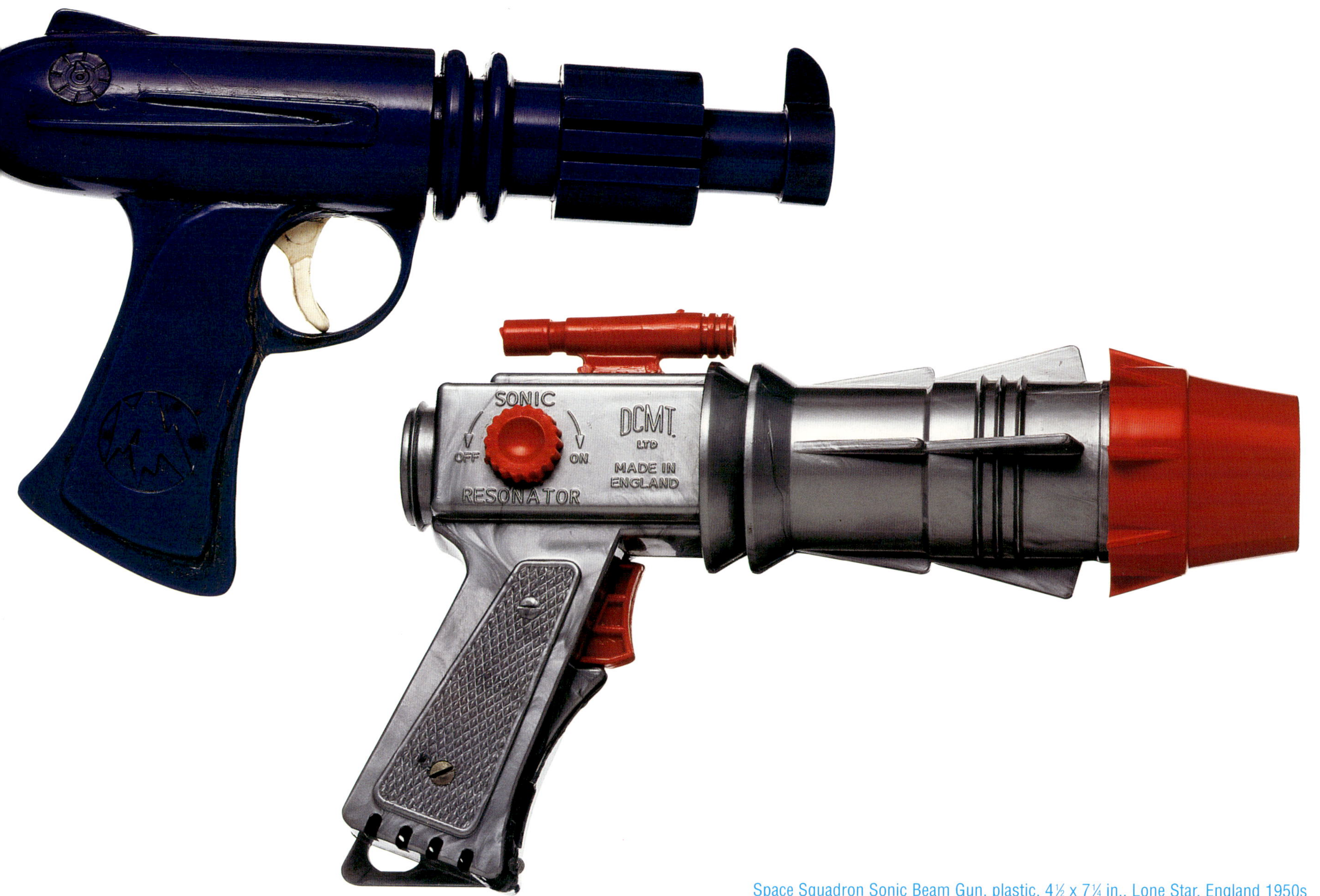

Space Squadron Sonic Beam Gun, plastic, 4½ x 7¼ in., Lone Star, England 1950s

Prototype Rex Mars Planet Patrol Rifle, plastic and tin, 7 x 26 in., Louis Marx Co., U.S.A. early 1950s

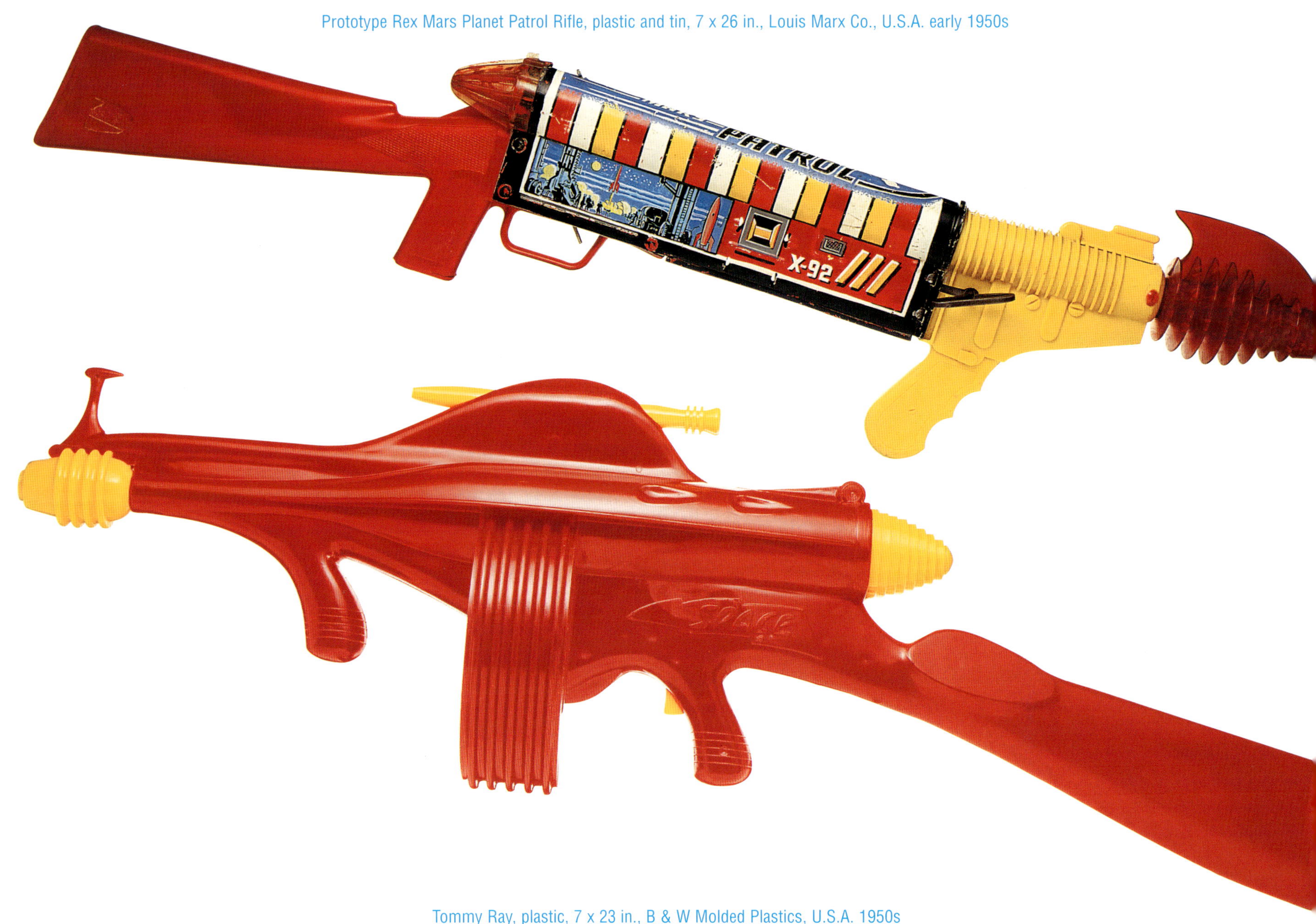

Tommy Ray, plastic, 7 x 23 in., B & W Molded Plastics, U.S.A. 1950s

Space Ship Water Guns, die-cast metal with rubber bulbs, 2 x 3 in., maker unknown, England 1950s

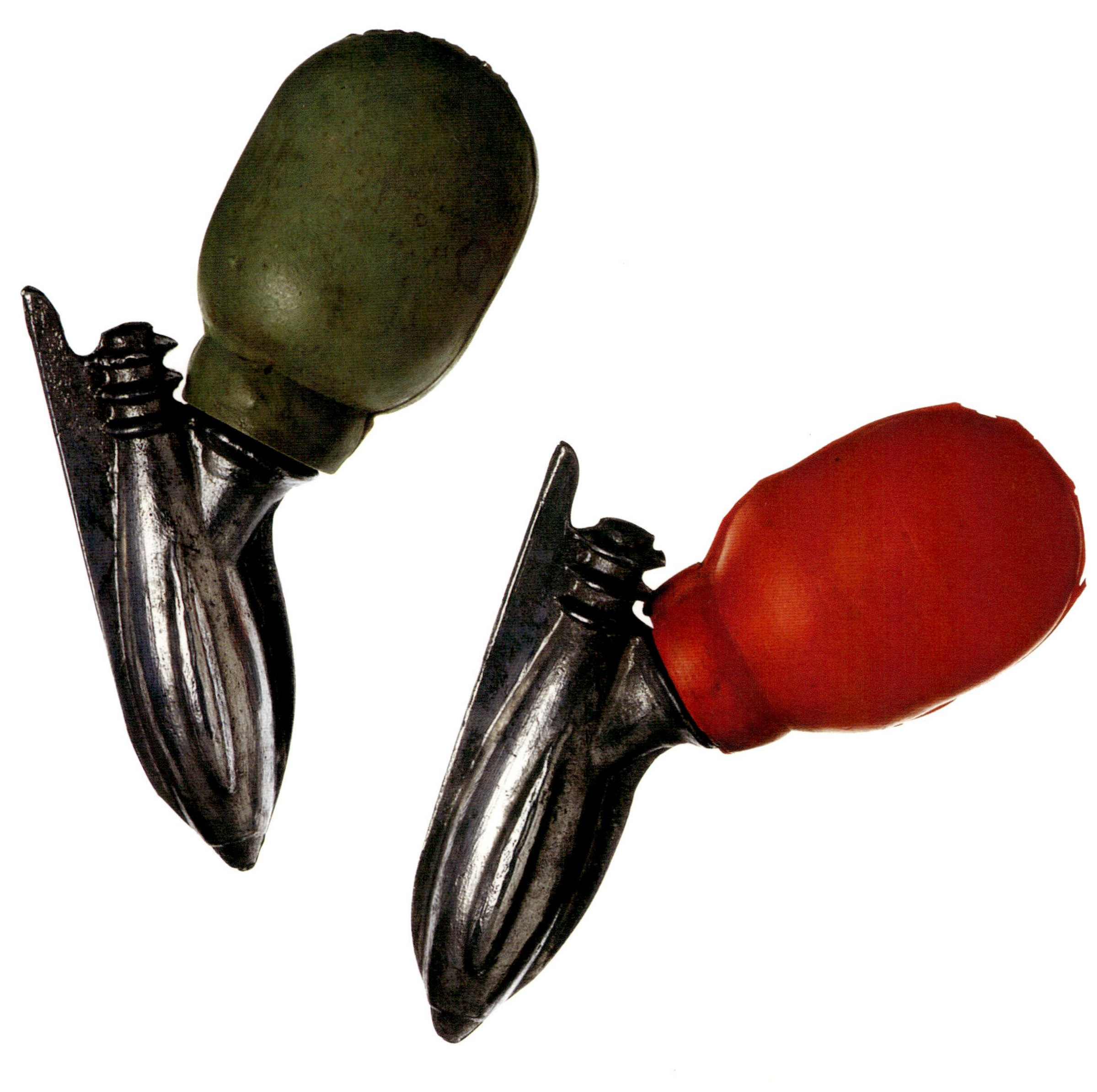

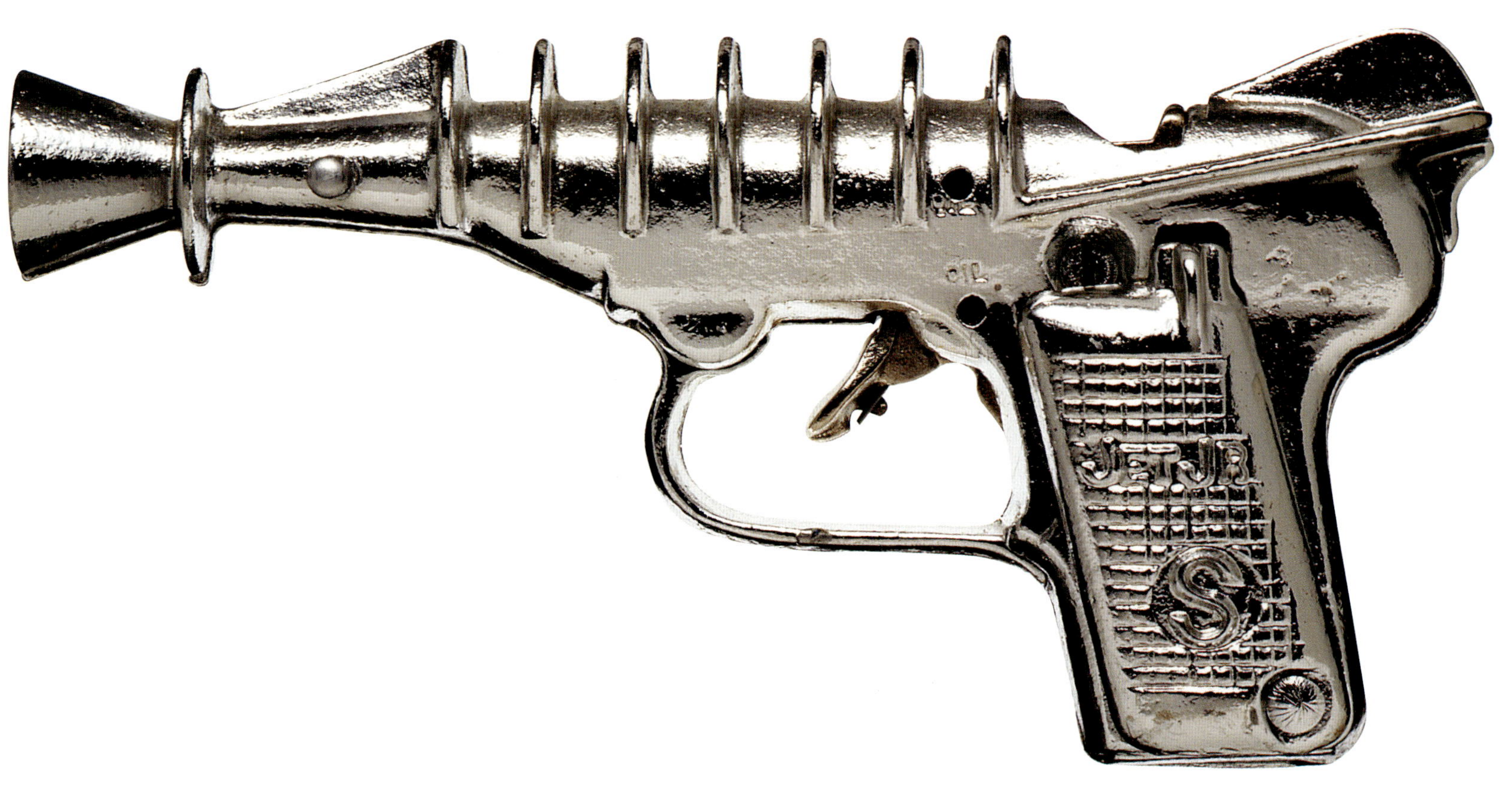
JET JR
S

Atomic Jet Gun, die-cast metal, 4½ x 7¾ in., The J. & E. Stevens Co., U.S.A. early 1950s

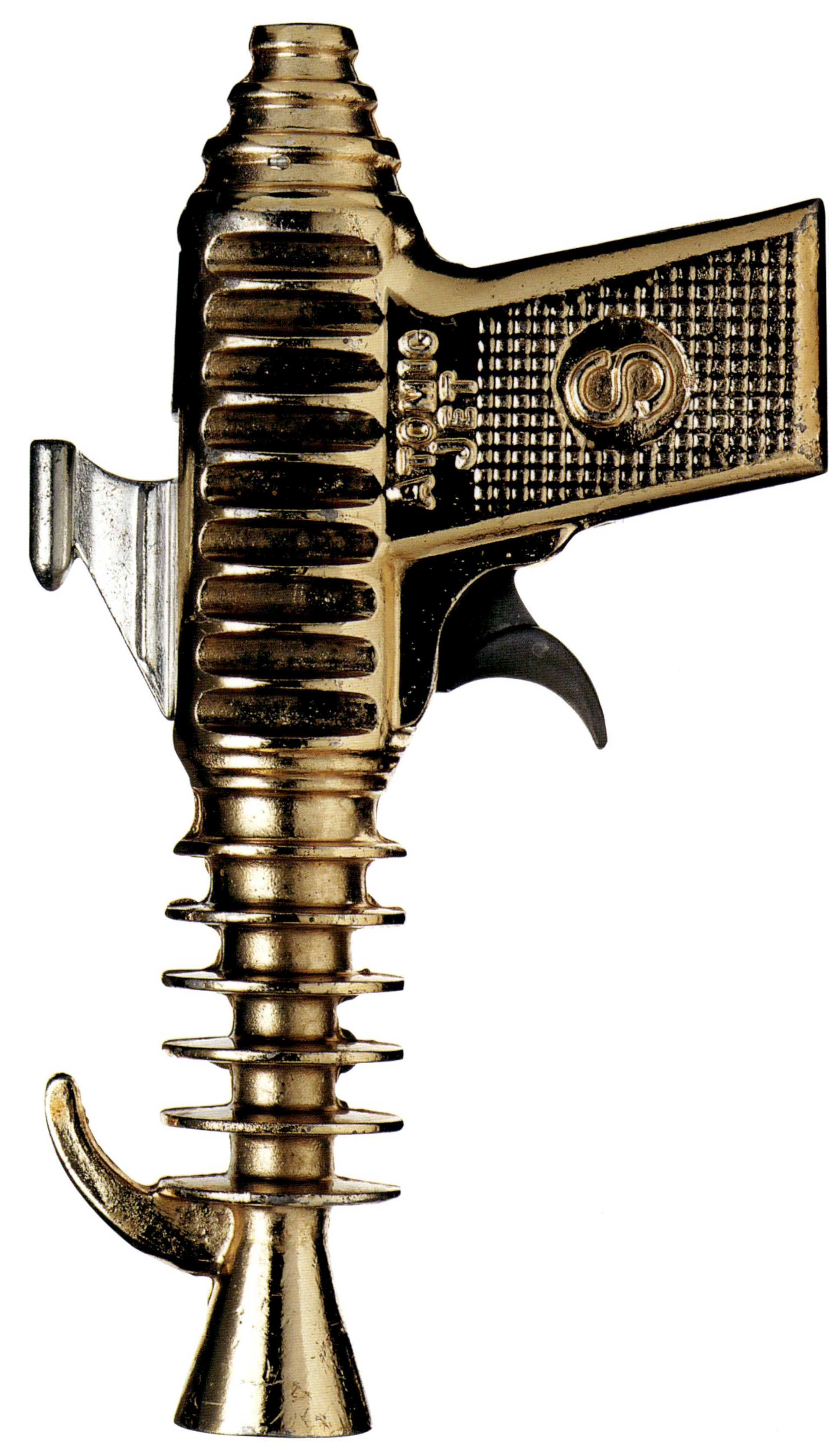

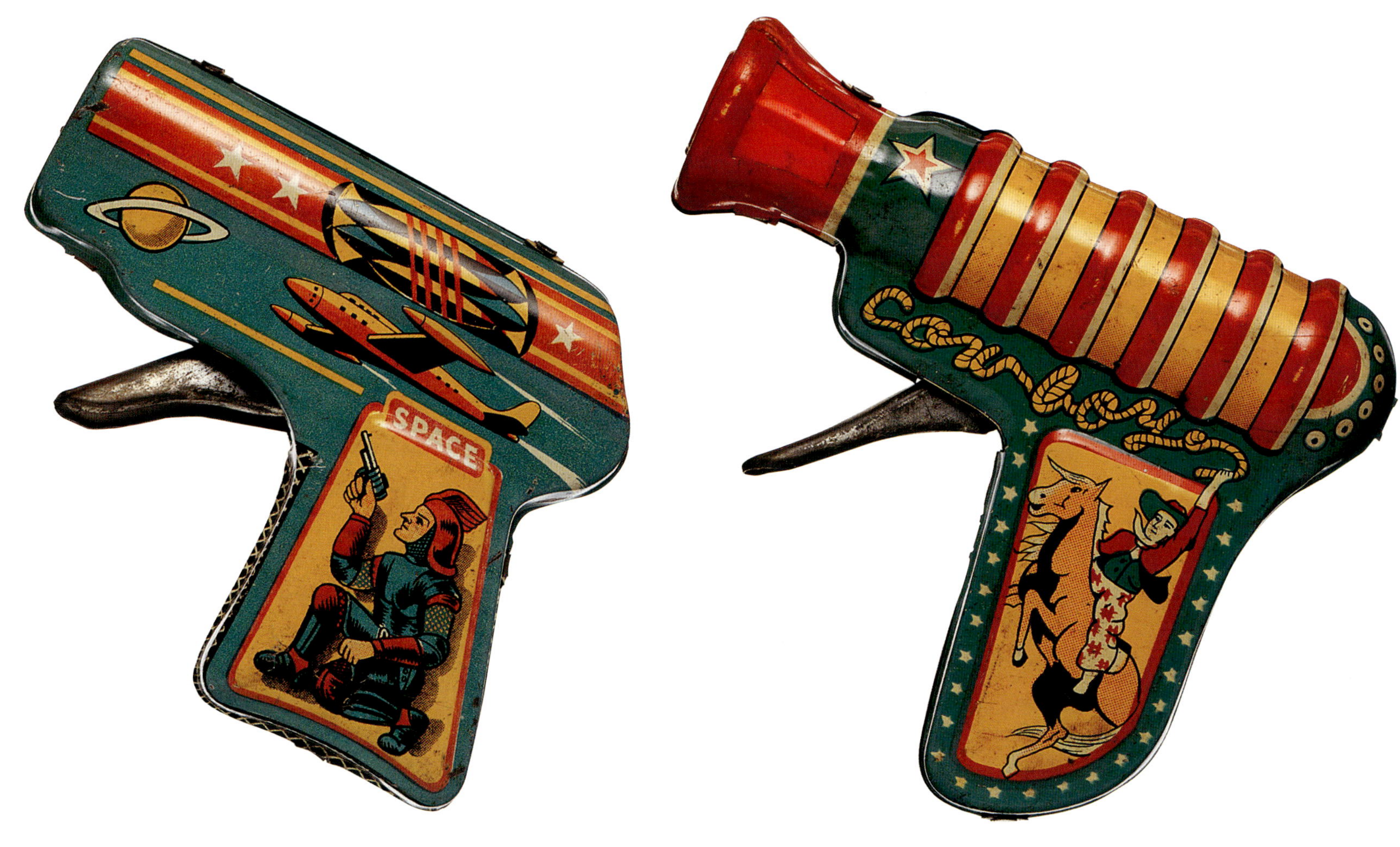

Space Gun, lithographed tin, 3 x 3½ in., maker unknown, Japan 1950s

Cowboy Space Gun, lithographed tin, 3¼ x 4 in., F.G., Japan 1950s

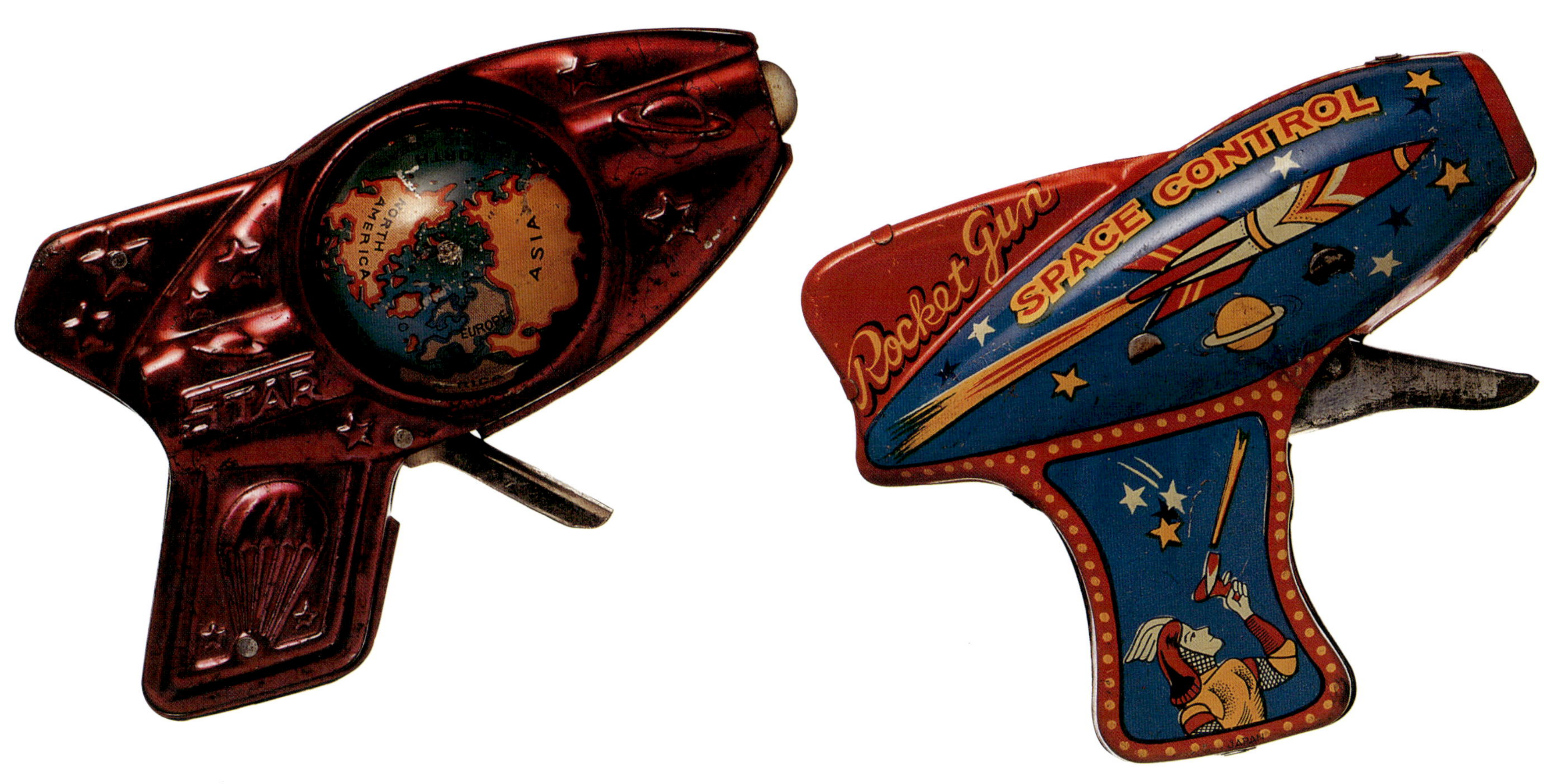

Star Globe Water Gun, painted and lithographed tin, 3 x 4½ in., maker unknown, Japan 1950s

Space Control Rocket Gun, lithographed tin, 3½ x 4 in., maker unknown, Japan 1950s

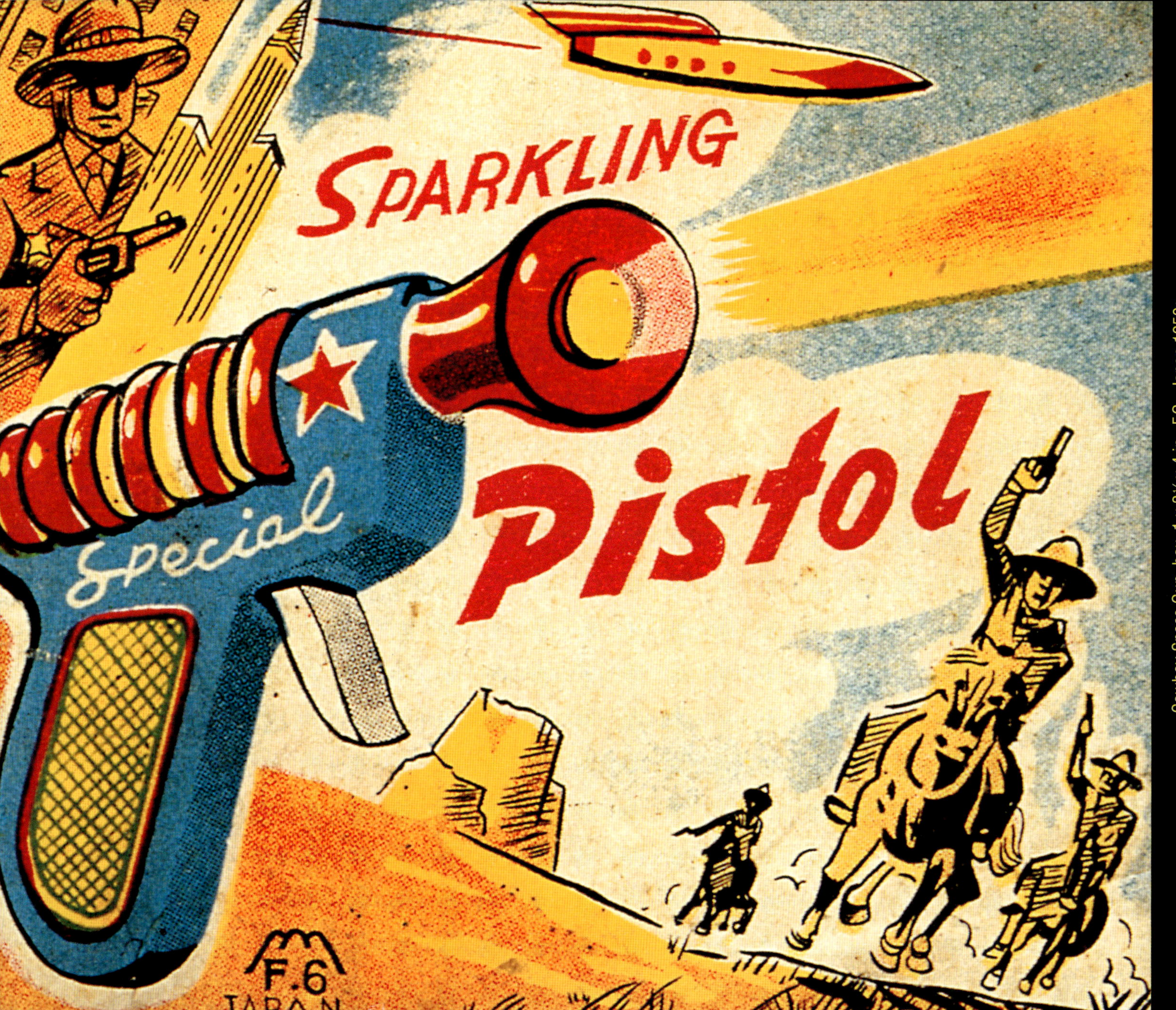

Cowboy Space Gun, box, 1 x 3¼ x 4 in., F.G., Japan 1950s
Flash Gordon Puzzle, 10¼ x 14½ in., Milton Bradley, U.S.A. 1951
Amazing Stories, magazine cover, 7 x 9¾ in., February 1952

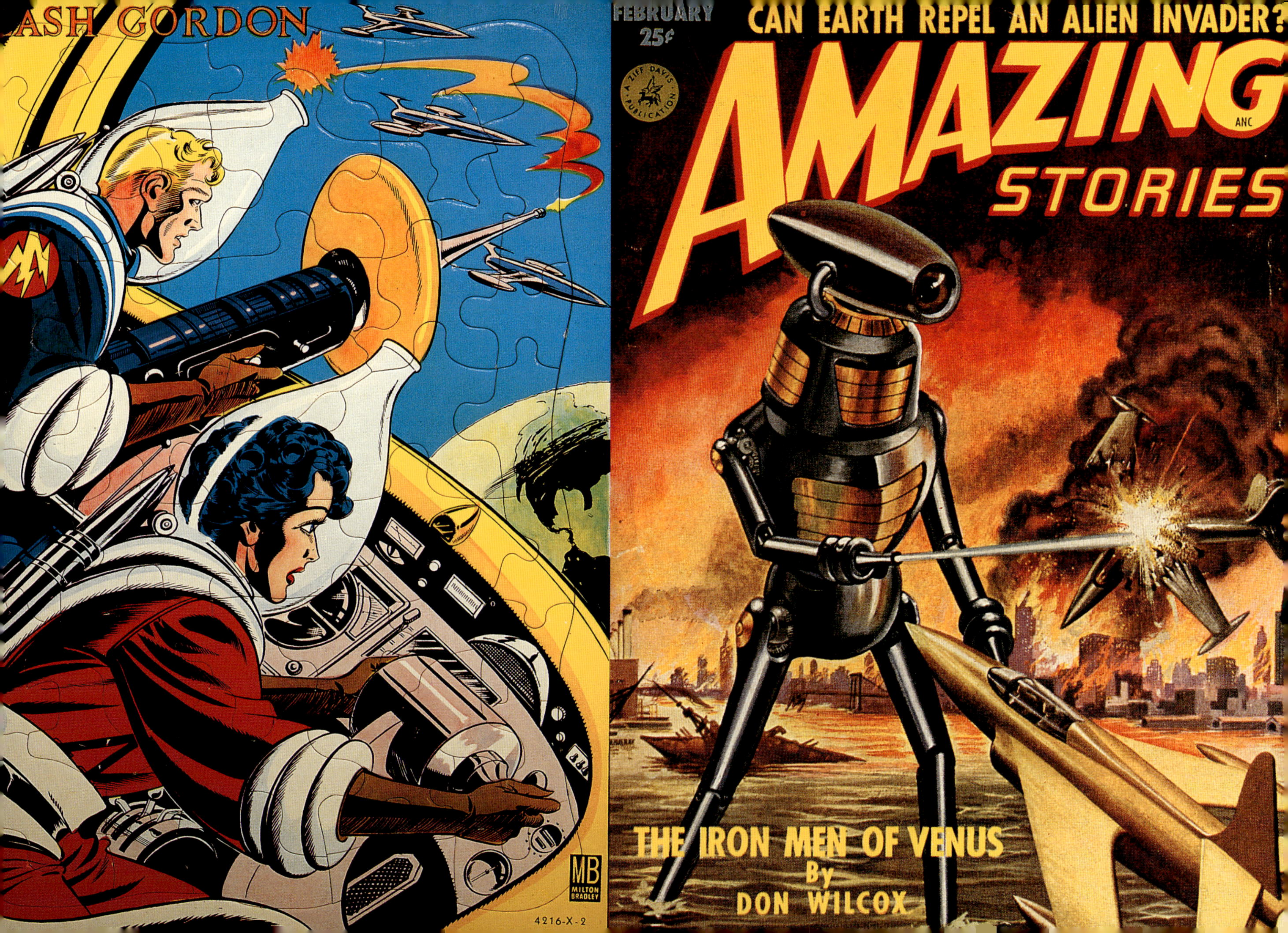
ASH GORDON
MB
MILTON BRADLEY
4216-X-2
FEBRUARY
25¢
CAN EARTH REPEL AN ALIEN INVADER?
A ZIFF DAVIS PUBLICATION
AMAZING
STORIES
THE IRON MEN OF VENUS
By
DON WILCOX

Dan Dare Planet Gun, plastic, 3¾ x 4¼ in., and box, 2 x 7 x 11 in., Merit, England 1950s

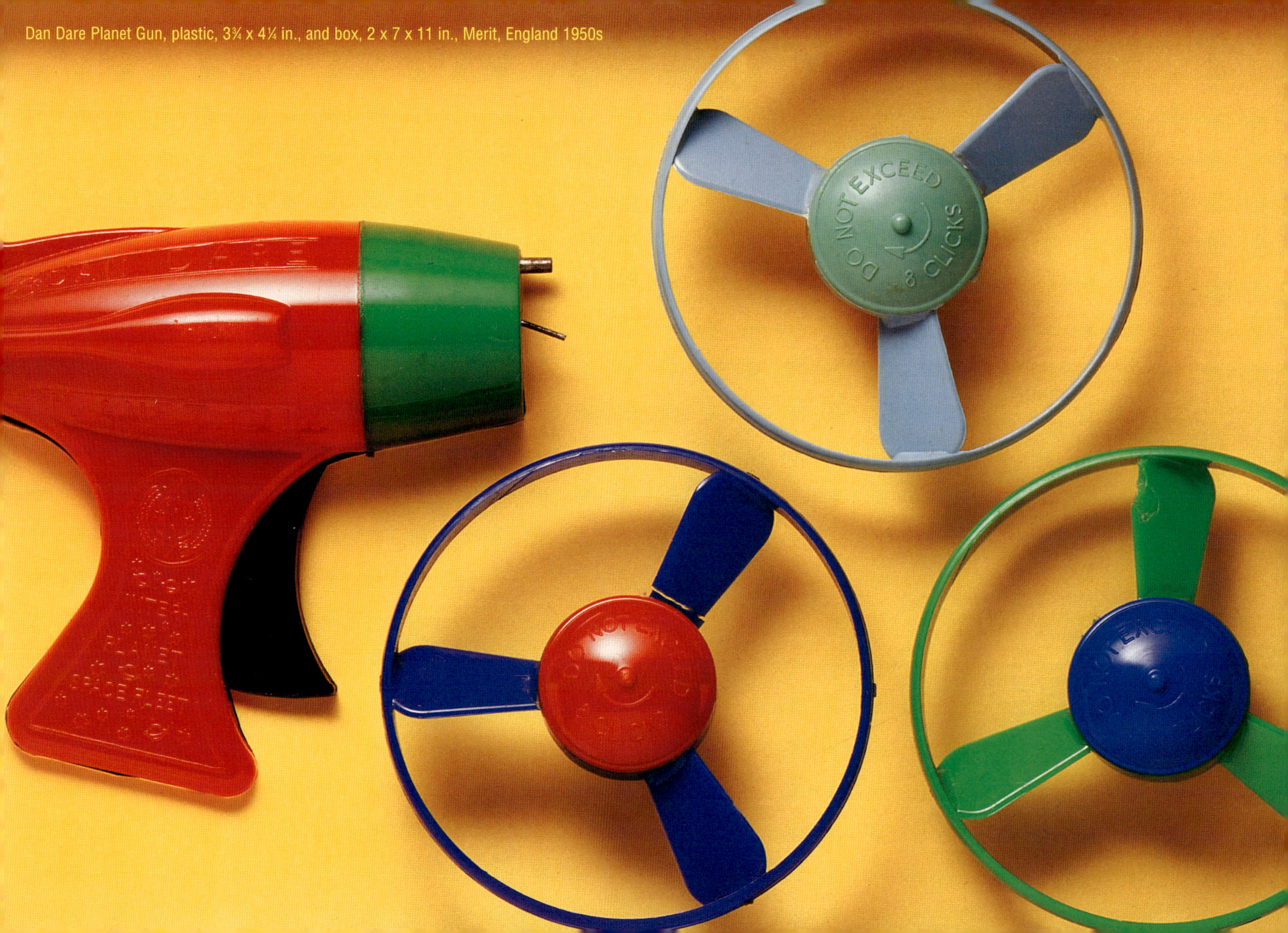

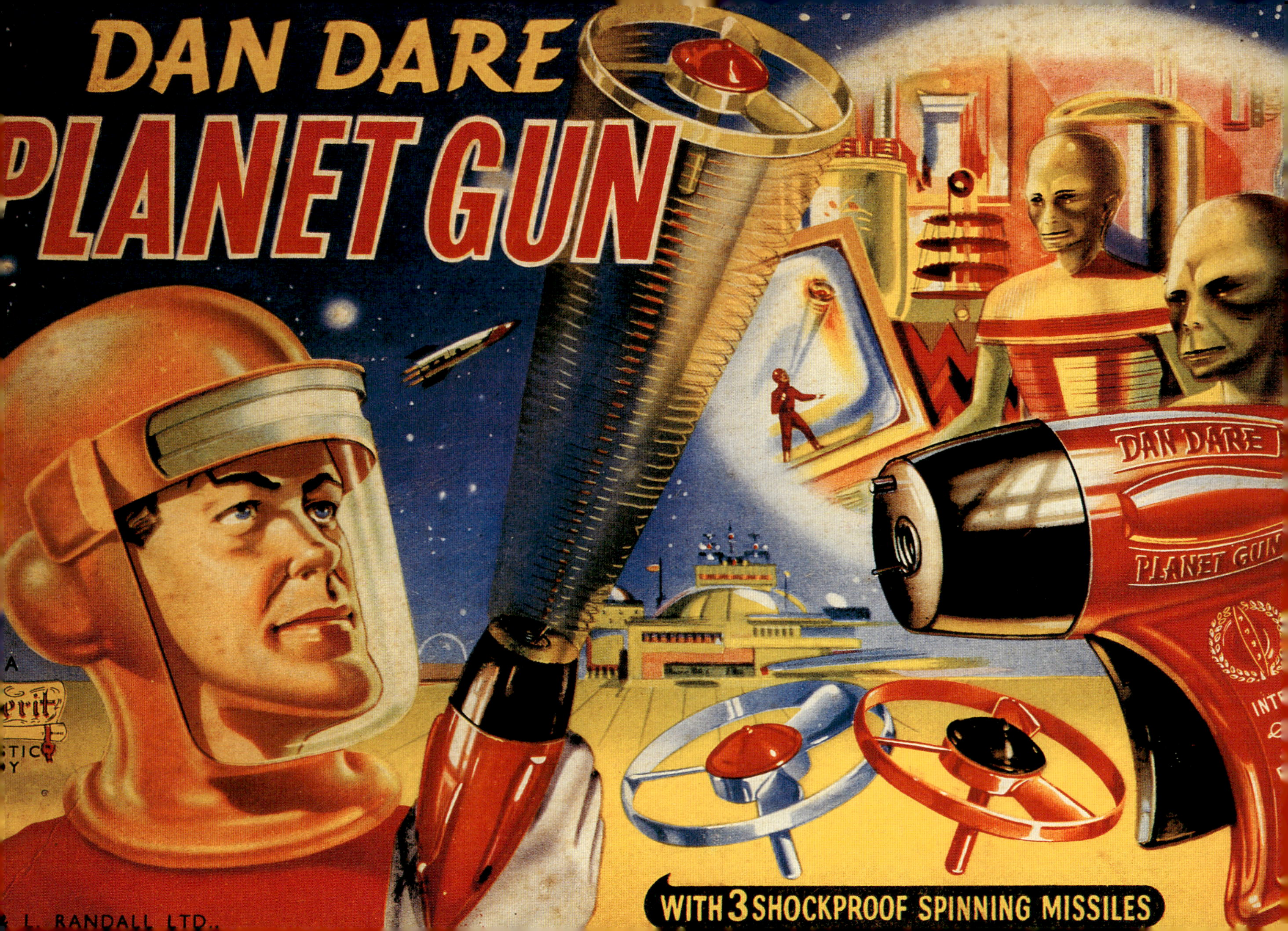
DAN DARE
PLANET GUN
DAN DARE
PLANET GUN
WITH 3 SHOCKPROOF SPINNING MISSILES
L. RANDALL LTD.

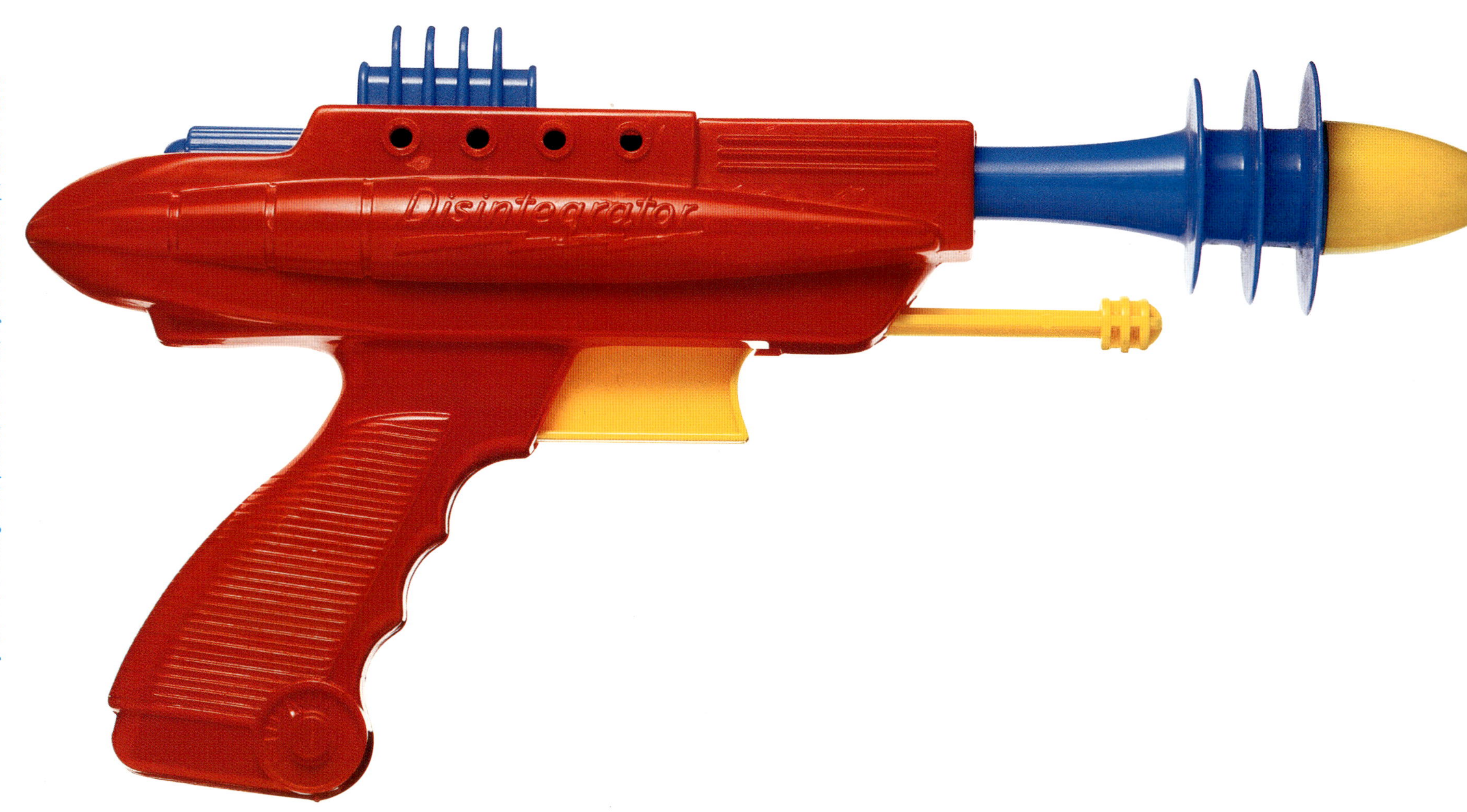

Pyrotomic Disintegrator, plastic, 5½ x 9 in., Pyro Plastics Corp., U.S.A. 1950s

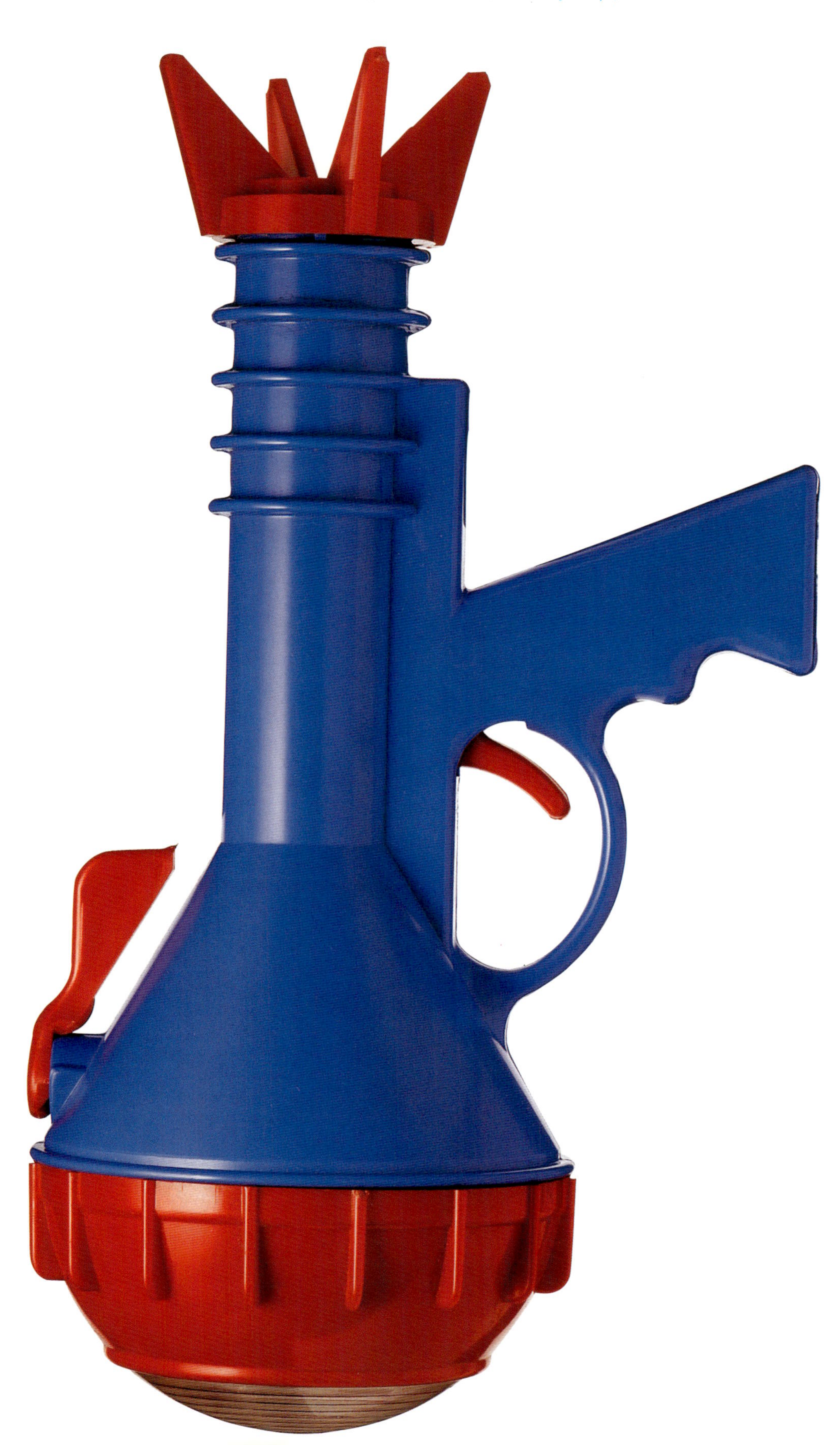

3-Way Futurama Ray Gun, plastic, 5 x 9 in., Ideal Toy Corp., U.S.A. 1951

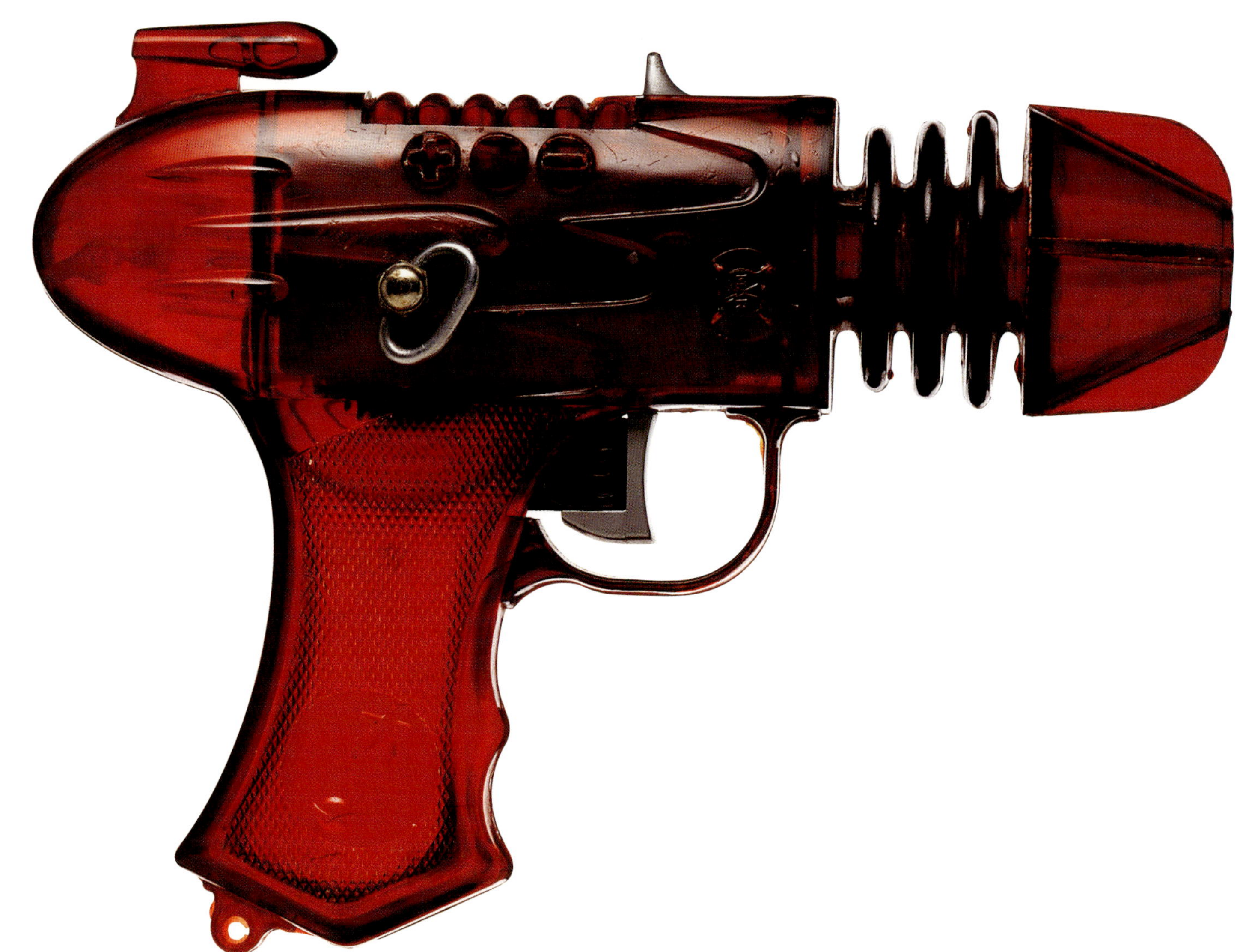

Rex Mars Planet Patrol Sparking Pistol, plastic, 5¼ x 6¼ in., Louis Marx Co., U.S.A. 1950s

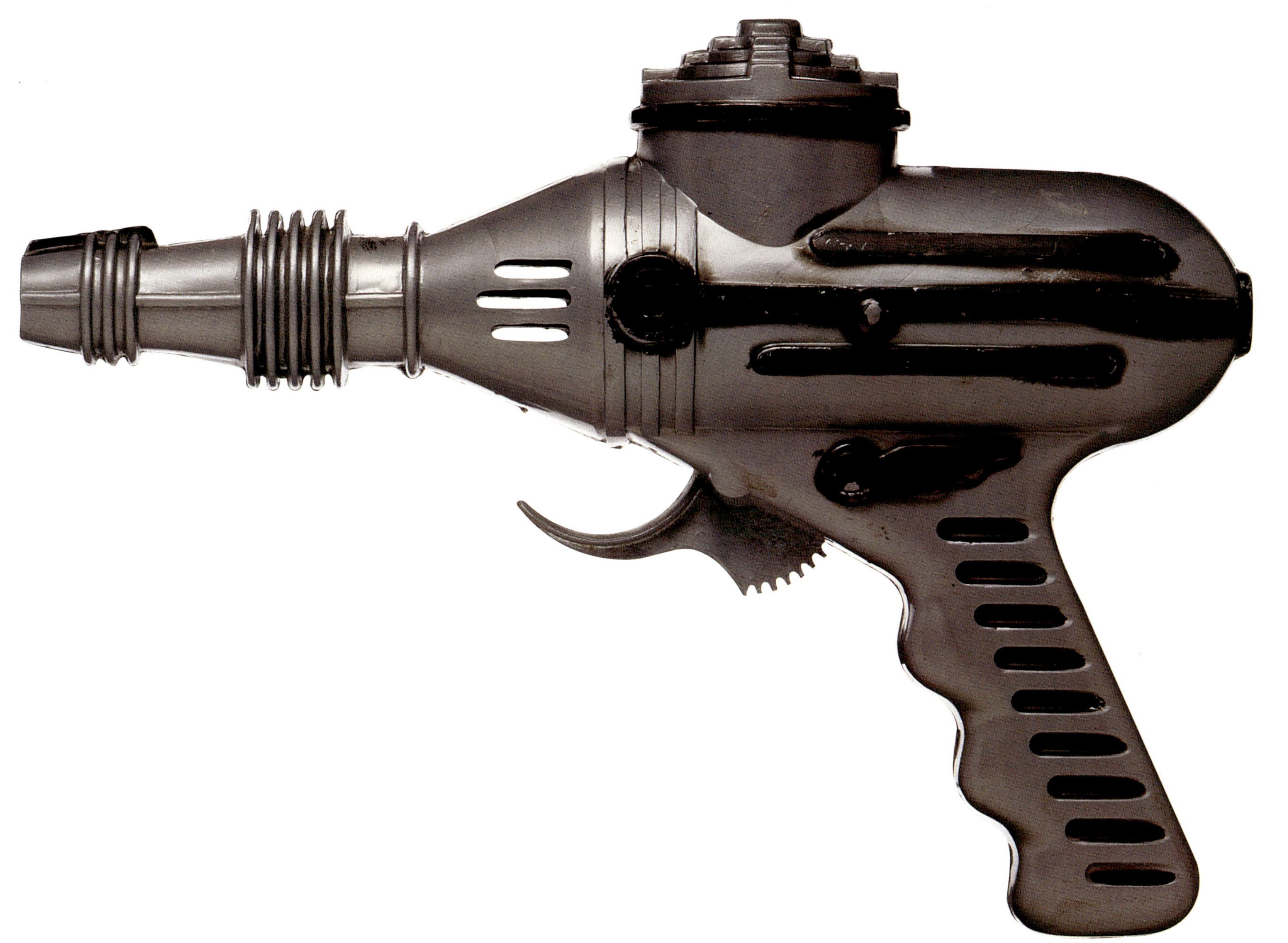

Ratchet Sound Gun, plastic, 5½ x 7 in., Ideal Toy Corp., U.S.A. 1950s

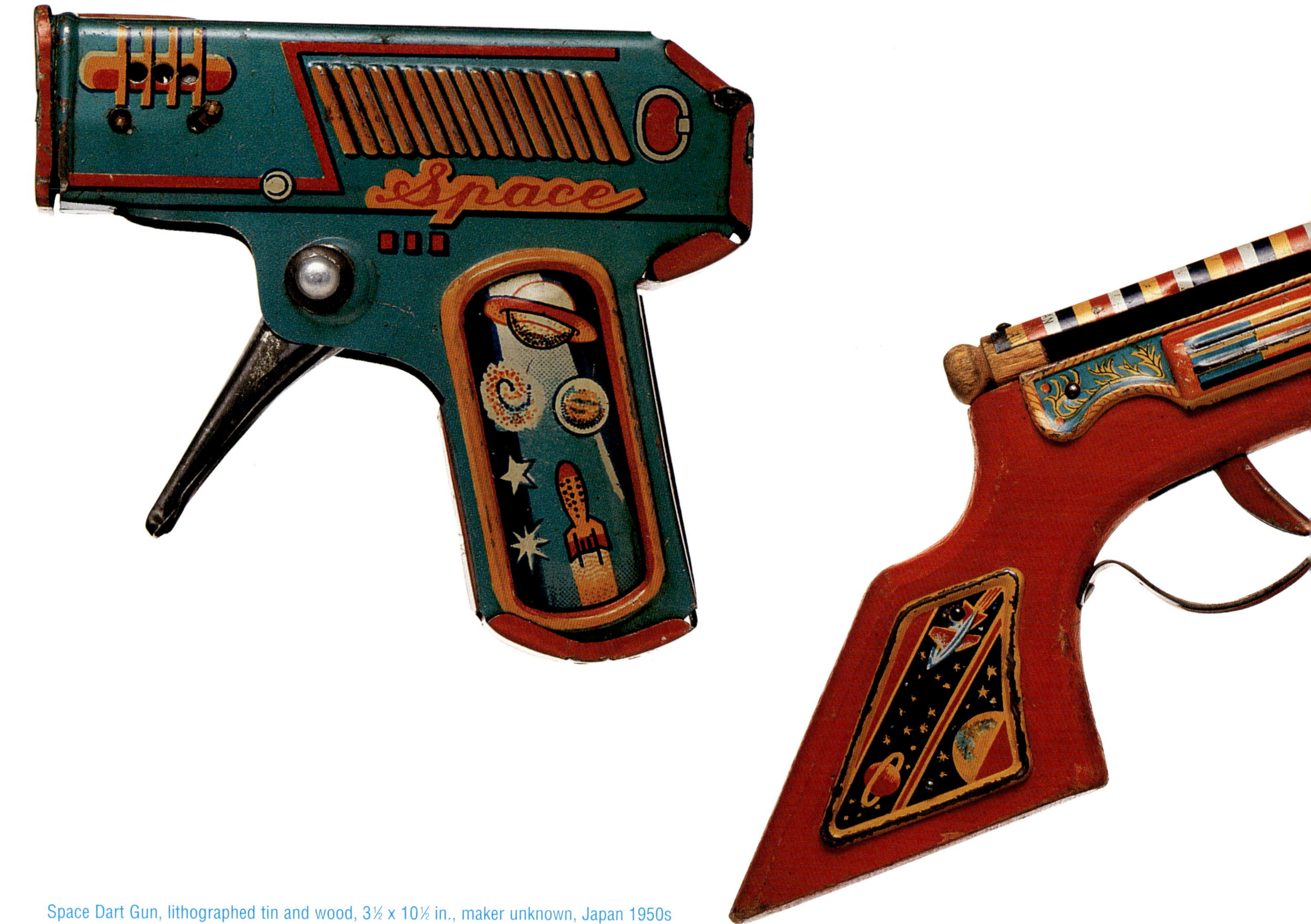

Space Gun, lithographed tin, 3 x 3½ in., SAN, Japan 1950s

Space Dart Gun, lithographed tin and wood, 3½ x 10½ in., maker unknown, Japan 1950s

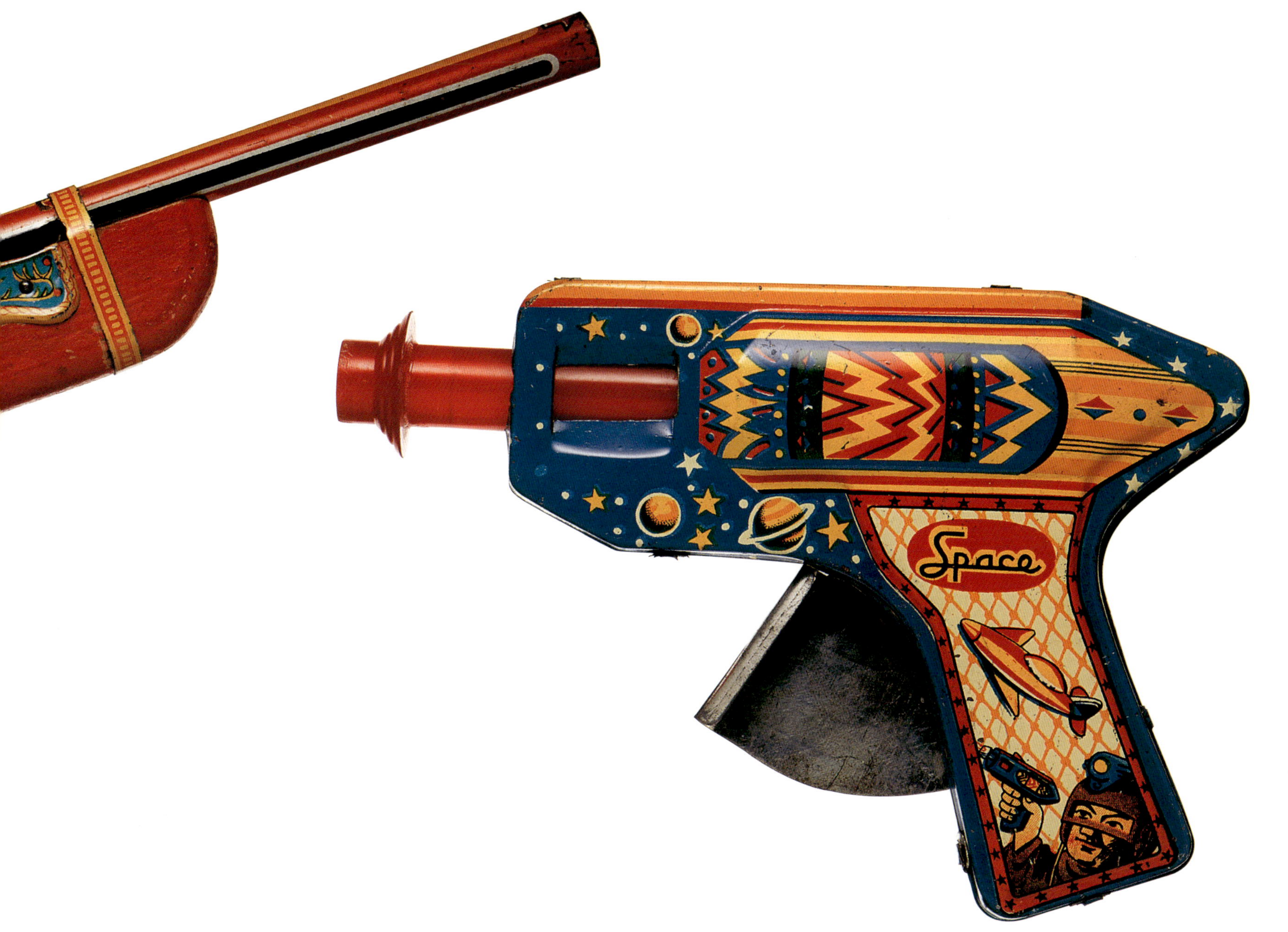

Space Gun, lithographed tin, 4 x 5½ in., maker unknown, Japan 1950s

Cap Firing Sub-Machine Gun, plastic, Ideal Toy Corp., U.S.A. 1953

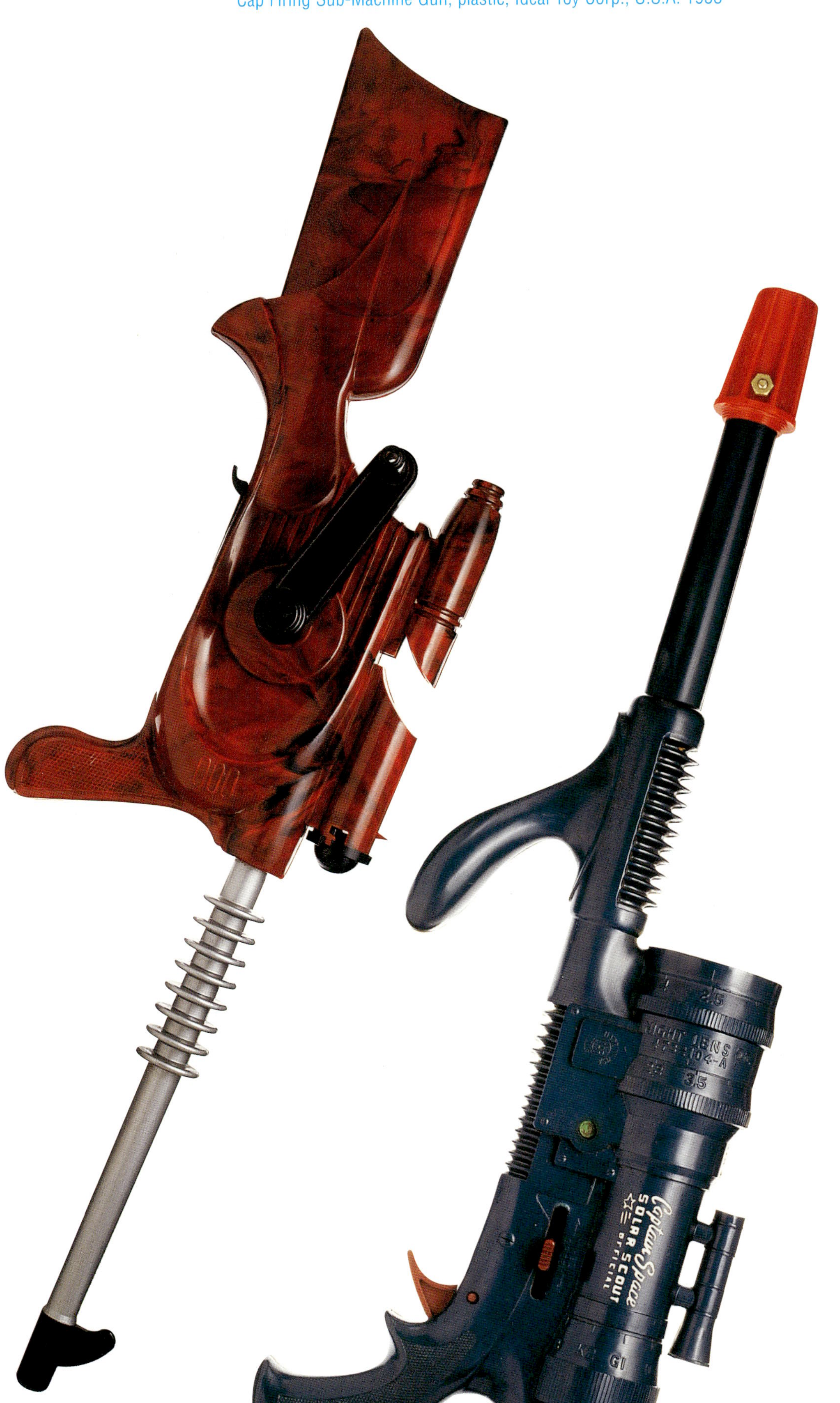

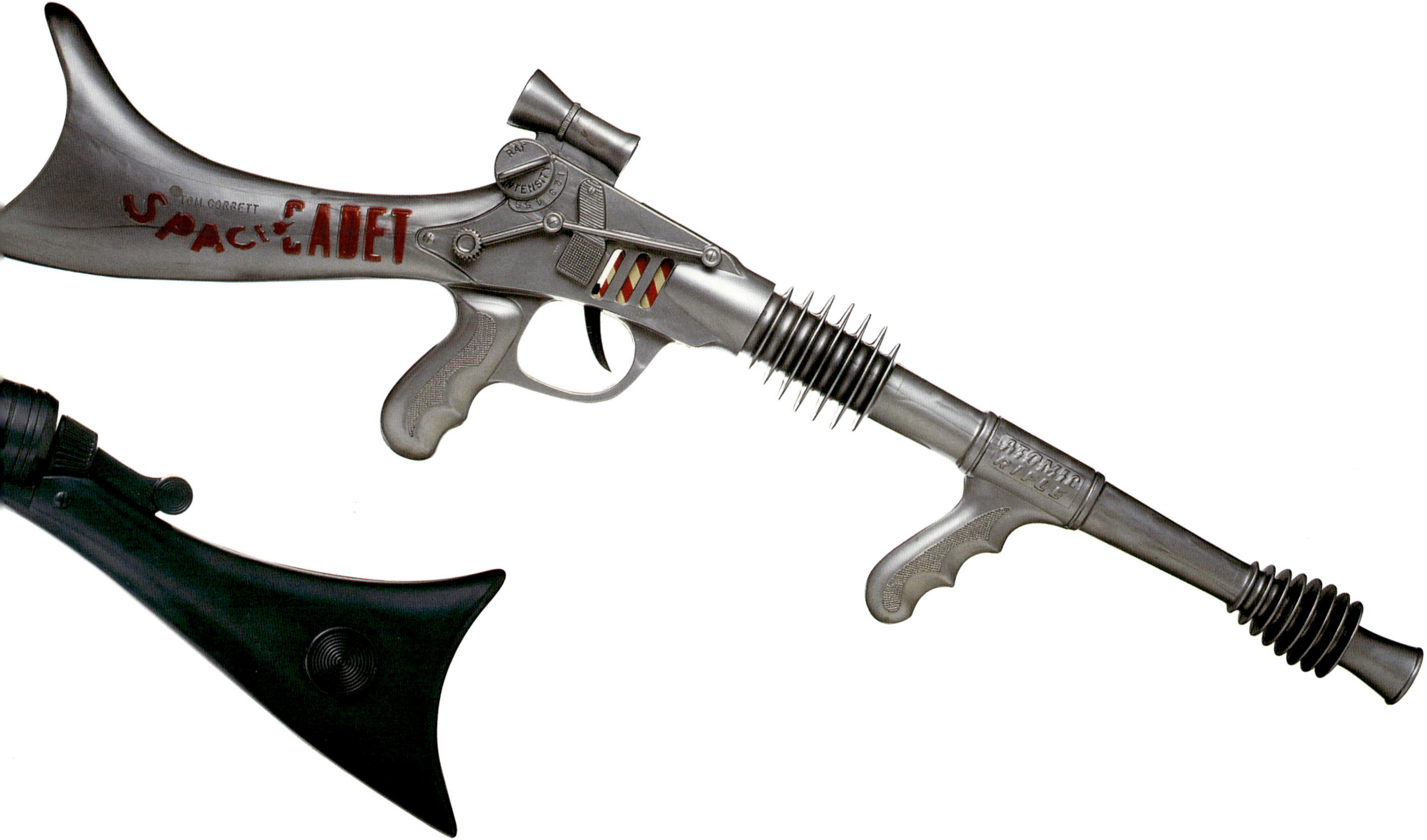

Tom Corbett Space Cadet Atomic Rifle, plastic, 6½ x 24 in., Louis Marx Co., U.S.A. 1950s

Captain Space Solar Scout, plastic, 7 x 26 in., Louis Marx Co., U.S.A. mid 1950s

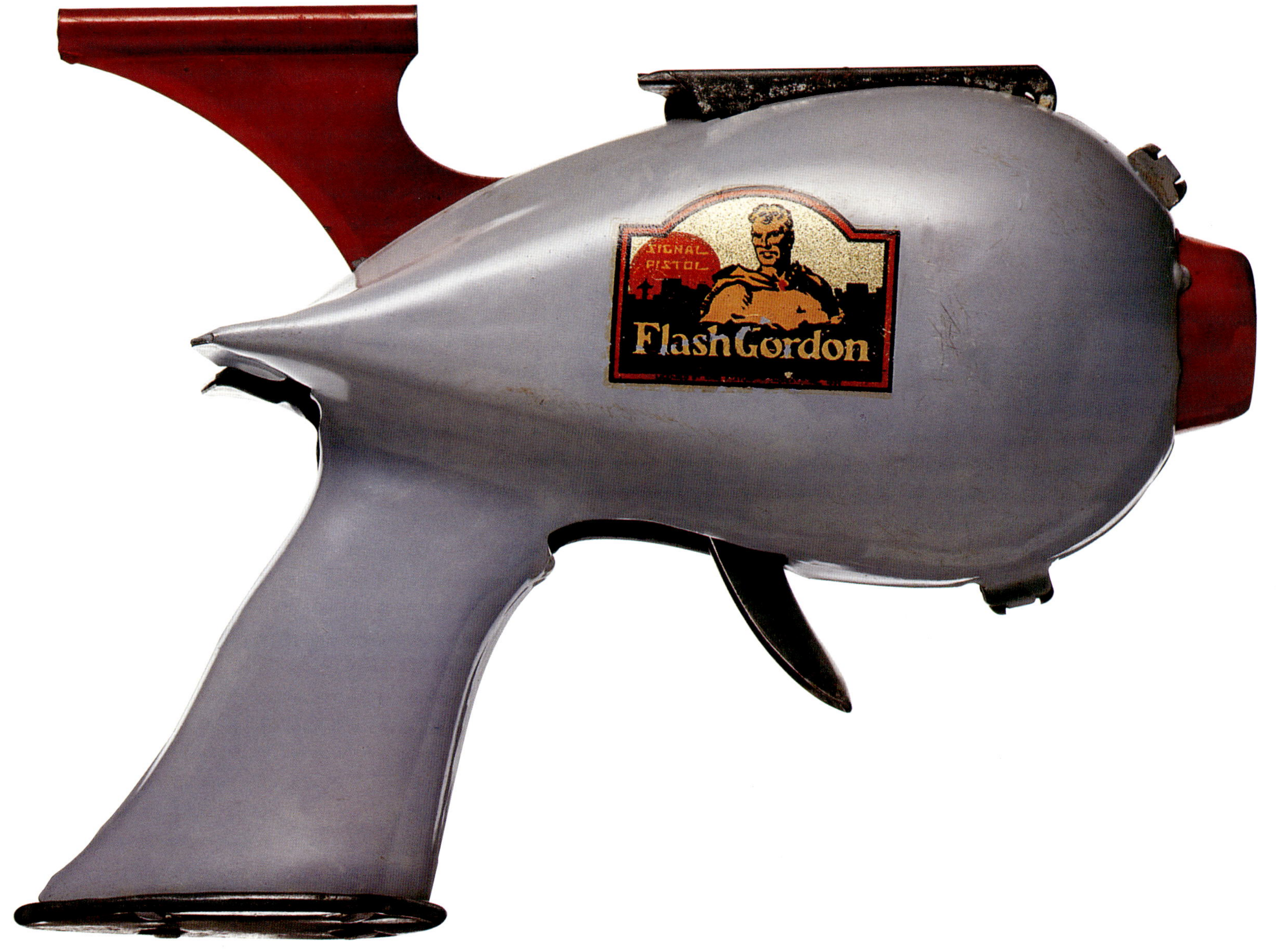

Flash Gordon Signal Pistol, pressed steel, 5½ x 6½ in., Louis Marx Co., U.S.A. mid 1950s

Atomic Disintegrator, die-cast metal, 5¼ x 7½ in., The Hubley Mfg. Co., U.S.A. 1954 and 1955

Space Gun, lithographed tin, 4½ x 7½ in., Daiya, Japan 1950s

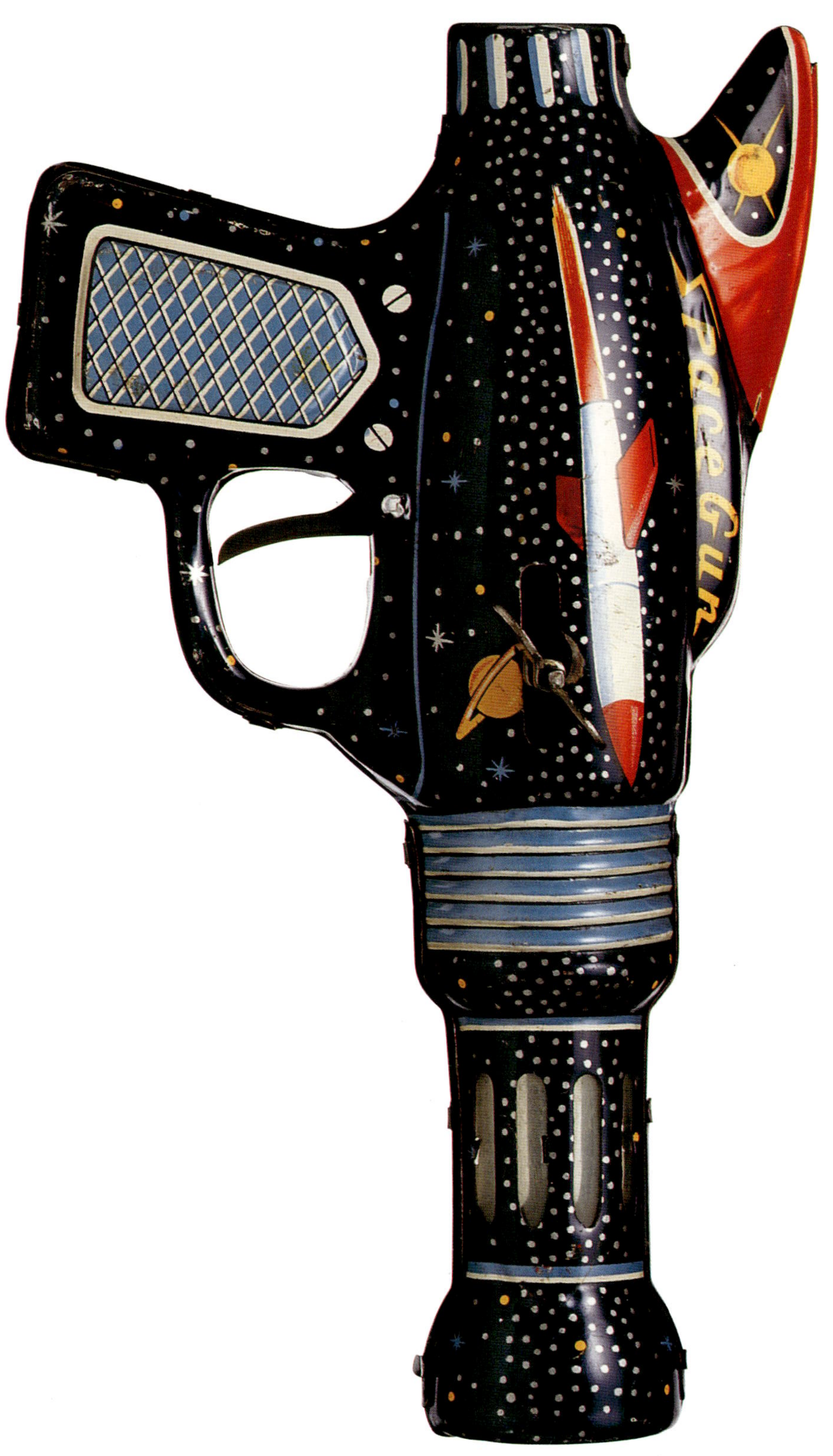

Cosmic Ray Gun, pressed steel, 5 x 8½ in., Ranger Steel Products Corp., U.S.A. mid 1950s

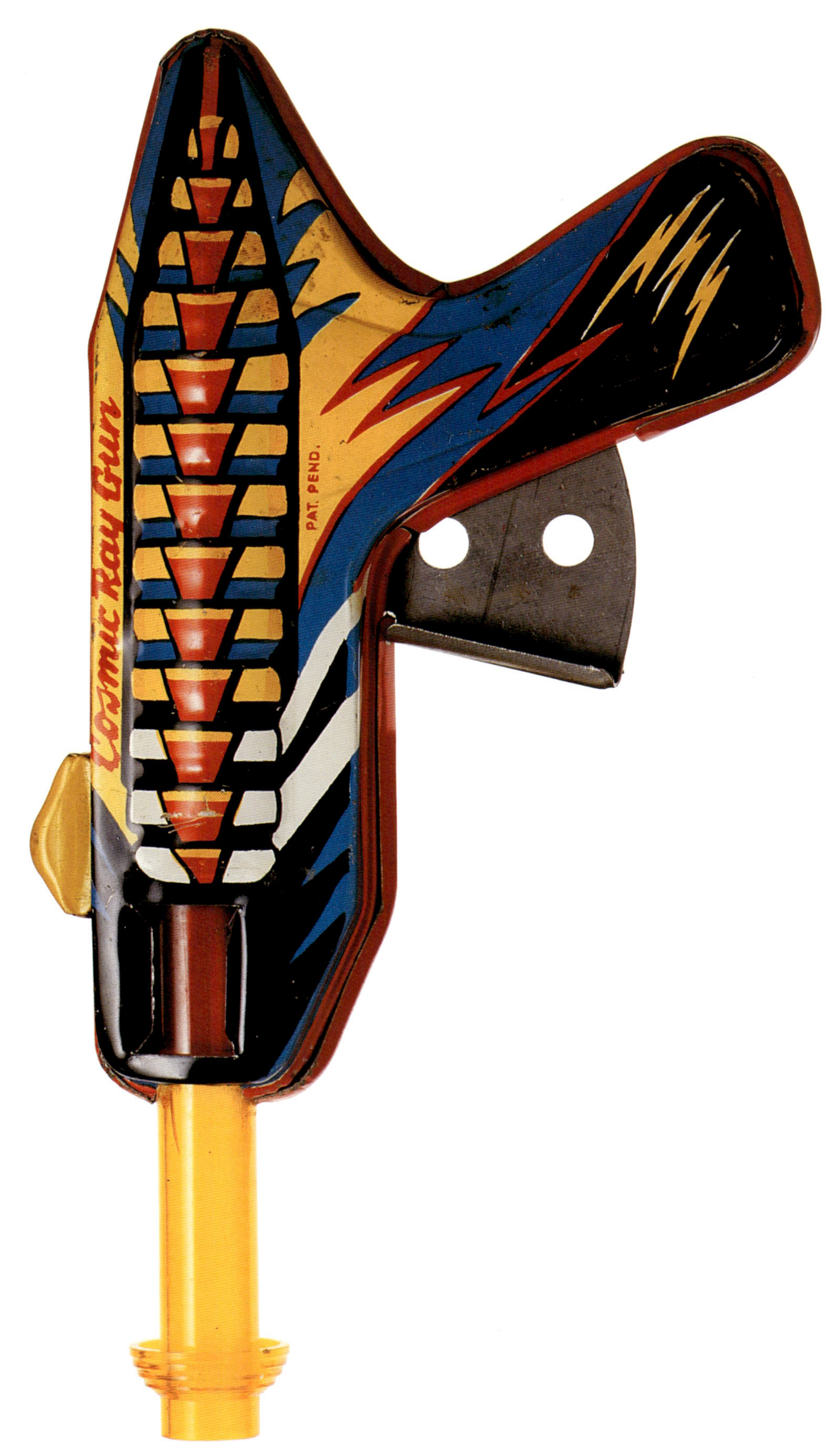

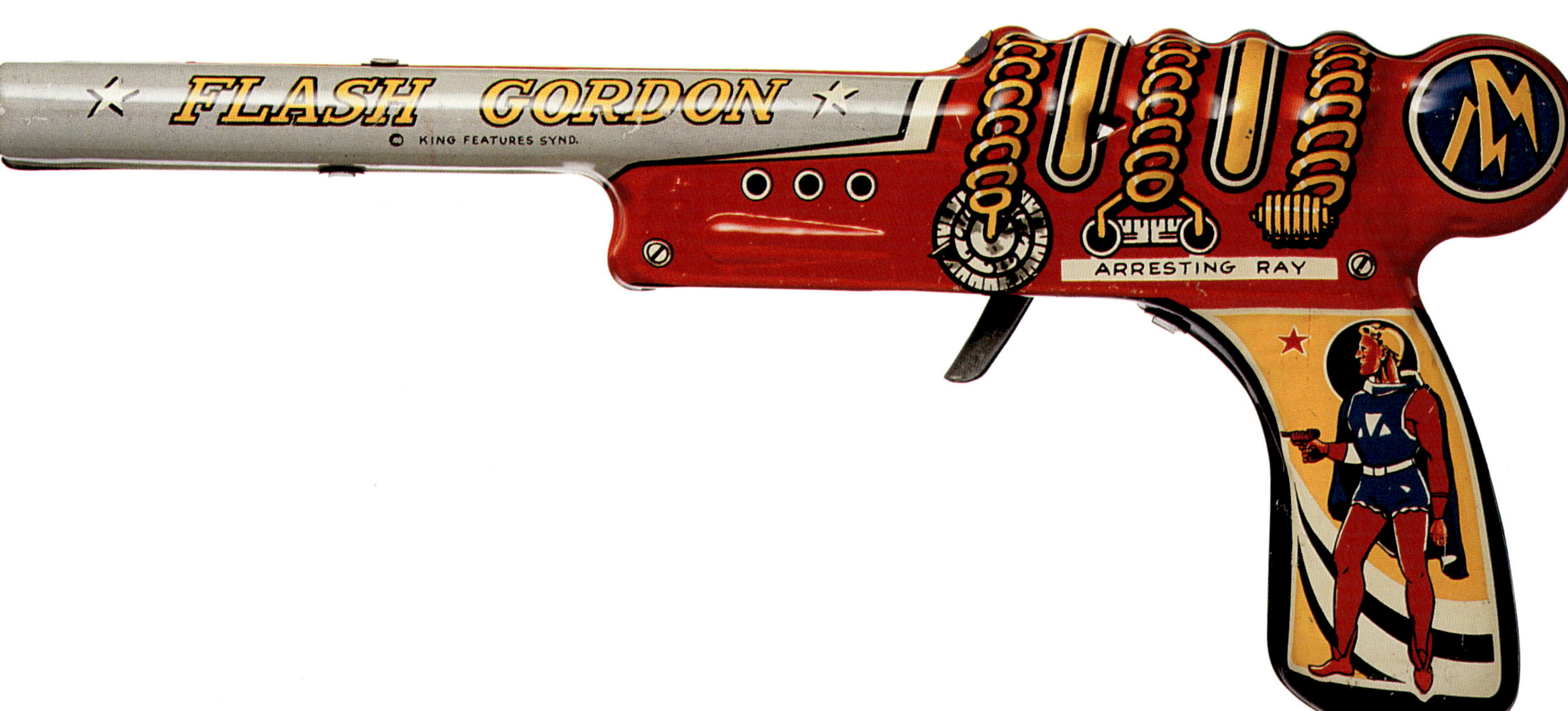
FLASH GORDON
© KING FEATURES SYND.
ARRESTING RAY

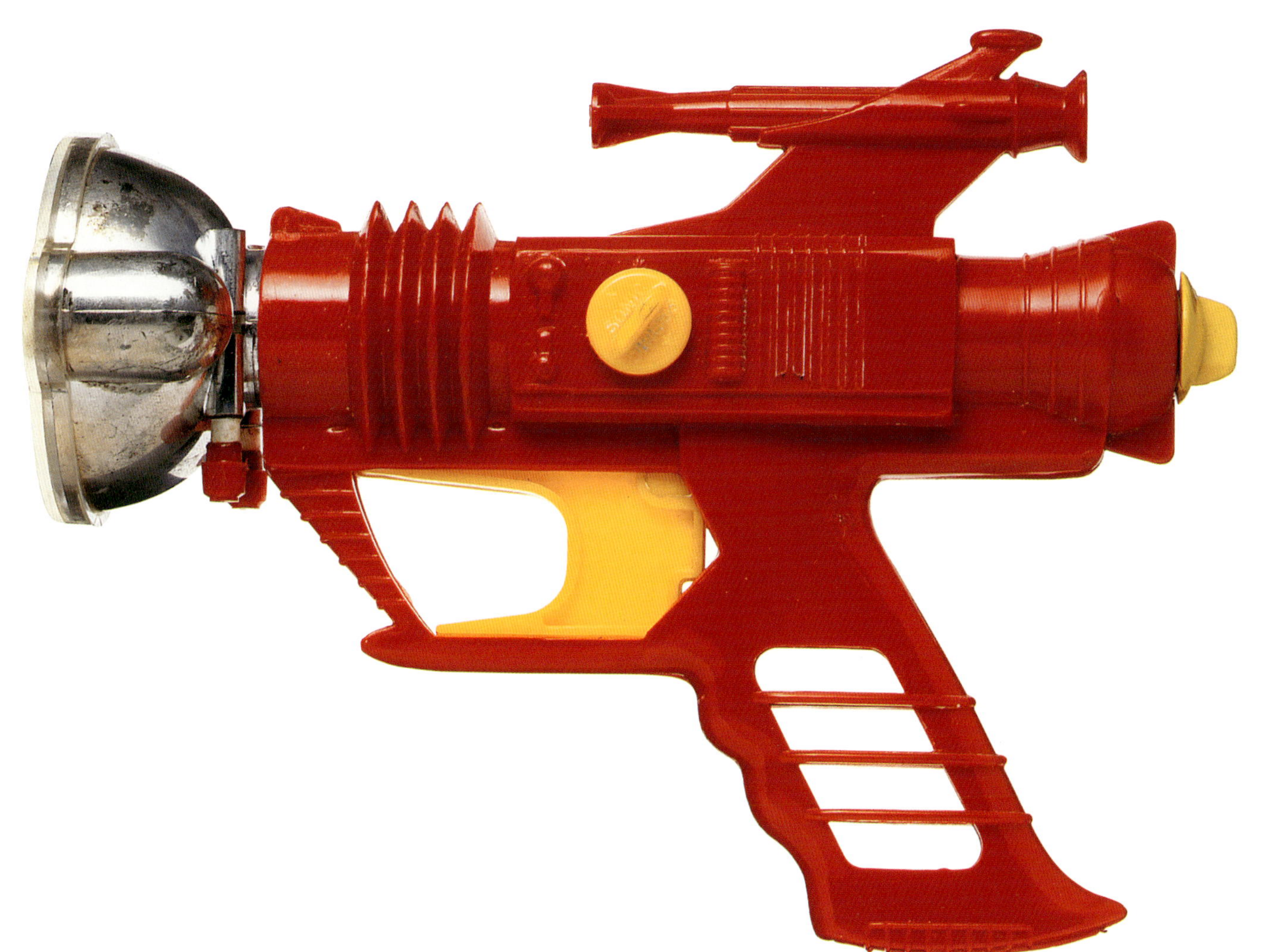

Dan Dare Cosmic Ray Gun, plastic, 4¾ x 6¼ in., Palitoy, England 1950s

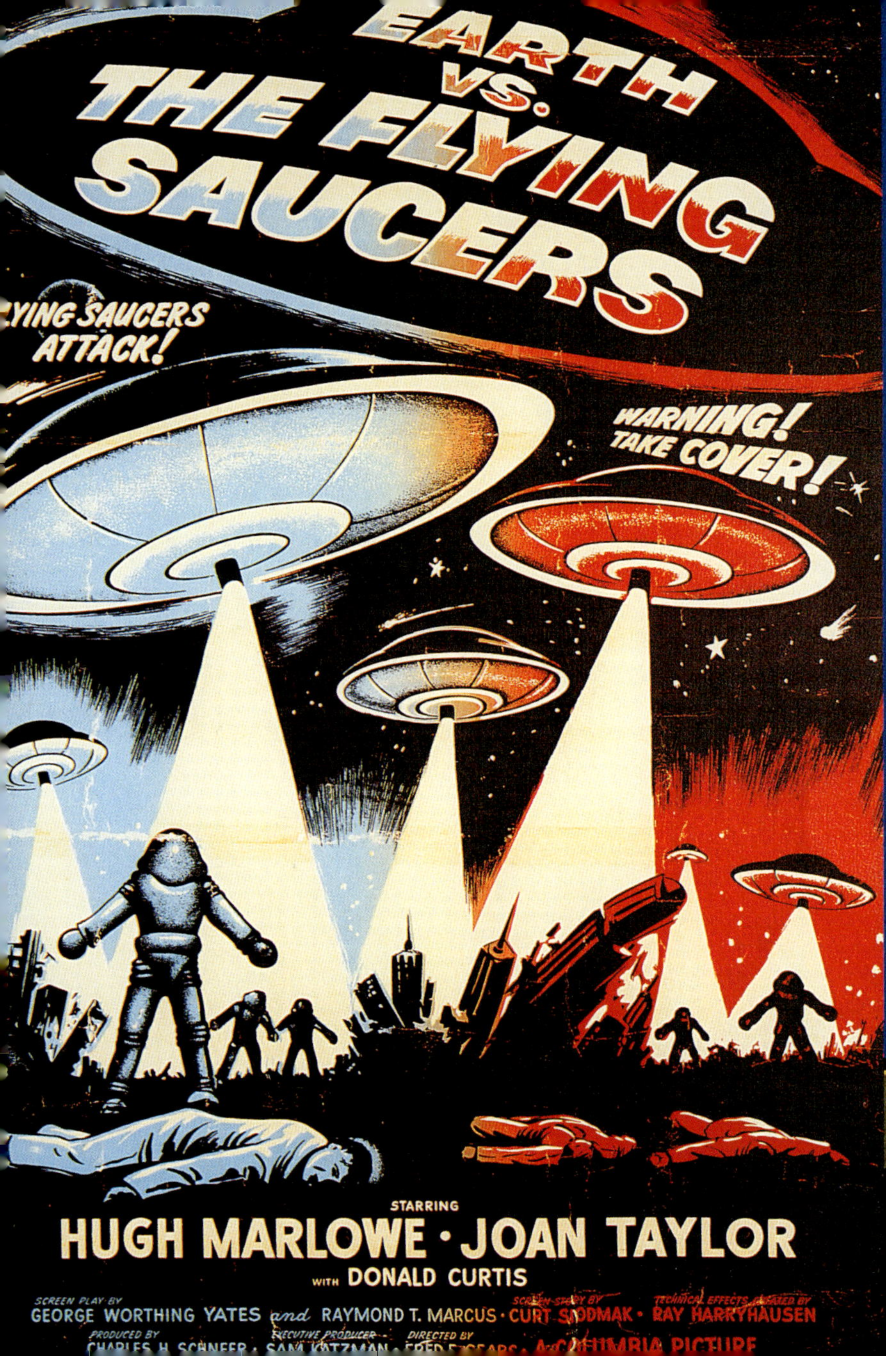

EARTH VS. THE FLYING SAUCERS

YING SAUCERS ATTACK!

WARNING! TAKE COVER!

STARRING

HUGH MARLOWE · JOAN TAYLOR

WITH DONALD CURTIS

SCREEN PLAY BY GEORGE WORTHING YATES and RAYMOND T. MARCUS · SCREEN STORY BY CURT SIODMAK · TECHNICAL EFFECTS CREATED BY RAY HARRYHAUSEN

PRODUCED BY · EXECUTIVE PRODUCER · DIRECTED BY

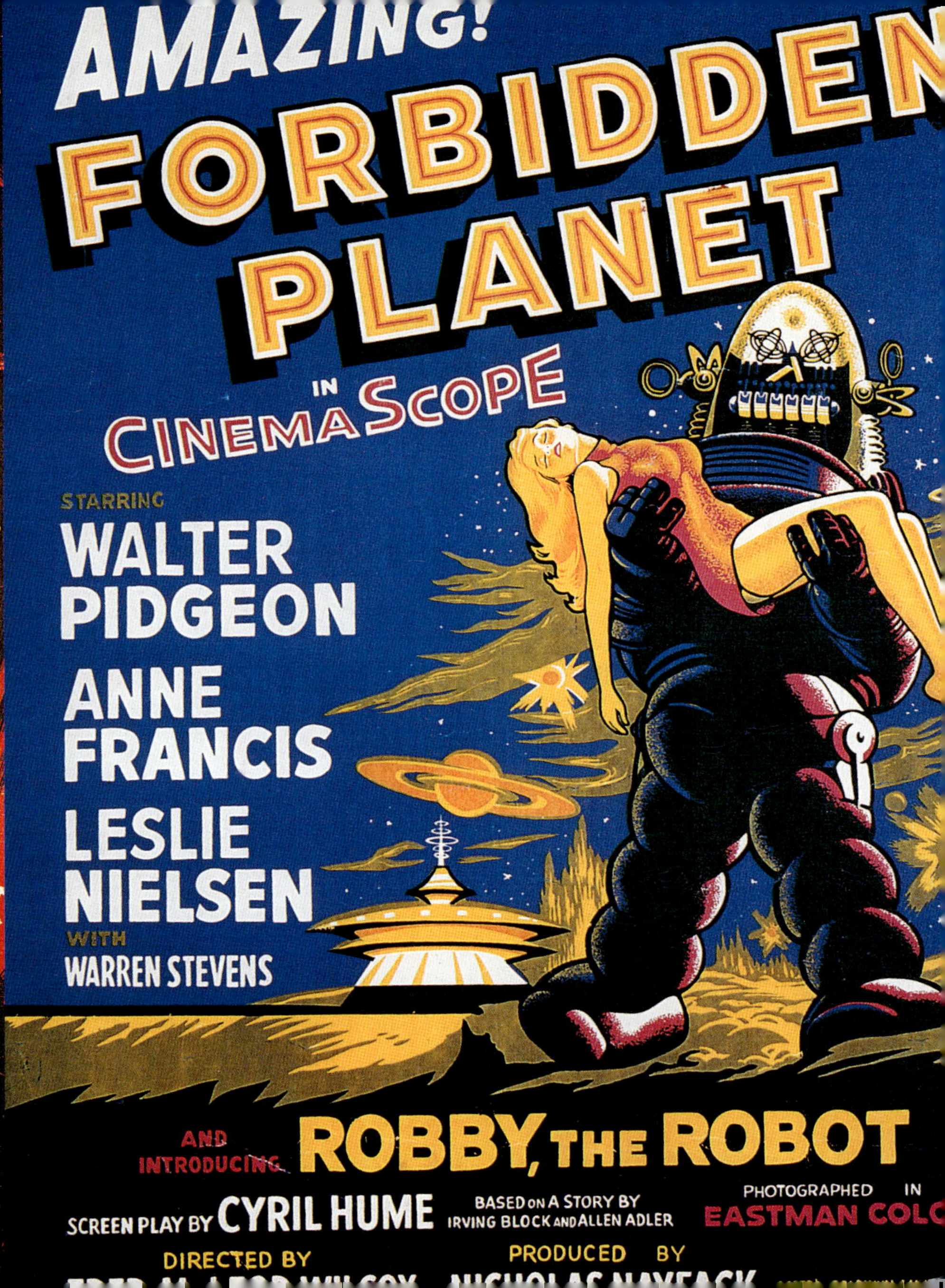

AMAZING!

FORBIDDEN PLANET

IN CINEMASCOPE

STARRING

WALTER PIDGEON

ANNE FRANCIS

LESLIE NIELSEN

WITH

WARREN STEVENS

AND INTRODUCING ROBBY, THE ROBOT

SCREEN PLAY BY CYRIL HUME

BASED ON A STORY BY IRVING BLOCK AND ALLEN ADLER

PHOTOGRAPHED IN EASTMAN COLO

DIRECTED BY

PRODUCED BY

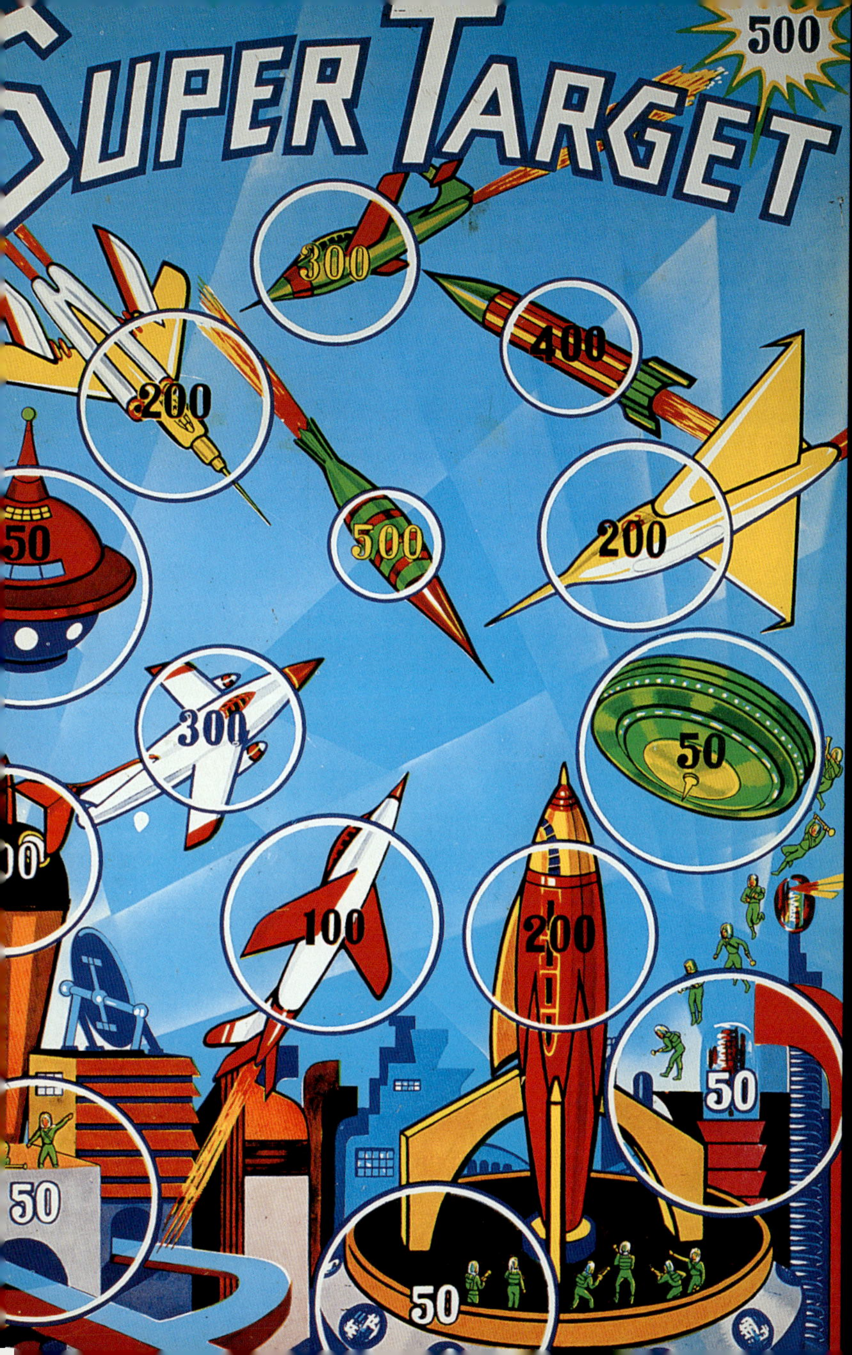

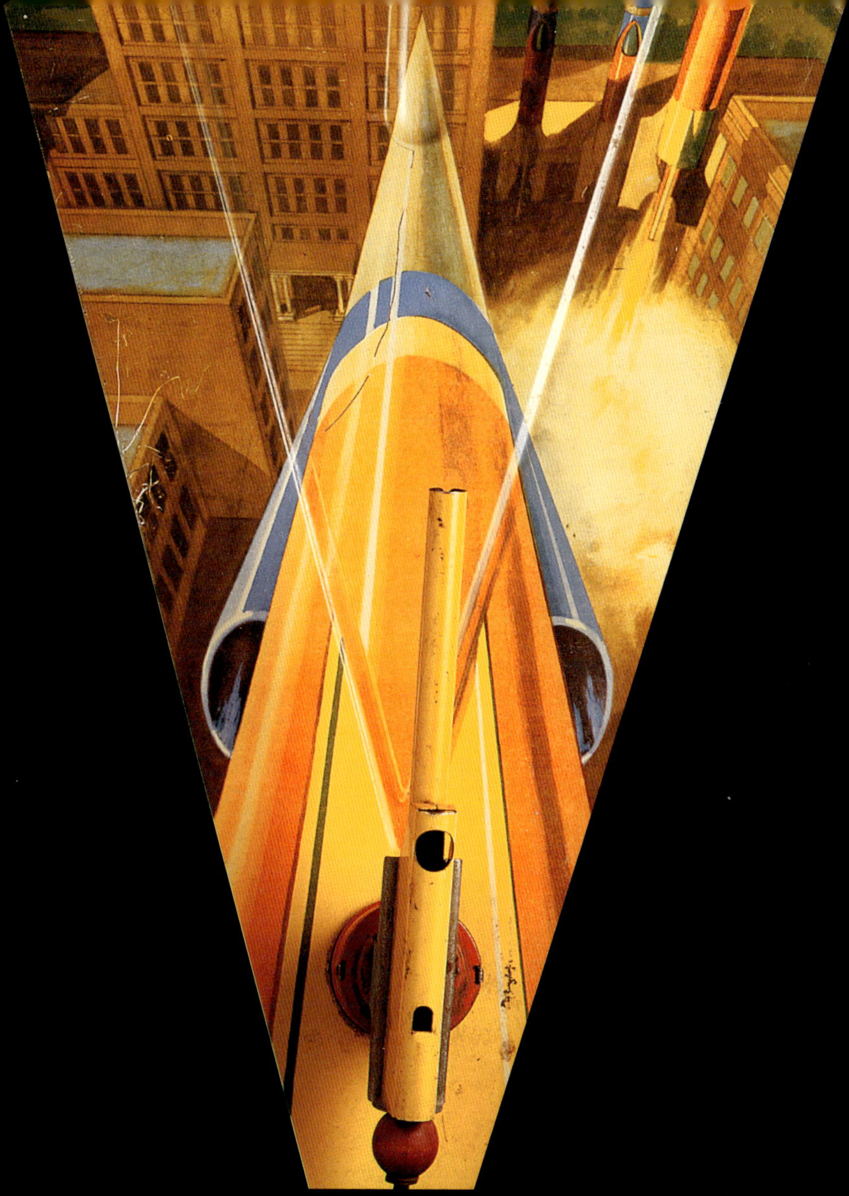

Earth vs. The Flying Saucers, movie poster, 10½ x 16¼ in., Columbia Pictures, U.S.A. 1956
Forbidden Planet, movie poster, 10½ x 14¼ in,. Metro-Goldwyn-Mayer Pictures, U.S.A. 1956
Super Target, game, 15 x 23 in., T. Cohn, U.S.A. early 1950s
Space Shooting Range, 10 x 15½ in., maker unknown, U.S.A. 1950s

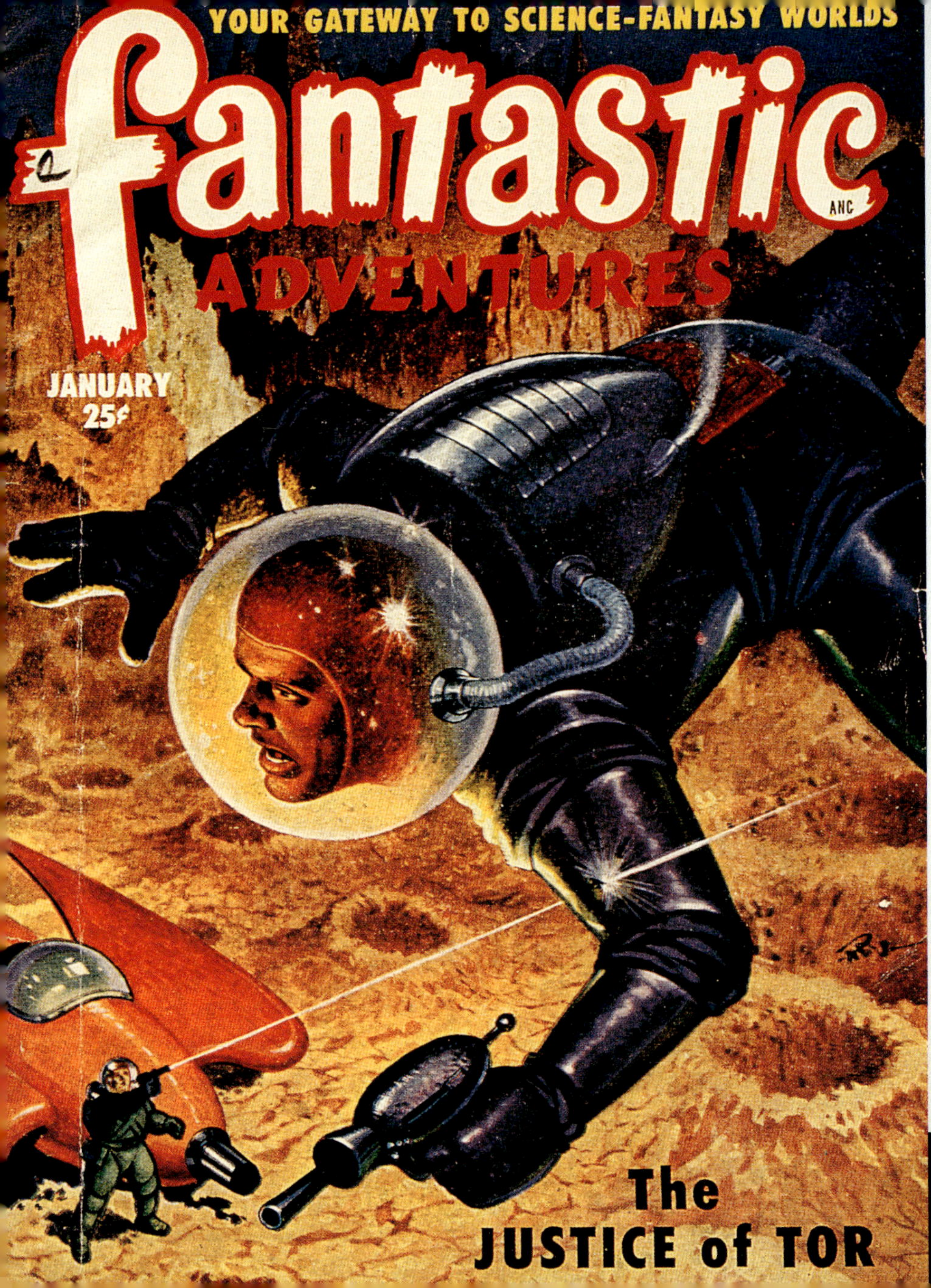

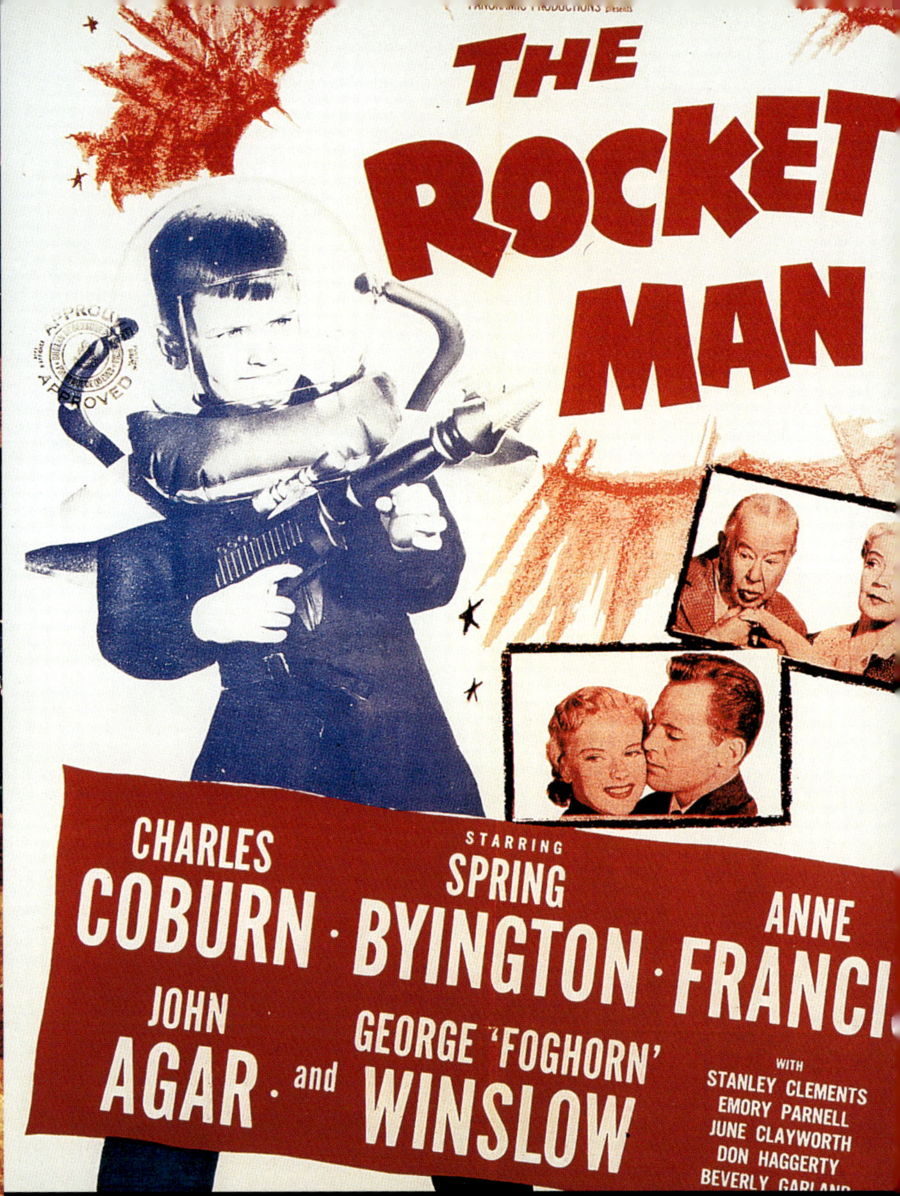

Fantastic Adventures, magazine cover, 7 x 9½ in., January 1951
The Rocket Man, movie poster, 10¾ x 16½ in., Twentieth Century Fox, U.S.A. 1954
Queen of Outer Space, movie poster, 10¾ x 13½ in., Allied Artists, U.S.A. 1958

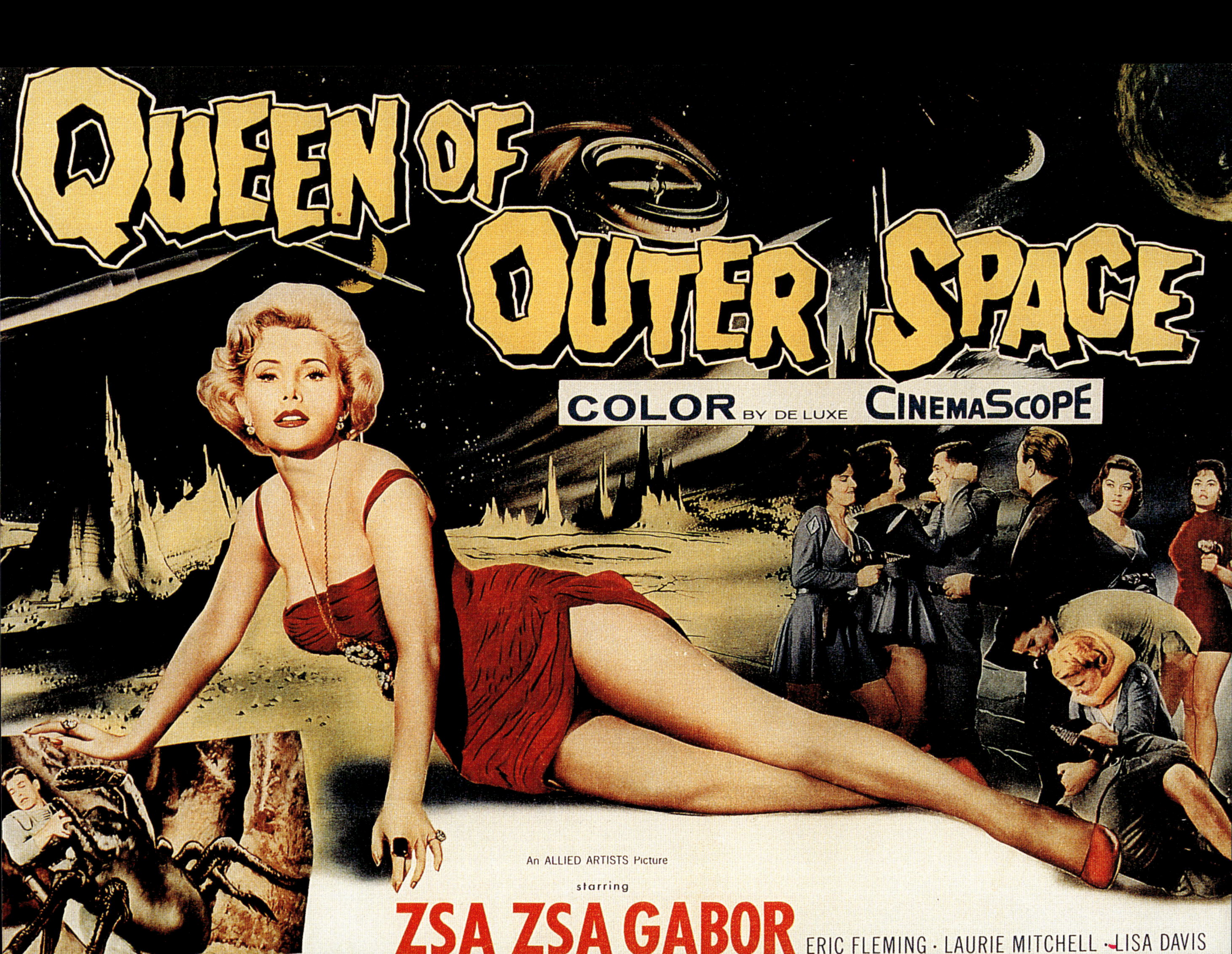
QUEEN OF OUTER SPACE
COLOR BY DE LUXE CINEMASCOPE
An ALLIED ARTISTS Picture
starring
ZSA ZSA GABOR
ERIC FLEMING · LAURIE MITCHELL · LISA DAVIS

Holster, 5¾ x 9½ in., Halco, U.S.A. 1950s, with Space Patrol Atomic Flashlight Pistol, Louis Marx Co.

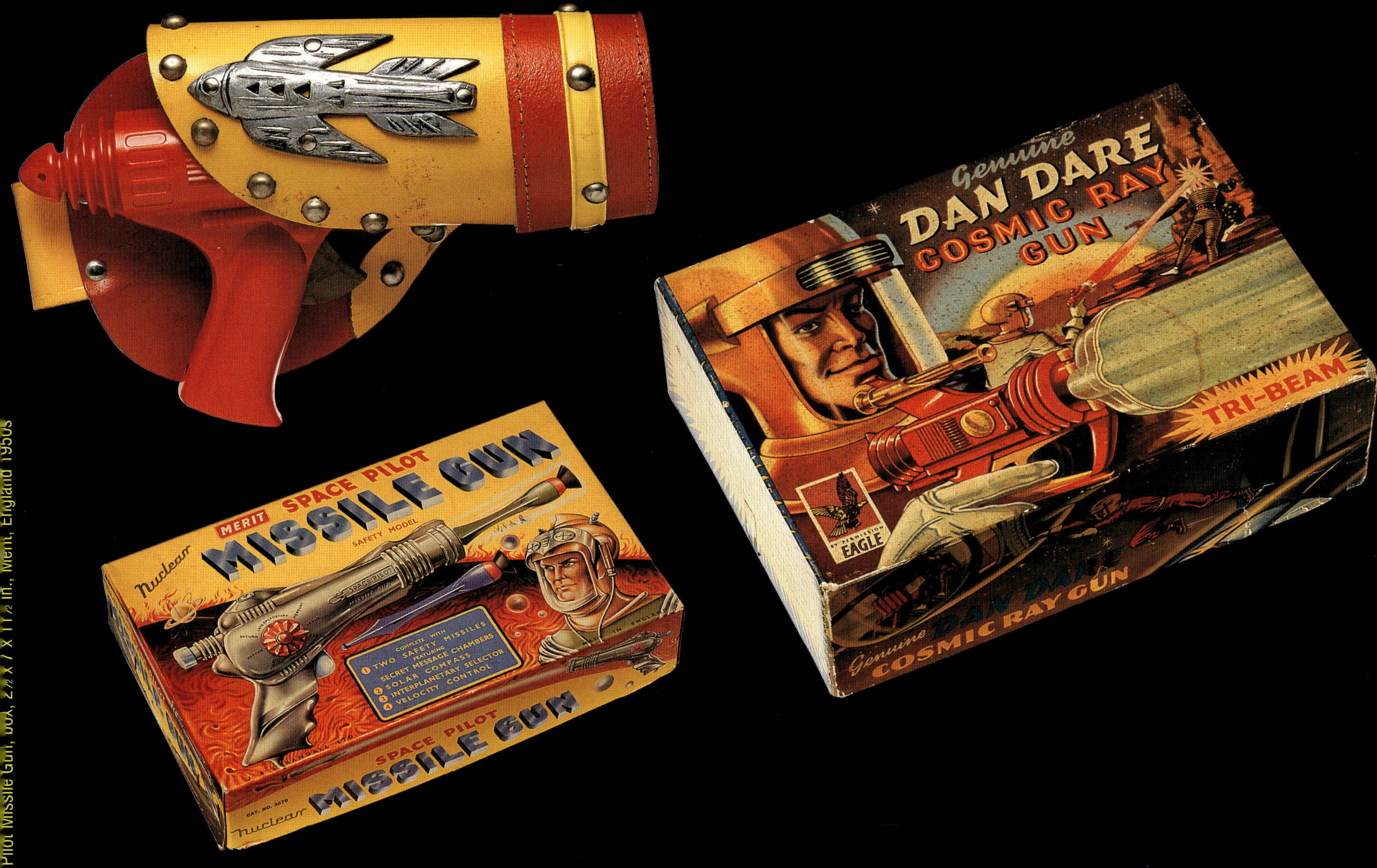

Space Pilot Missile Gun, box, 2½ x 7 x 11½ in., Merit, England 1950s

Dan Dare Cosmic Ray Gun, box, 3¼ x 7¼ x 10 in., Palitoy, England 1950s

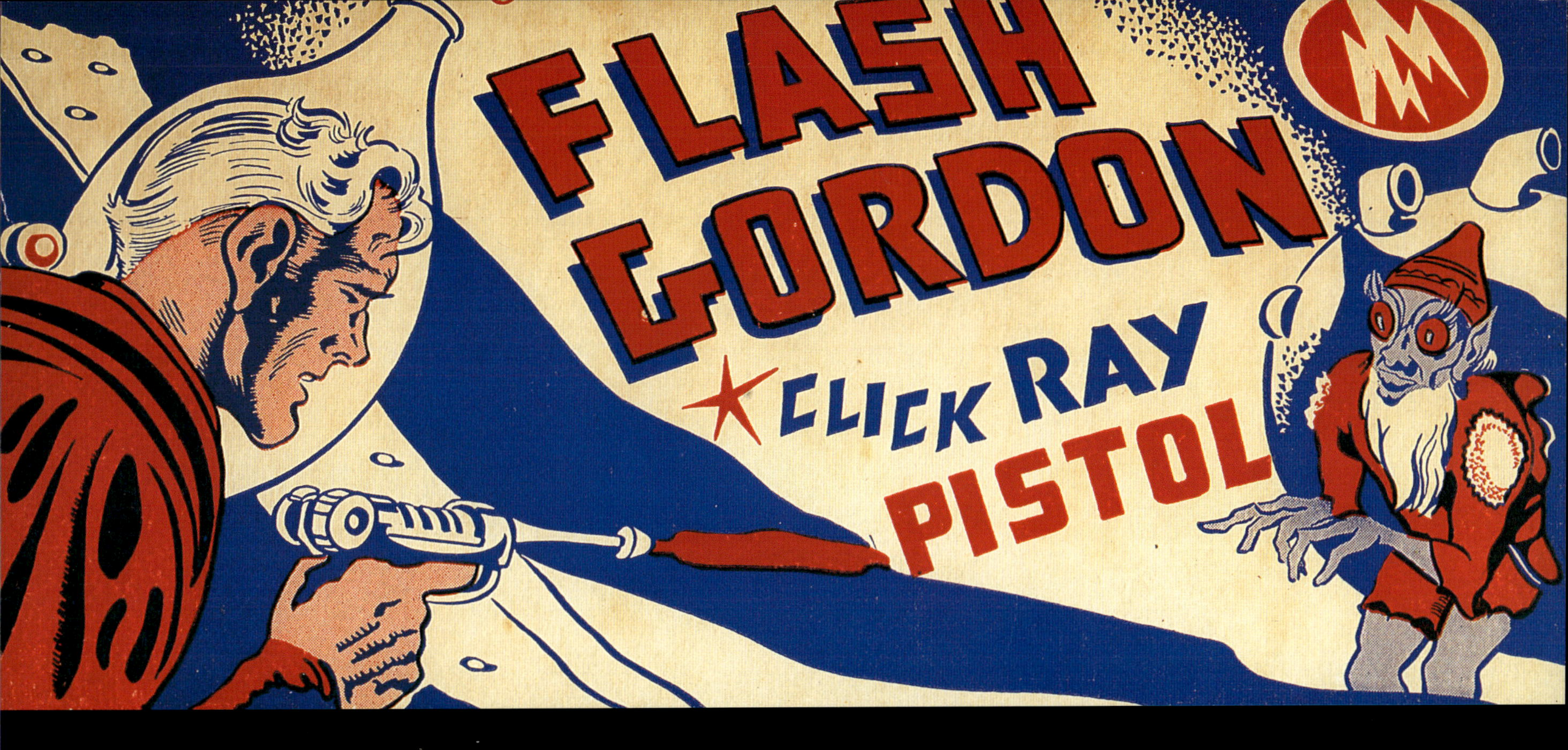
FLASH GORDON
CLICK RAY
PISTOL

Atomic Gun, lithographed tin and plastic, 4¼ x 8¾ in., Haji, Japan 1960s

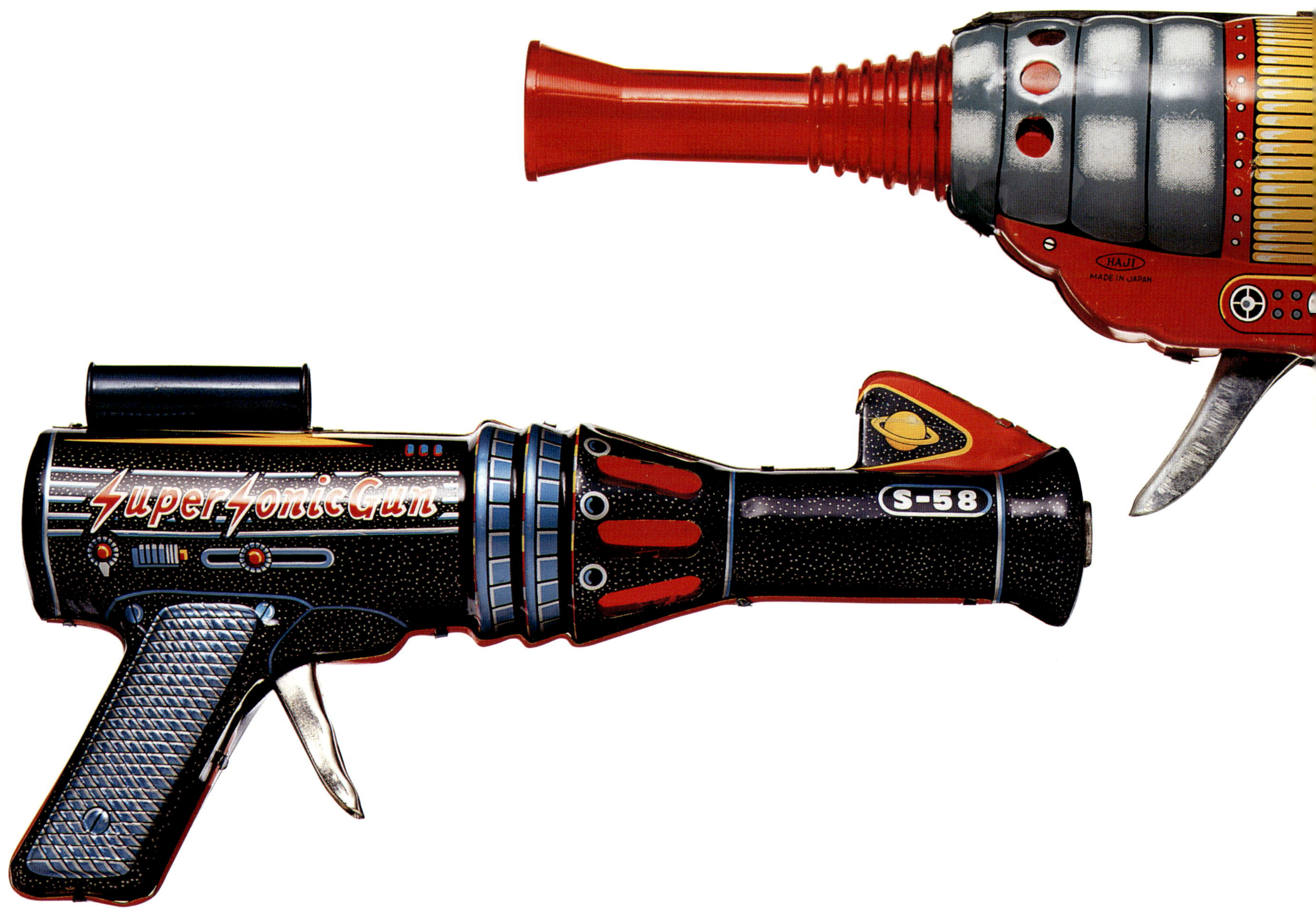

S58 Super Sonic Gun, lithographed tin, 4¾ x 9½ in., Daiya, Japan 1960s

Baby Space Gun, lithographed tin, 3½ x 5¾ in., Daiya, Japan 1960s

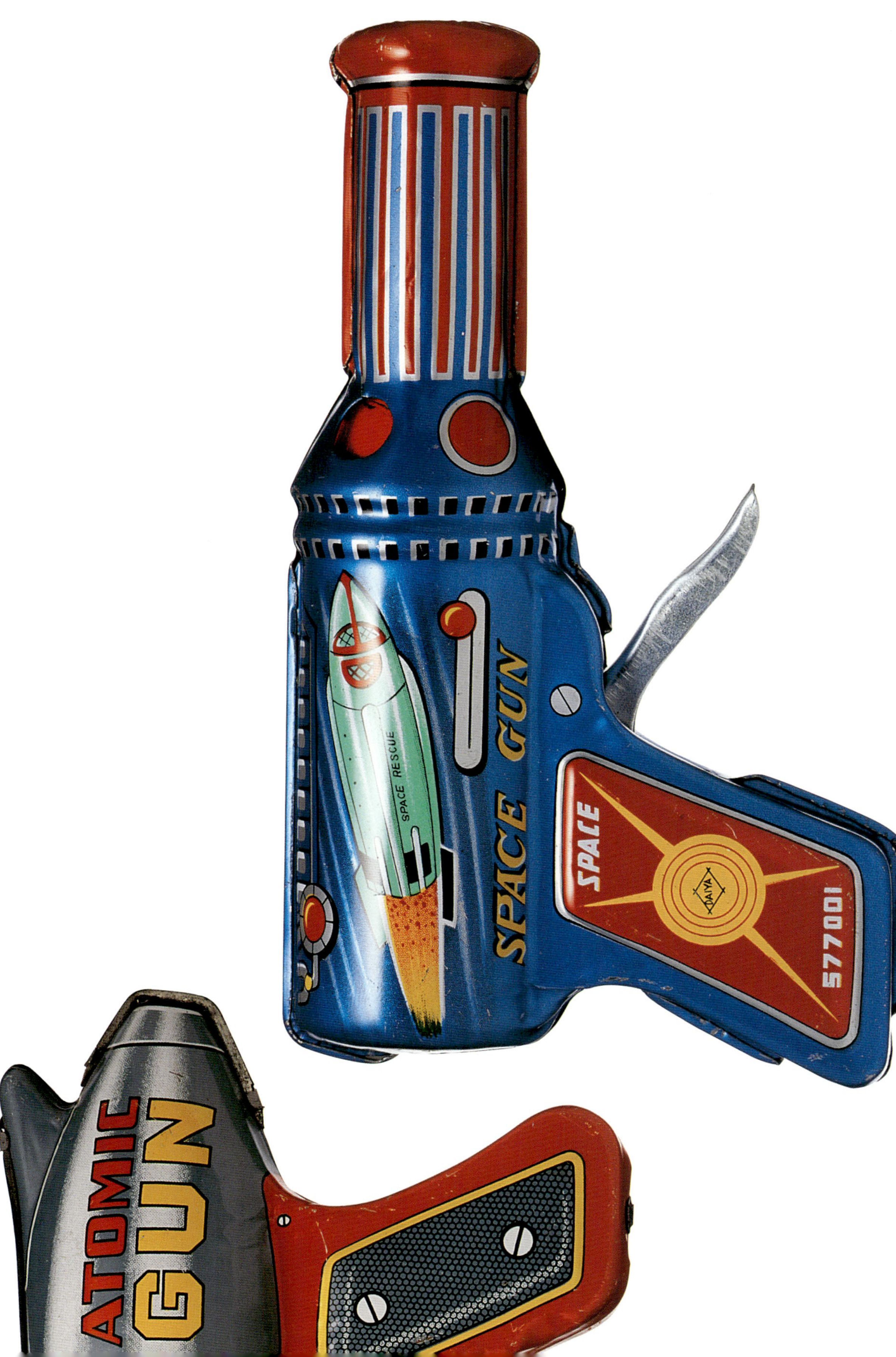

Space Gun, lithographed tin and plastic, 5½ x 9 in., maker unknown, Japan 1960s

Space Gun, lithographed tin, 4¼ x 7 in., Toy Hero, Japan 1960s

Space Gun 45, lithographed tin and plastic, 4½ x 9¾ in., K.O., Japan 1960s

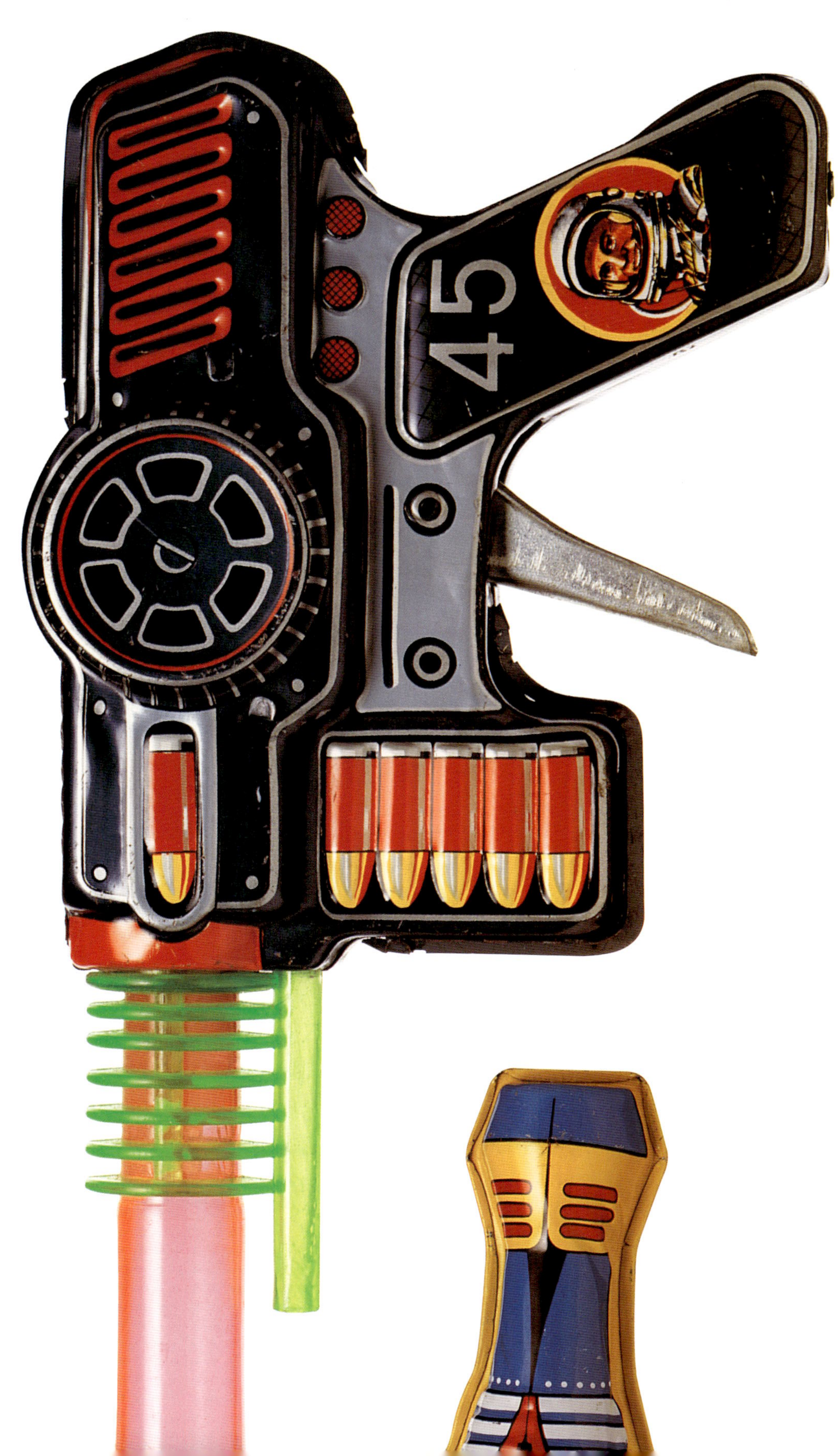

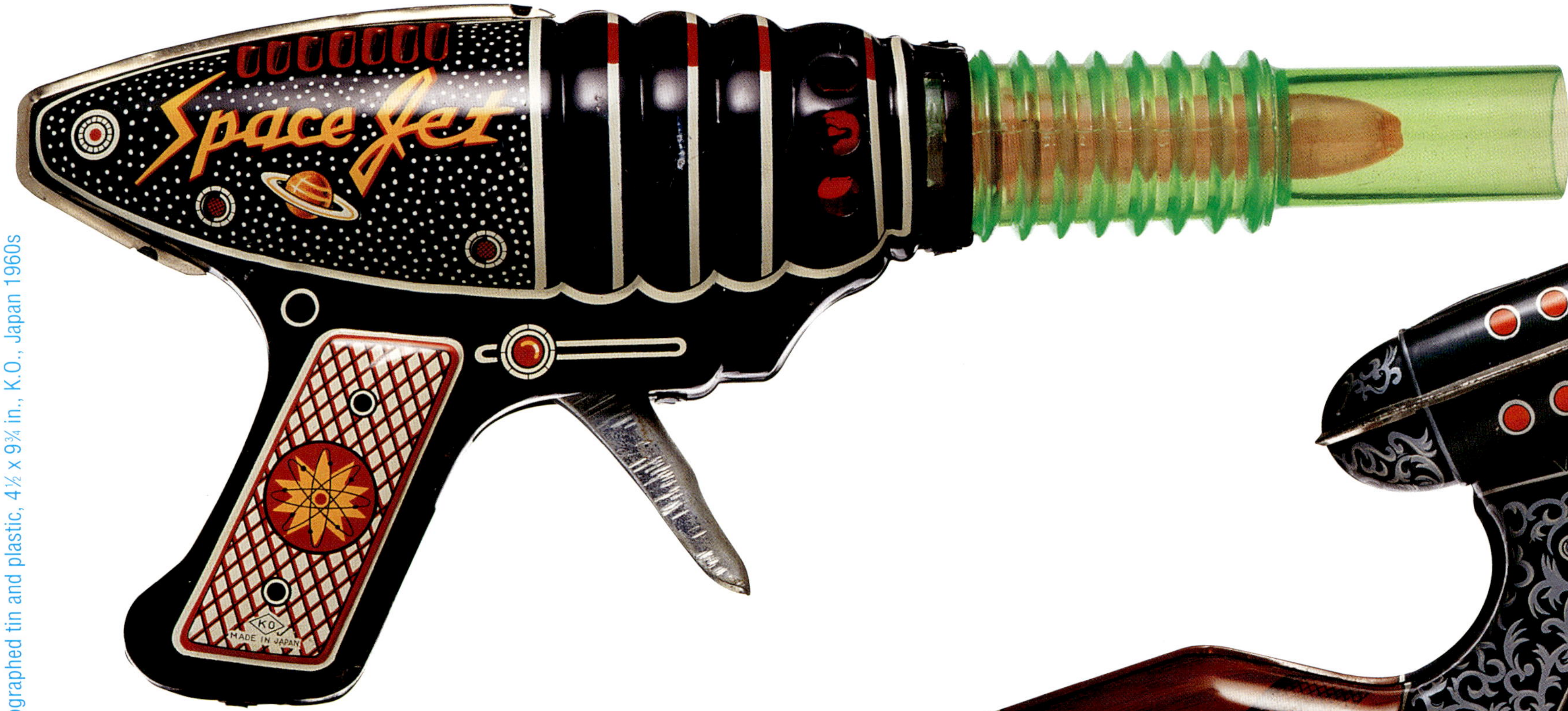

Space Jet, lithographed tin and plastic, 4½ x 9¾ in., K.O., Japan 1960s

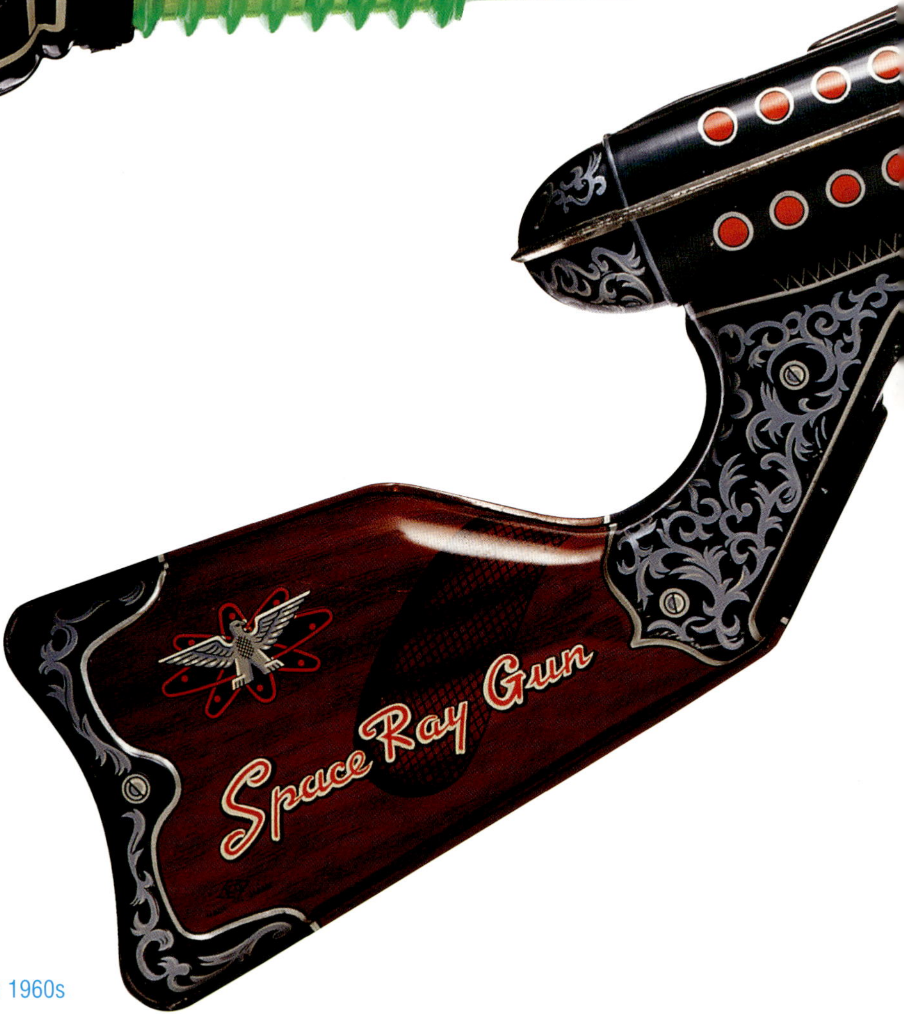

Space Ray Gun, lithographed tin and plastic, 5 x 15 in., K.O., Japan 1960s

Super Sonic Space Gun, lithographed tin, 4 x 7¼ in., Daiya, Japan 1960s

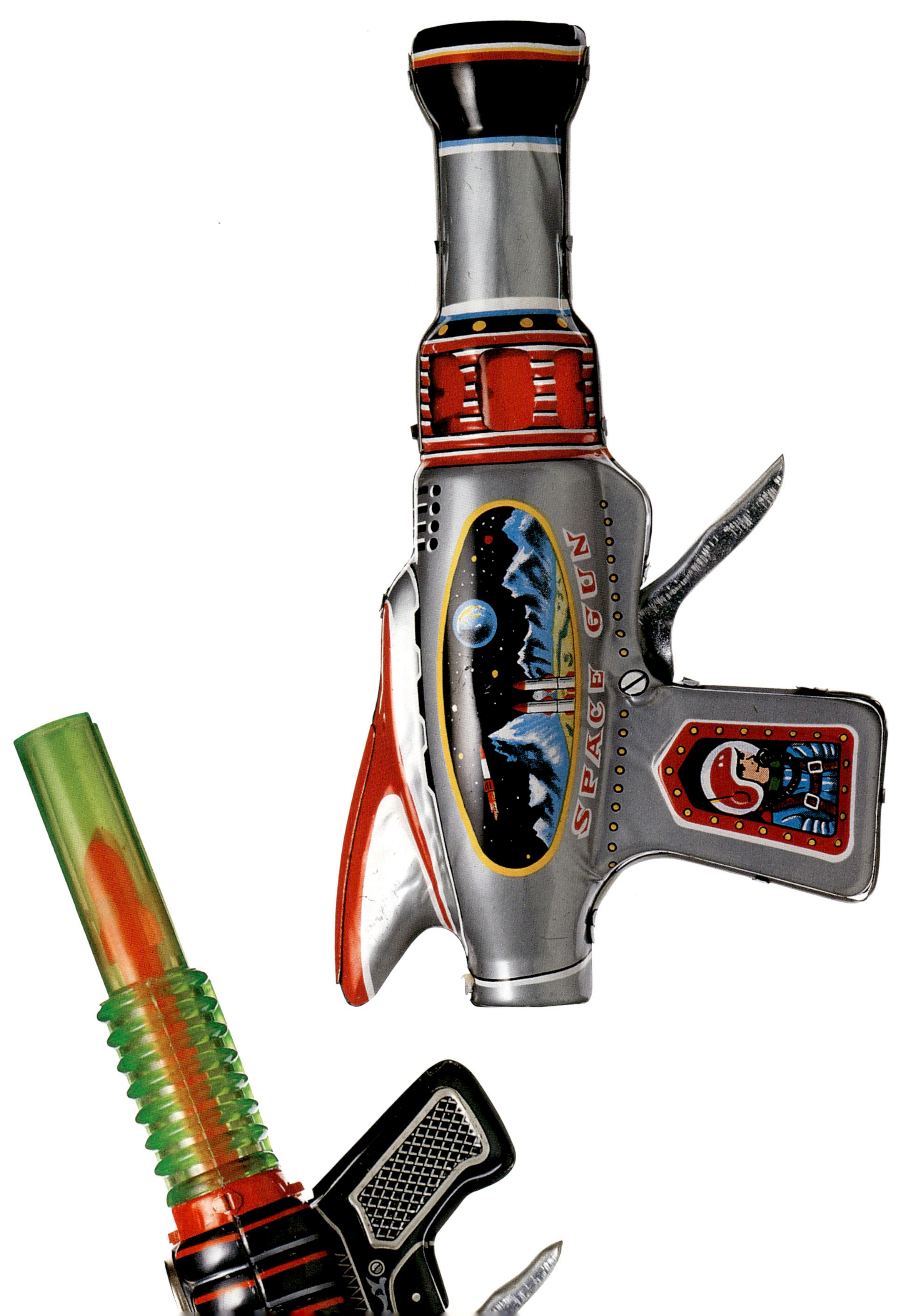

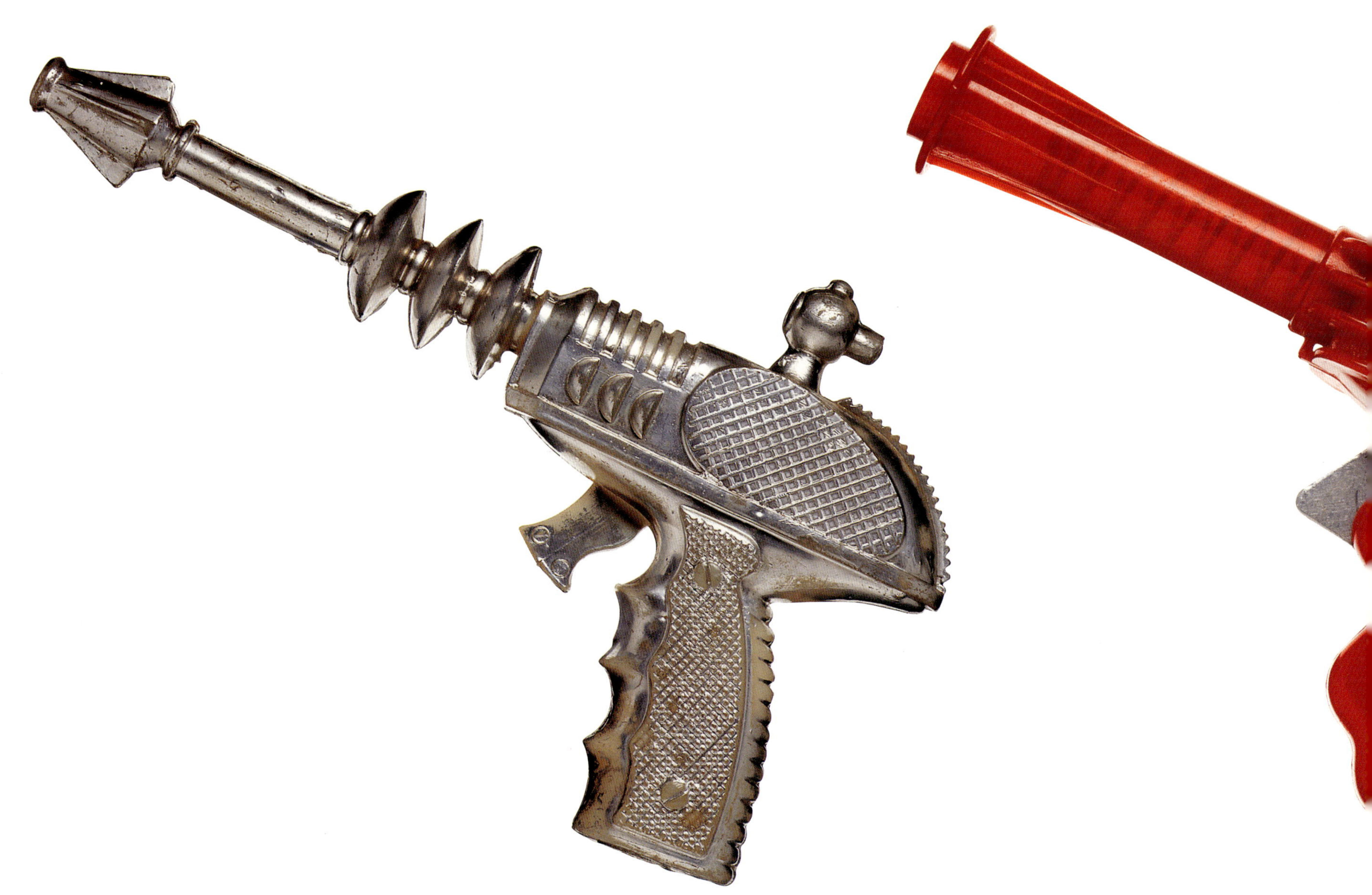

Space Gun, plastic, 6 x 10 in., maker unknown, France 1960s

Space Gun, plastic, 3½ x 4¾ in., Geyper, Spain 1960s

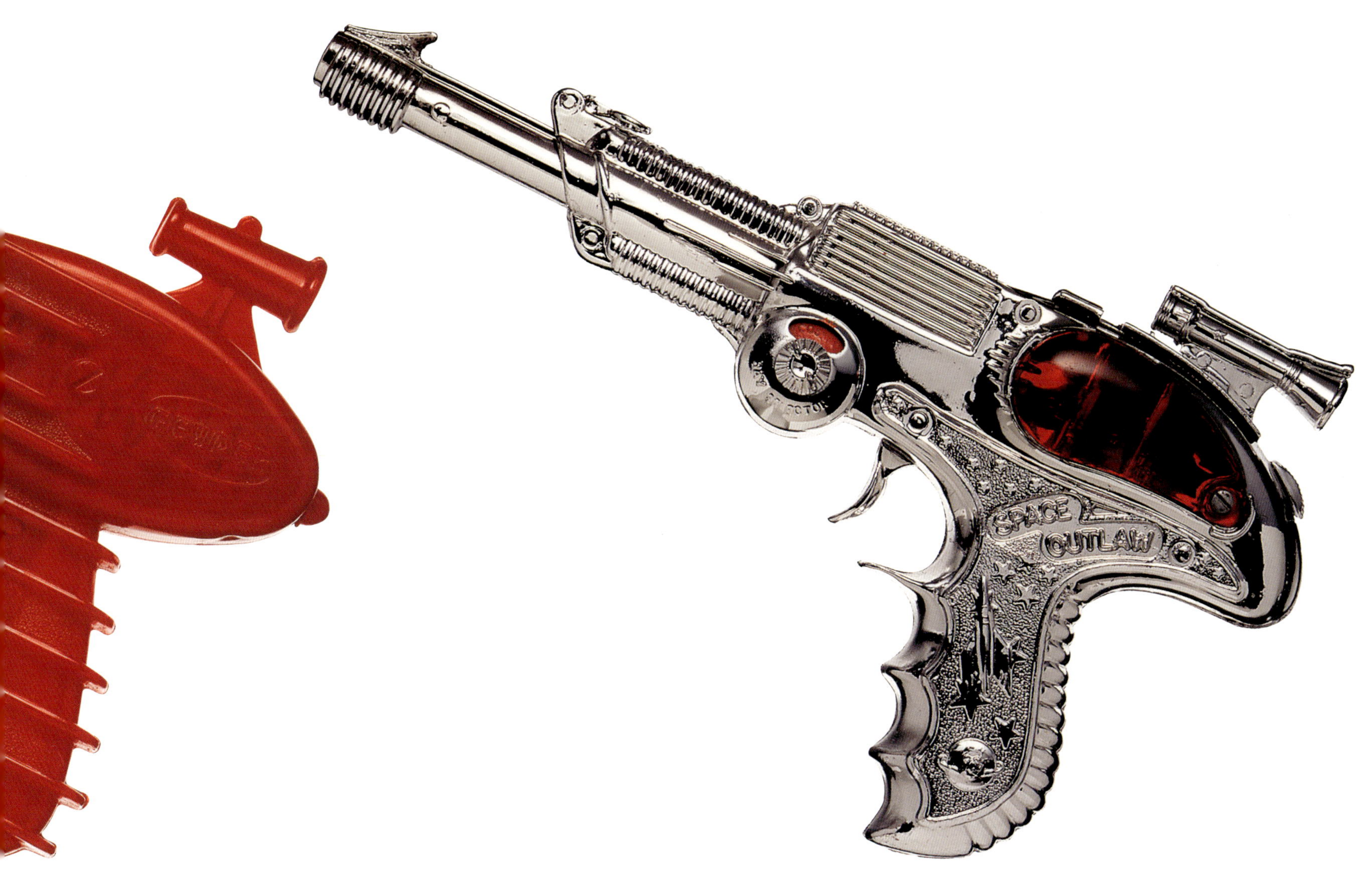

Space Outlaw Gun, die-cast metal, 5½ x 9¾ in., B.C.M., England 1960s

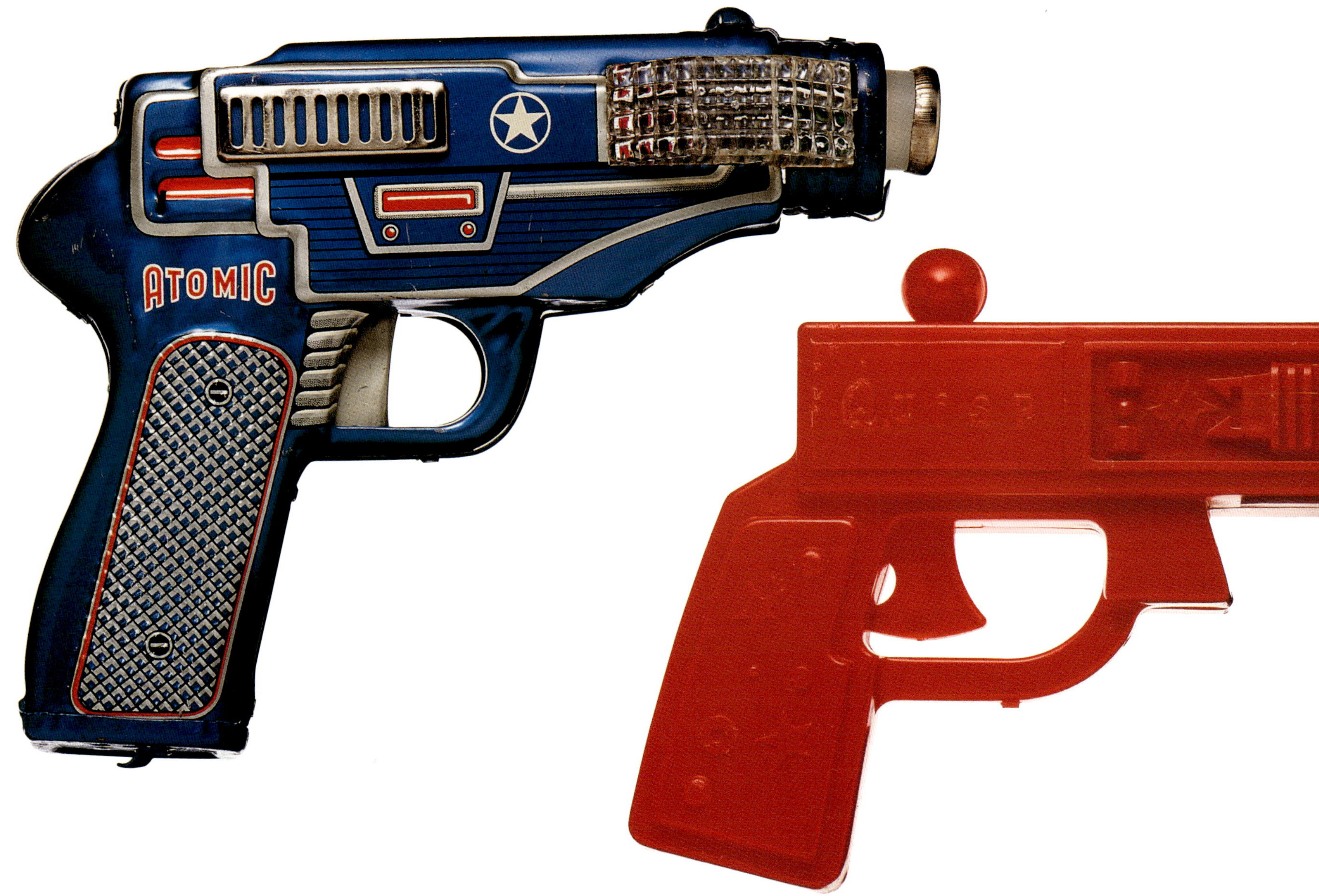

Atomic Space Pistol, lithographed tin and plastic, 5½ x 7 in., T.N., Japan, 1960

Quisp Cosmiclouder Space Gun, plastic, 4¾ x 7½ in., Quaker Cereal, U.S.A. 1960s

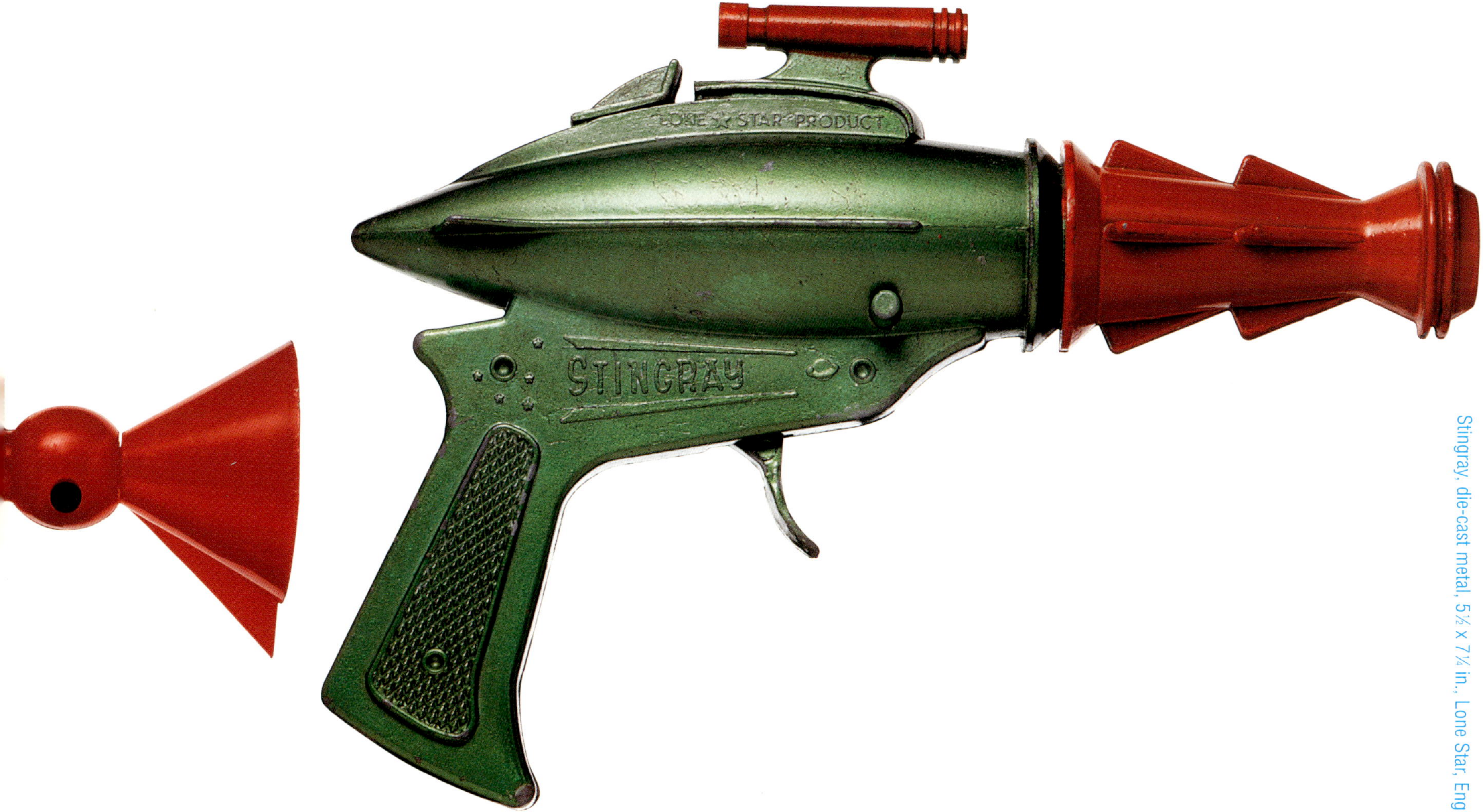

Stingray, die-cast metal, 5½ x 7¼ in., Lone Star, England late 1960s

Space Rifle, lithographed tin, 2¾ x 11¾ in., maker unknown, England 1960s

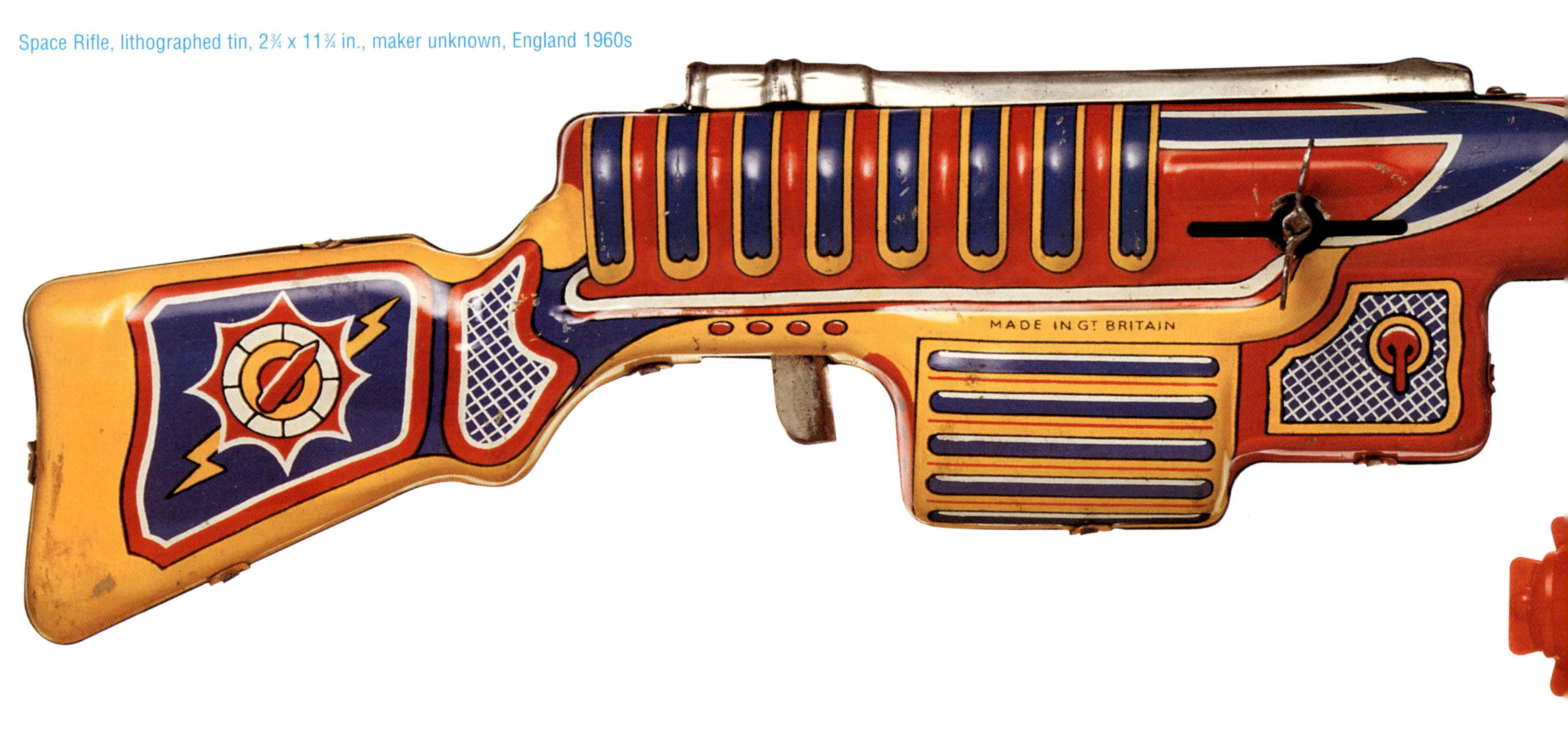

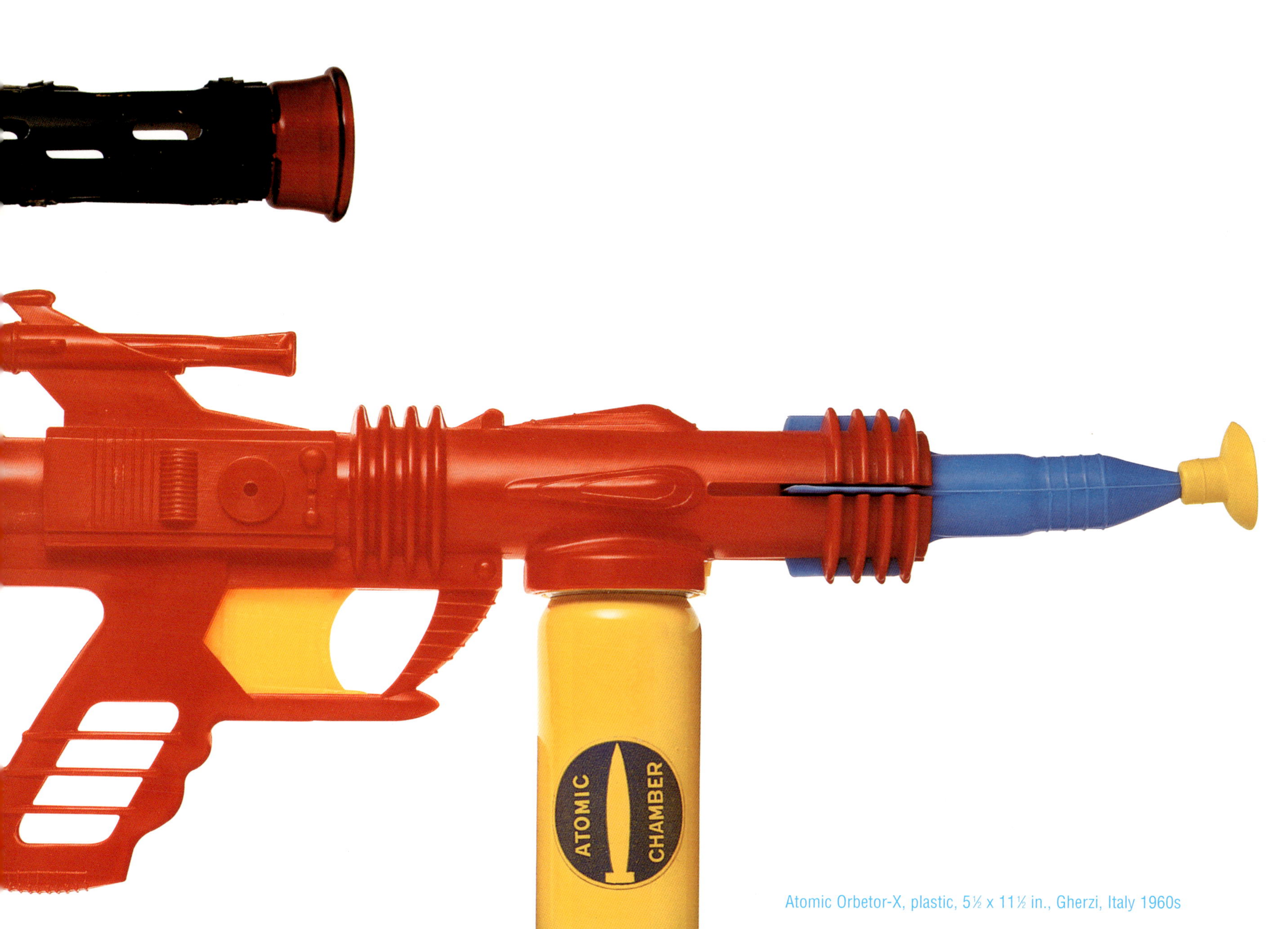

Atomic Orbetor-X, plastic, 5½ x 11½ in., Gherzi, Italy 1960s

atomic orbetor-x®

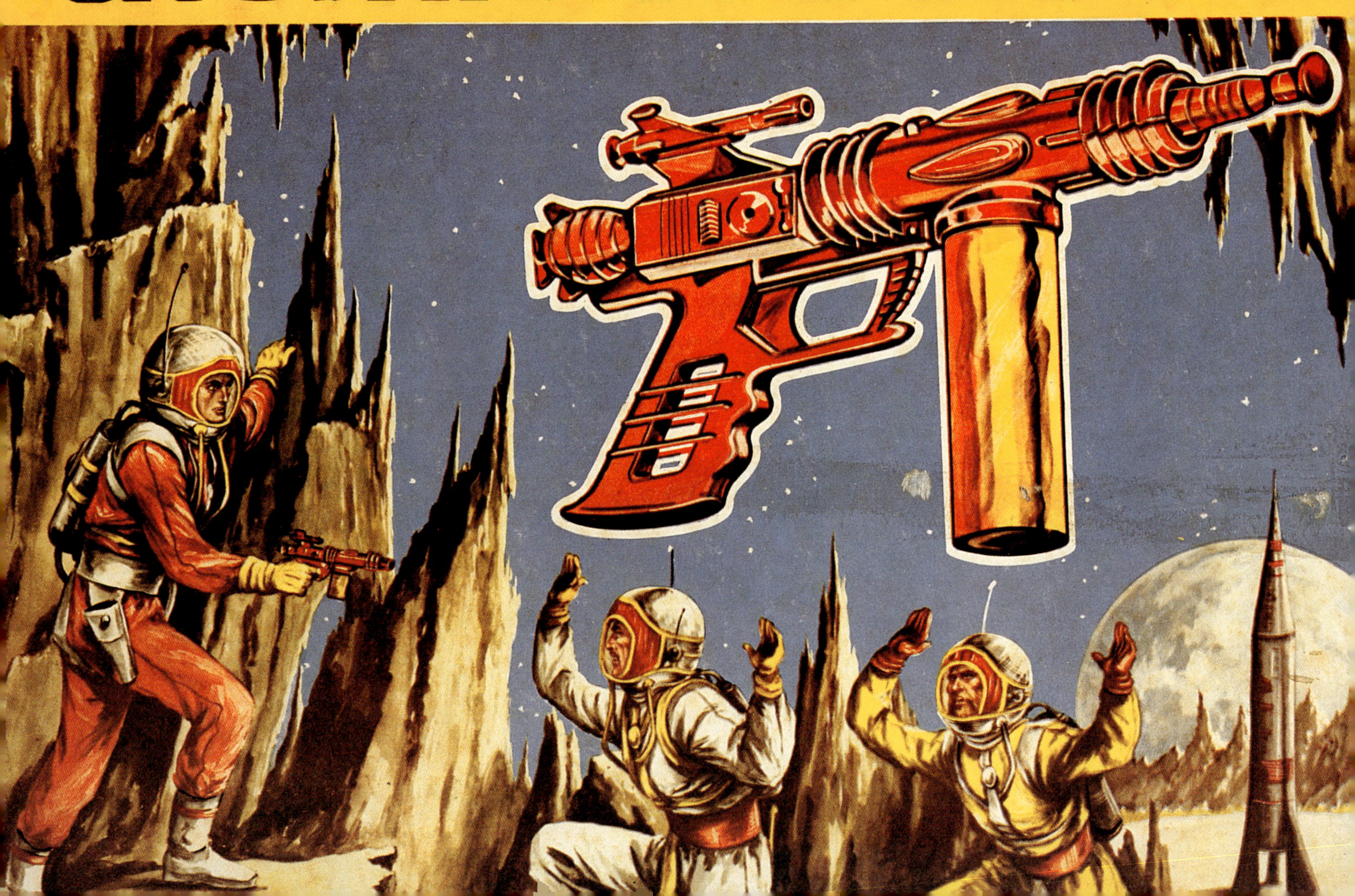

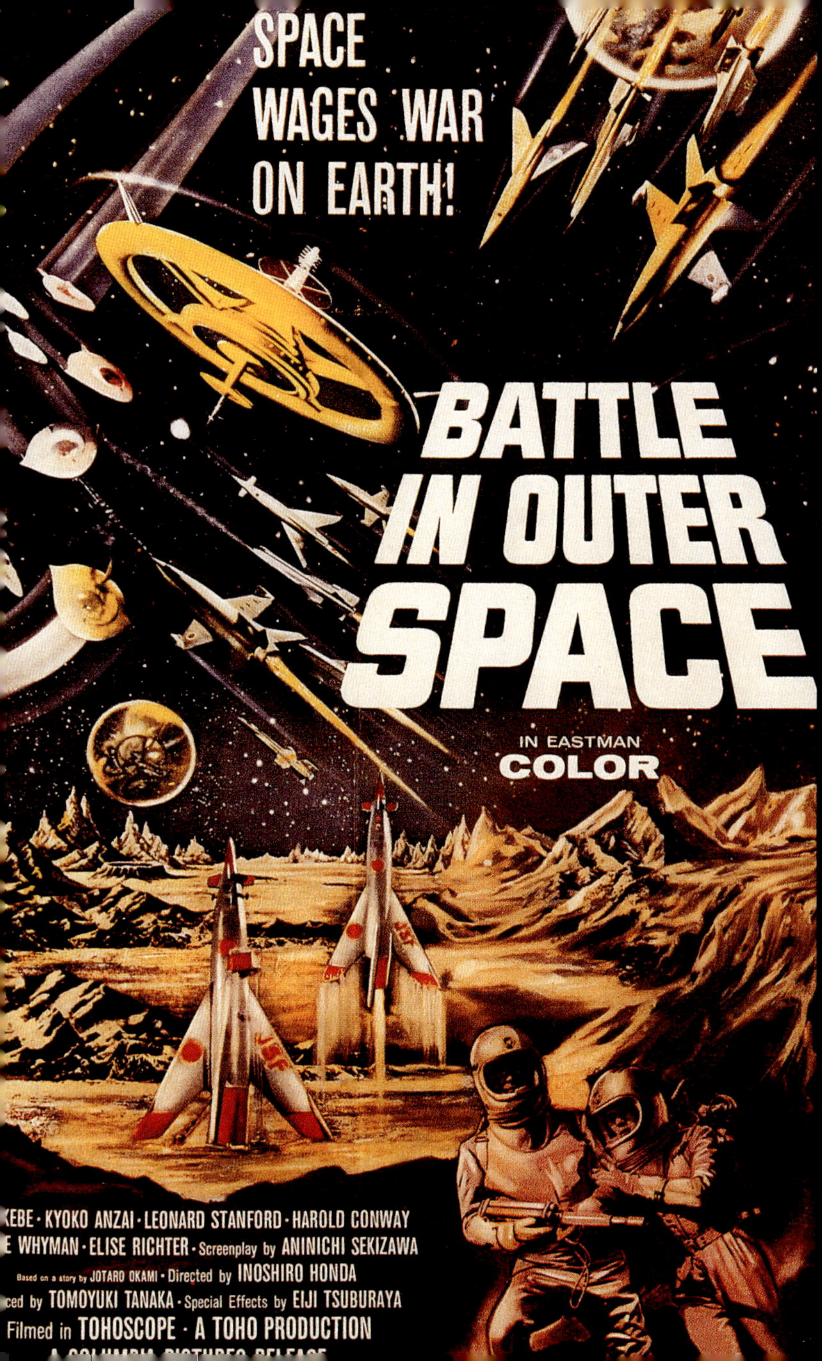

SPACE WAGES WAR ON EARTH!

BATTLE IN OUTER SPACE

IN EASTMAN COLOR

KEBE · KYOKO ANZAI · LEONARD STANFORD · HAROLD CONWAY
E WHYMAN · ELISE RICHTER · Screenplay by ANINICHI SEKIZAWA
Based on a story by JOTARO OKAMI · Directed by INOSHIRO HONDA
ced by TOMOYUKI TANAKA · Special Effects by EIJI TSUBURAYA
Filmed in TOHOSCOPE · A TOHO PRODUCTION

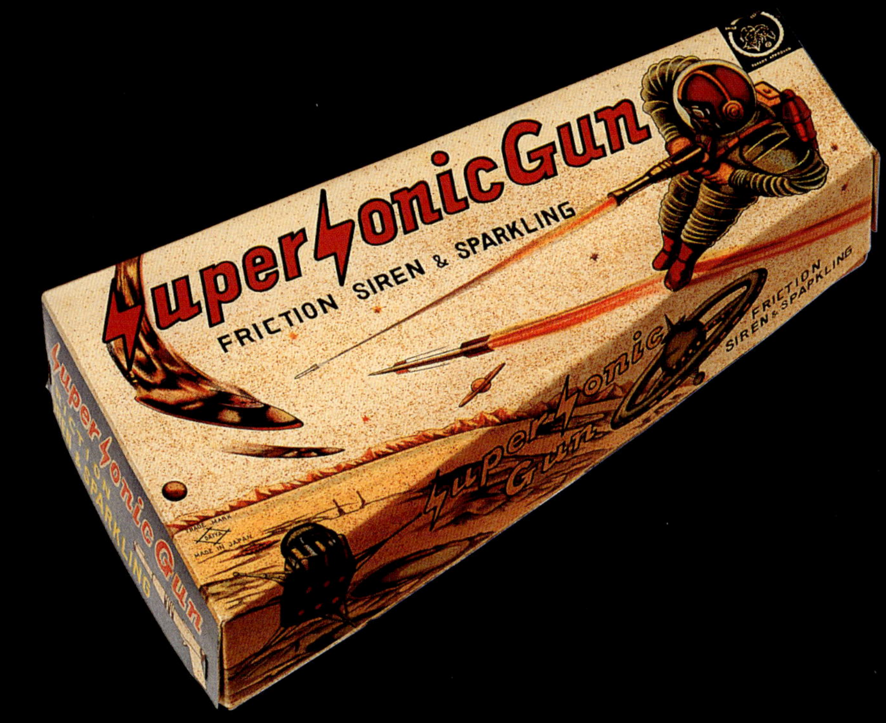

Atomic Orbetor-X, box, 1¾ x 9 x 11½ in., Gherzi, Italy 1960s
Battle in Outer Space, movie poster, 16½ x 10¾ in., Columbia Pictures, U.S.A. 1960
Super Sonic Gun, box, 2 x 5 x 9½ in., Daiya, Japan 1960s

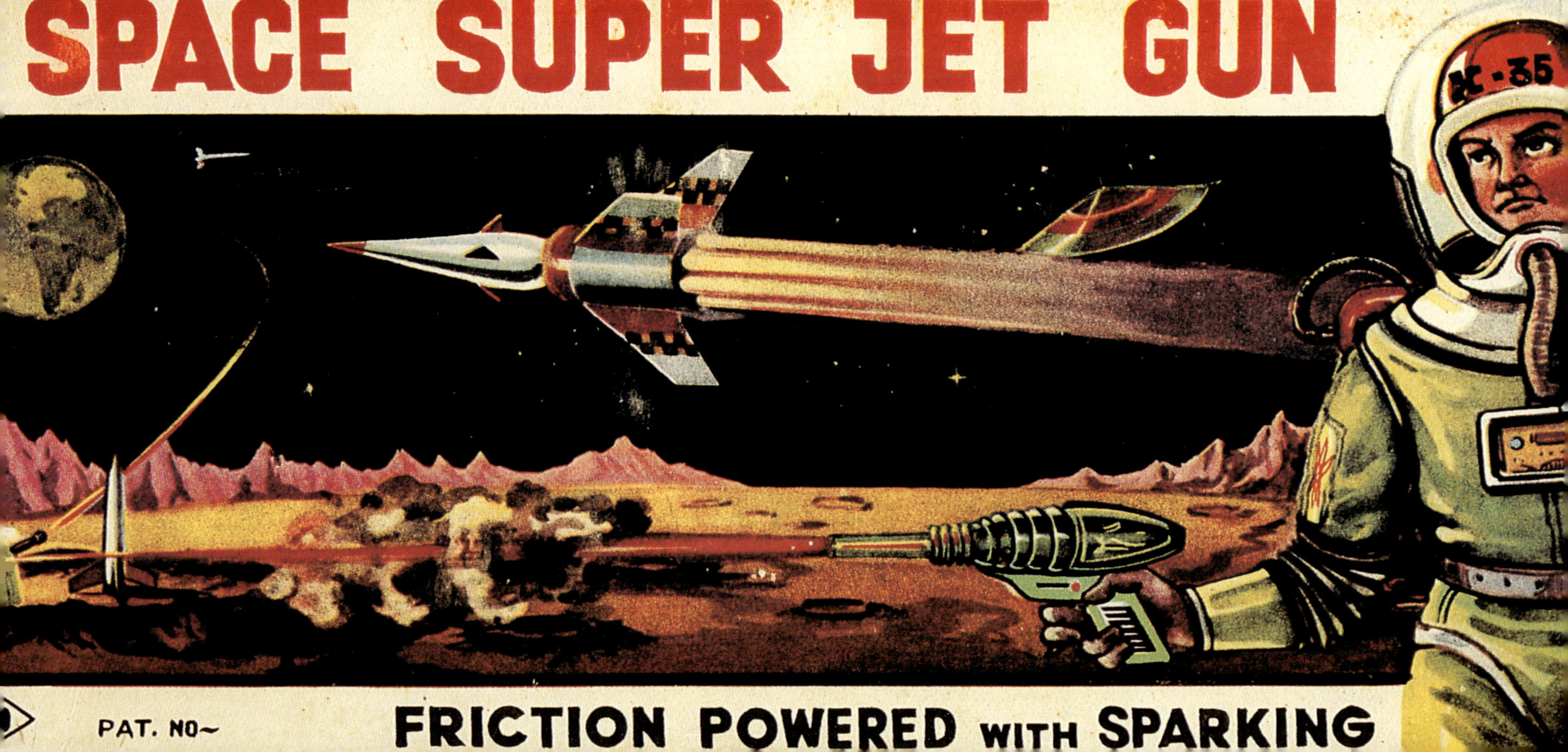

SPACE SUPER JET GUN
X-35
PAT. NO~
FRICTION POWERED WITH SPARKING

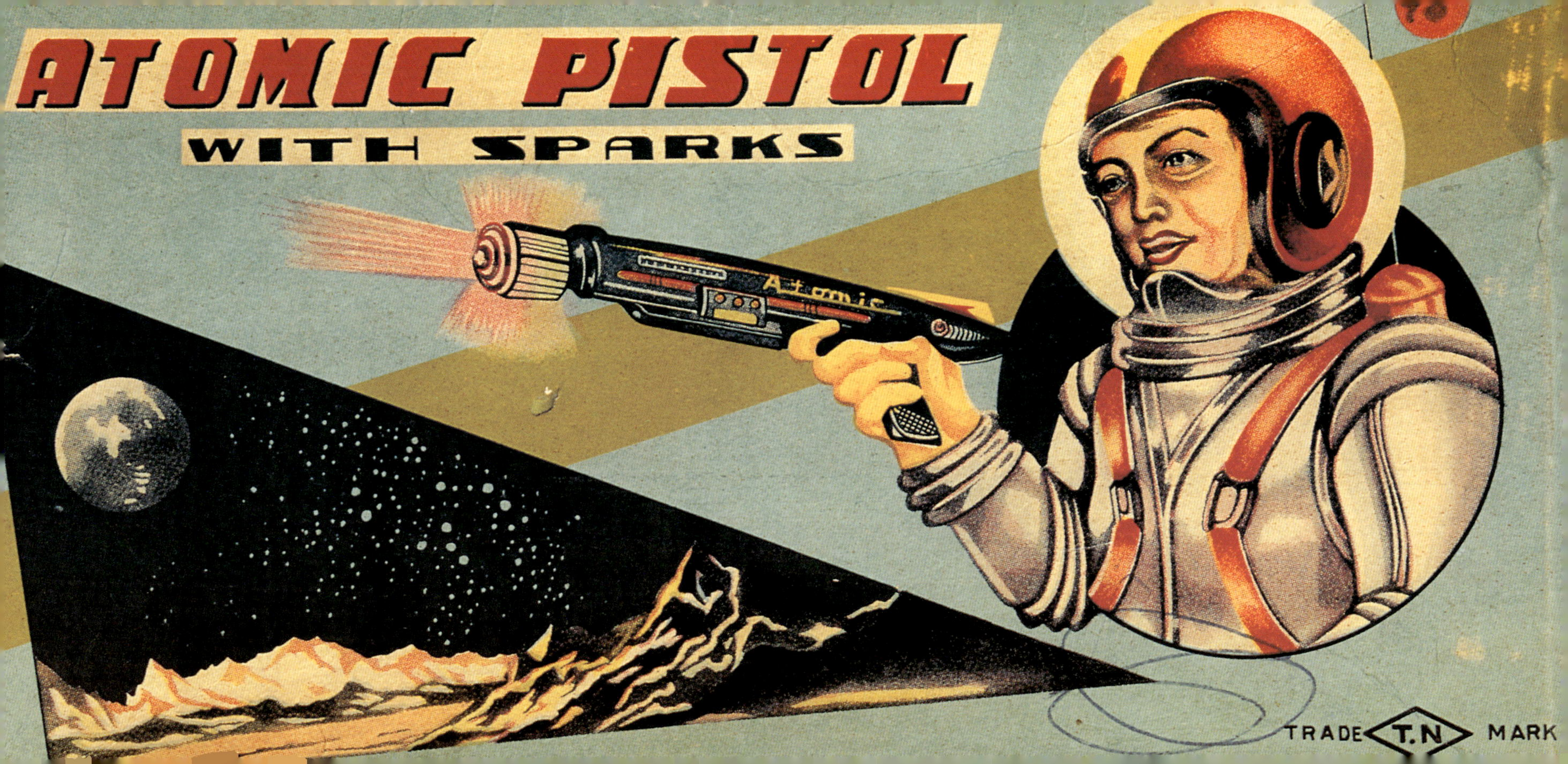
ATOMIC PISTOL
WITH SPARKS
Atomic
TRADE T.N MARK

TOY RAY GUN SOURCES

Website

Metcalf, Eugene W. *Toy Ray Guns.* http://www.toyraygun.com. Presents images of hundreds of toy ray guns and related items like holsters, space helmets, and space suits. Explores the aesthetic meaning, history, and cultural significance of these toys. A forum for interactive discussion and information exchange on the topic of toy ray guns.

Books

Cross, Gary. *Kids Stuff: Toys and the Changing World of American Childhood.* Cambridge: Harvard University Press, 1997. A fascinating social history of toys and their relationship to changing conceptions of childhood. Particularly interesting information on space toys and Buck Rogers.

Hake, Ted. *Hake's Price Guide to Character Toy Premiums*, Timonium, MD: Gemstone Publishing, Inc. 1996. Includes ray gun premiums in a number of sections. See particularly the sections on Buck Rogers, Captain Video, Flash Gordon, Space Patrol, and Tom Corbett Space Cadet.

Kitahara, Teruhisa. *Yesterdays Toys: Robots, Space Ships, and Monsters.* San Francisco: Chronicle Books, 1989. Includes six pages of color photographs of toy ray guns and their boxes.

Lesser, Robert. *A Celebration of Comic Art and Memorabilia.* New York: Hawthorn Books, 1975. A beautifully illustrated history and production list of great comic book and media characters from the late 19th century through the 1950s. The best information on Buck Rogers available.

Payton, Crystal and Leland. *Space Toys: A Collector's Guide to Science Fiction and Astronautical Toys.* Sedalia, Missouri: Collector's Compass. 1982. An early book on space toys. Includes a section on space guns.

Sansweet, Stephen J. *Science Fiction Toys and Models, Vol 1.* New York: Star Log Press. 1980.The first book on space toys. Includes many types of toys including some great illustrations of space guns.

Schneider, Stuart. *Collecting the Space Race.* Atglen, PA: Schiffer Publishing Lt. 1993. A complete guide to collecting space-related artifacts. One of the many sections focuses on ray guns.

Singer, Leslie. *Zap: Ray Gun Classics.* San Francisco: Chronicle Books. 1991. The first book on ray guns. Beautifully illustrated. Includes toys from the 1930s through the present.

LENDERS

Every attempt has been made to secure proper credit information on the images used in this book. However, it was not always possible to locate the original sources of ownership. We apologize for any oversights. The numbers listed below refer to the page numbers and position of the item.

Ray Amati 8, 9, 10, 15, 16, 17, 18 bottom left, 18–9, 20, 21, 23, 35 (badges)

David Greeman 74, 100

Dennis Merritt 33, 62 left, 62 right, 63 left, 64 top

Barbara Moran 68 left, 69 right, 84

Michael Schneider 65, 68 right, 69 left, 70, 76, 77, 78, 78–9, 79, 102 left, 102 right

Richard Thomas 38, 56–7, 64 bottom, 67, 75, 80, 80–1, 81, 89 right

Private Collection 11, 12, 13, 14, 18 top left, 19 left, 19 right, 22, 24, 25, 26, 26–7, 27, 28, 29, 30, 31, 32, 34 left, 34 right, 35 center, 36, 37, 39, 40, 41, 42, 43, 44, 45, 46 left, 46 right, 47, 48, 48–9, 49, 50 top left, 50 bottom left, 50 right, 51 left, 51 right, 52, 53, 54 left, 54 right, 55 left, 55 right, 56, 57, 58, 58–9, 59, 60, 60–1, 61, 63 right, 66, 71 left, 71 right, 72, 73, 82, 83, 85, 86, 87, 88 left, 88 right, 89 left, 90 left, 90 right, 91, 92 top left, 92 bottom left, 92 right, 93, 94, 94–5, 95, 96, 96–7, 97, 98, 98–9, 99, 100–1, 101, 103, 104, 105, 106, 107 left, 107 right, 108 109

Eugene W. Metcalf is Professor of Interdisciplinary Studies at Miami University in Ohio. A renowned scholar in the fields of American art and material culture, he has written and lectured extensively on folk, self-taught, and vernacular art. His authored works include seminal writings on the politics of African-American art, the social meaning of American folk art collecting, and the myth of the Self-Taught artist. He is co-editor of the major critical volume *The Artist Outsider: Creativity and the Boundaries of Culture*. Metcalf is also an avid collector of toy ray guns and the creator of an internationally acclaimed website devoted to ray guns and their role in the popular imagining of outer space.

As co-owner of the Ricco/Maresca Gallery in New York City, Frank Maresca is among America's most distinguished collectors and dealers of Outsider and Self-Taught art. He has co-authored several books published by Alfred A. Knopf, among them: *A Certain Style: The Art of the Plastic Handbag*, with Robert Gottlieb, *Bill Traylor: His Art, His Life*, *American Primitive*, *American Self-Taught: Drawings and Paintings by Outsider Artists*, and *William Hawkins: Paintings*, all co-authored with Roger Ricco. Maresca is also well known as a fashion photographer, and his work has appeared in *Vogue*, *Harper's Bazaar*, and *Town and Country*.

Charles Bechtold's photographs have been the highlight of numerous fine art books published by Alfred A. Knopf, among them *Bill Traylor: His Art, His Life*, *American Self-Taught: Drawings and Paintings by Outsider Artists*, and *William Hawkins: Paintings*. He was also a contributing photographer in the book *Passionate Visions of the American South*. His photographs also grace the pages of *Bill Traylor: Observing Life*, and *Charles A.A. Dellschau 1830–1923*, both produced by Ricco/Maresca Gallery. Bechtold lives in New Jersey and is a graduate of the School of Visual Arts in New York City.

ACKNOWLEDGMENTS

This book was written and compiled with the help of many friends. Leslie Singer shared his ray gun knowledge and enthusiasm in countless phone calls and E-mail messages. Ray Amati helped organize the "Buck Rogers" material in this book and loaned many of the toys presented in it. David Greeman, Dennis Merritt, Barbara Moran, Michael Schneider, and Richard Thomas generously loaned toys to be photographed. George Newcomb, of Plymouth Rock Toy Company, caught factual errors in the text and checked the dates of manufacture and maker's names for the toy guns presented here. Leonard Nimoy graciously shared a personal experience. Finally, Joanne Cubbs carefully edited the text of this book, giving it a "zap" it certainly would have lacked otherwise. Thank you.

Fotofolio, Inc.
561 Broadway, New York, New York 10012
Fotofolio: Martin Bondell, Juliette Galant, Ron Schick, Cindy Williamson, Justine Keefe
Printed in Korea
Library of Congress Catalog Card Number: 99-64972
ISBN: 1-58418-004-8 (hardcover)

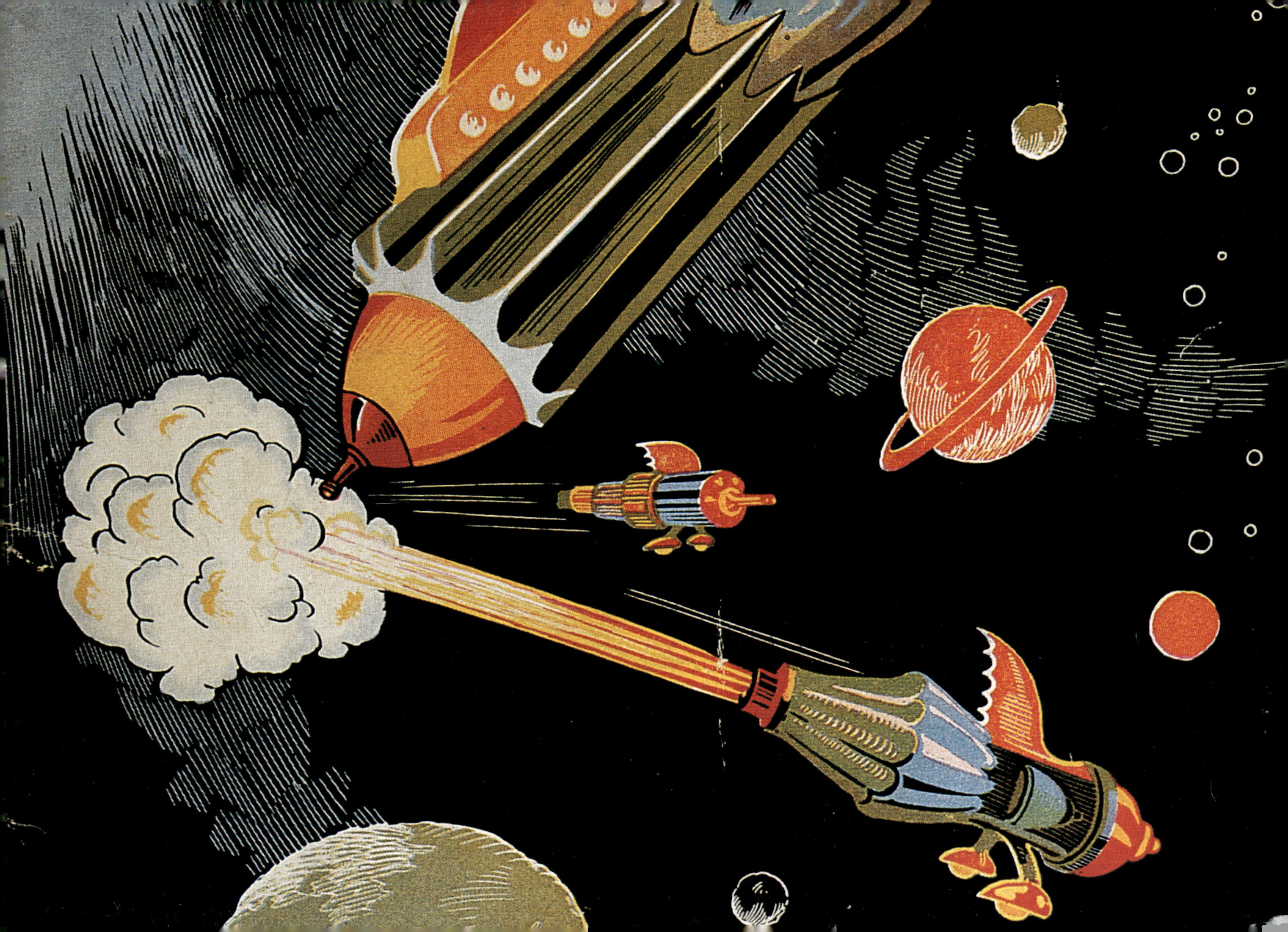